INSIDE THE
MUSLIM
BROTHERHOOD

INSIDE THE
MUSLIM
BROTHERHOOD

YOUSSEF NADA
WITH DOUGLAS THOMPSON

metro

Published by Metro Publishing
an imprint of John Blake Publishing Ltd
3 Bramber Court, 2 Bramber Road,
London W14 9PB, England

www.johnblakepublishing.co.uk

www.facebook.com/Johnblakepub   facebook

twitter.com/johnblakepub   twitter

First published in hardback in 2012

ISBN: 978-1-85782-687-6

British Library Cataloguing-in-Publication Data:

A catalogue record for this book is available from the British Library.

Design by www.envydesign.co.uk

Printed in Great Britain by CPI Group (UK) Ltd

1 3 5 7 9 10 8 6 4 2

© Text copyright Youssef Nada and Douglas Thompson 2012

Papers used by John Blake Publishing are natural, recyclable products made
from wood grown in real forests. The manufacturing processes conform
to the environmental regulations of the country of origin.

Every attempt has been made to contact the relevant copyright-holders,
but some were unobtainable. We would be grateful if the
appropriate people could contact us.

'*When the sky is torn apart,*
When the stars are scattered,
When the seas burst forth,
When graves turn inside out,
Then each soul will know what it has done
And what it left undone…'

The Judgment Day denouement, from the 82nd sura of the Koran

For all who struggle for justice and dignity

'*When you touch the humanity in the human, it will wake up, even if it was dormant, even if it was dead. When you touch the humanity it rises up.*'

Youssef Nada, 2012

Contents

CONTENTS

BOOK TWO: BEYOND REASON

INTRODUCTION

'All the world's a stage, and all the men and women merely players: they have their exits and their entrances; and one man in his time plays many parts, his acts being seven ages.'

William Shakespeare, *As You Like It*

H e is an acrobat with thought and languages, and in a world engulfed by ambiguities we can all benefit from interpreters. The enlightened message from Youssef Nada at its simplest – and most provocatively – is to live and let live. He is for overall justice and democracy and has risked his life in the struggle for it.

An exiled Egyptian, Youssef Nada tells everyone he has been honoured to be a member of the Muslim Brotherhood (*al-Ikhwan al-Muslimeen*) for more than 60 years. It is *the* most controversial, influential and potent of all Islamist 'organisations' throughout the world. Many nations feared that, as despotic regimes toppled like dominoes, there would be an Islamic mirror of Iran throughout the Middle East. As the Shah of Iran's departure in 1979 led to the return of the Ayatollah Khomeini and a huge backlash against the West, it was argued events heralded a much bigger twenty-first-century Islamist revolution. And world turmoil.

In America on 30 January 2011, one-time US Republican party presidential aspirant Mike Huckabee told his nation: '*If, in fact, the Muslim Brotherhood is underneath much of the unrest, every person who breathes ought to be concerned.*'

No one publicly questioned that statement. Of course, much of the world did not know who or what the Muslim Brotherhood was. Newt Gingrich, American Presidential contender in 2012 and the former US House Speaker, presumably did. On 6 February 2011, he told the CNN television network that reaching out to the Muslim Brotherhood to help resolve the Egyptian crisis was a bad idea: '*The Muslim Brotherhood is a mortal enemy of our civilisation, they say so openly, their way is Jihad, their method is death.*'

Youssef Nada, unsurprisingly, has a more even-minded view of things, although to some Islamists his thoughts will be revolutionary, possibly heretic. His mission is for Sunni and Shia, Muslim, Christian and Jew, West and East, man and woman, to live alongside each other in peace. He has a vision of a Mediterranean pact whereby Europe and the Arab world can build a future together: his 'Marco Polo Solution'. He has an understanding of what's turned the world into an arena of often heart-stopping brinkmanship; of the round-the-clock apprehension about who'll blink first.

Youssef Nada and I began talking about this book a long time before the stirrings of what became known as 'The Arab Spring'. I had spent two years compiling an investigative dossier for a prominent family in the region, and became intrigued by the Muslim Brotherhood and the story of their away-from-the-spotlight international negotiator – the enigmatic Youssef Nada.

Until now he had been the mystery inside the heart of the Middle East mystery; the part of the puzzle no one could place; that final part of the jigsaw, out of reach like a wisp of smoke on the horizon. He liked it that way. It was safer. Events, as you will quickly realise, changed his profile. The timing was perfect for our collaboration, and following private introductions and many meetings in which we tested our motives and suitability for working together, we began.

Neither of us realised how events would interrupt and inform us. At times it was exasperating but it was always exciting. I sat with Youssef Nada as he was consulted on revolution in Egypt, the end of Gadaffi, and continually in the desperate search for an answer to the massacres in Syria. Problems in other areas – Saudi Arabia and Yemen, Iran and Iraq – surfaced every day. It was an astonishing lesson in diplomacy and world politics. If Youssef Nada has one guiding mantra it is that the participation of political Islam in the running of the Arab nations was the only way forward to establish legitimacy and democracy.

Youssef Nada had lost his freedom of self-will and exiled himself from Egypt half-a-dozen years after the establishment in 1952 of the nationalism regime of Colonel Gamal Abdel Nasser and a return to Pharaonic culture. Nasser and the clones that followed – Anwar Sadat and Hosni Mubarak – behaved like Pharaohs and expected to be treated as deities. With numbered overseas bank accounts.

The distinguished and readable Naguib Mahfouz, the Arab world's only Nobel Laureate in Literature and author of the books which comprise the *Cairo Trilogy*, said that Nasser's ousting of King Farouk had stolen the '*the property of the few and the liberty of all*'.

Indeed, for more than 60 years of rampant corruption a military cabal has in every sense plundered all around the banks of the Nile. It's taken a painfully slow time, but the people of Egypt, the standard bearer in Arab politics, began fighting to get that liberty. The young of Egypt and throughout the Middle East have no interest in a stability simply to accommodate America's interests. The aspirations of an increasingly educated Arab world require new and delicate handling.

Youssef Nada has a hard, clear, lucid, vision. He cannot promise answers, yet he would offer possible solutions through the ideas and philosophy he has lived to all his life as an ambassador of reason, a peacemaker. And also as the *de facto* foreign minister for a quarter of a century of the Muslim Brotherhood group, whose membership thrives not only in the Middle East and Far East but with pivotal positions in America, the UK, and throughout continental Europe.

He maintains almost all that is written or broadcast about the Muslim Brotherhood is not correct, causing resentment and trouble. He found that out abruptly after the 9/11 attacks on America when he was trapped in the spotlight: this man who'd controlled a business empire worth billions of US dollars was branded a global financial terrorist and listed as such by America and the United Nations Security Council.

President George W Bush named him as 'Al Qaeda's banker'. He, it was said publicly, was 'the godfather of all evil'. He remained blacklisted by America in 2012, though delisted by the United Nations Security Council. He has never been charged with anything, anywhere. What had gone before him prepared him for this personal catastrophe. It is a unique, fascinating life he talks about and one which points to some solutions for the world's future.

During three years of investigations and many, many months of face-to-face conversations, Youssef Nada has never avoided a question or given a less than frank answer. From this we can tell his story in his own words as well as from the events which so reluctantly forced him from the shadows into the spotlight.

There are those who will not believe what he says or will twist his words. I have approached this book as an open and fair-minded reporter rather than a commentator or author operating with an agenda – I've read many of the dozens of such books which exist and much of the endless electronic essays and statements – from one side of the fence or another. I've talked to many people, some of whom believe the Muslim Brotherhood wants to murder all of us in our beds and others who believe they are the acceptable face of Islam. Almost all endorse the selflessness of Youssef Nada in his life's work. I have one caveat for my own impartiality.

As he insists, we are all human and as such I admit I believe him to be a good and honest man. I have let Youssef Nada explain his life and philosophy as much as possible in his own words, for they dramatically reflect his life's determination. Some of it is trenchant: Palestine and Israel cannot exist as two states; Muslim religious scholars have not used their brains since the 12th century; ruling Muslim states – Saudi Arabia, the United Arab Emirates (UAE) and others – by family inheritance is a betrayal of Islam and Muslims; Muslim women can discard the burqa and still be decent – and go into politics.

He believes those following the rigid Salafist interpretation of Islam cannot survive in the 21st century; extremists have hijacked Sharia law; and, vitally, Muslims must negotiate and avoid violence. They must live as well as die in the way of God.

Youssef Nada is a man who will never give up. He's a man who'd look the Devil in the eye until the Devil blinked – no matter what guise Satan took.

Douglas Thompson, Cairo, 2012

PROLOGUE: DESERT RATS

'It is better to light a candle than to blame the dark.'

Anon

CAIRO, NOVEMBER 1954

He stumbled off the train into the confusion of Misr Station at the end of the railway line which for more than 60 years had brought passengers from Alexandria to Cairo seeking opportunities, and comfort from family and friends.

Comfort wasn't available for 23-year-old Youssef Nada: simply staying alive would be welcome enough. The young man had some hope. The guard he'd been handcuffed to for the dry, dusty and cramped four-hour journey knew his family. Maybe there was a chance of survival. He hadn't see it in the eyes of the soldiers who'd roughly escorted him from his family home in a pleasant, green suburb of Alexandria, only a short walk from the Mediterranean Sea, or now in the behaviour of the guards preparing to take him and their other, tougher captives to military prison. The noise was overwhelming. The shouts of the army men, their tunics soaked in sweat, were full of anger and ricocheted around the station like bursts of bullets.

Youssef Nada, a tall, wiry agricultural student, had heard terrifying tales about the evil concentration camp – Abbasia Military Prison – after Gamal Abdel Nasser became the power of, and in, Egypt and outlawed the Muslim Brotherhood, which a teenage Nada had joined six years earlier. There were many such stories, each more scary than the next.

Membership of the Muslim Brotherhood (*al-Ikhwan al-Muslimeen*) – and a dictatorial crackdown after an 'assassination attempt' on President Nasser which was linked to Mahmoud Abdel Latif, also a Brotherhood member – led to Nada being escorted into the desert on the outskirts of Cairo. He stood at the open gate of the military building, home of what was to be a never-ending jailhouse horror.

'They took us directly from the train to the military compound. On the gate three words were written beneath the name of the prison. The message spelled out the treatment we could expect: Discipline, Behaviourism and Correction. They put us in lines and between every line of prisoners was a stretch of soldiers with whips. Suddenly, the leader screamed and every soldier lashed the prisoner next to him with a whip. The commander screeched again and stared at the prison sign. We were ordered to look at it. Read it. Repeat it. Read it and repeat it.

'The soldiers began their business – thrashing us, flaying the skin from our backs and legs and arms. One giant of a man, a boxer and a sporting hero, jumped at the soldiers and knocked one down. Four others turned on him. The big man was very strong and tough and fought back with all his being. About two dozen soldiers turned from us and attacked the boxer. I looked at him moments later and he was but a piece of blood and meat.'

The prisoners were told they had been 'taught a lesson' and were forced, bleeding and cut, inside the compound, consigned to the military from the control of the Ministry of Interior to the Ministry

Defence. Then the soldiers started the paperwork of confinement. They said that it all must be written down: your name, your father's name, mother's name, your address, your sister's, brother's, their husbands and wives – so they knew who they were whipping and killing.

'We had to get on our knees in the muddy water and put our hands up on a wall in front of us. From behind they cut off all our hair with clipper machines. They buzzed our heads and whipped our bodies. We were left kneeling in the blistering sun. If your hands came down, so did the guard's hand with a whip in it. It went on for hours. Bodies were taken away. We didn't know where. In the prison I saw people being tortured to death with inhuman means in ways which even the Devil could not invent.

'The excrement of the prisoners went into barrels and filled to the top. A man with his hands and legs tied was hung above a barrel by his shoulders from a crane device in the ceiling. If he didn't say what they wanted they'd dip him in it again and again and again…dip him in the human waste and whip him until he talked the words they wanted to hear. Sometimes they just found fun in routine humiliation. One prisoner was hanged with the crane and asked to swear insults at the Supreme Guide of the Brotherhood. He refused until he was dipped in the barrel and gulping the waste.

'The guards seemed to take a special pleasure in their work. The officers always put the Brothers in the hands of a group of ignorant and illiterate peasant soldiers. They used them for tasks which didn't need brains.'

One particular guard confronted Nada, berating him: 'You are a fool. You are Brotherhood. You want to come in power. Do you think the government is an easy job? We are in the government and we are here all day and night hitting you. We are in power but we have no rest. We work all the time hitting you. And you want to have a job which has no rest?'

Nada said there were special cells with the door opening out, not in. 'The prison officials closed it with bricks and cement 70 centimetres high: when you opened the door to come in you had to step up. The cell was filled with water and ice blocks, so freezing you couldn't stand up. Some prisoners gave up after five minutes. Some, if they were strong, managed to stay for one hour.'

After the cell ordeal the interrogations began. 'They tied men to crosses and whipped them and worked on them, cutting them with small knives. Pieces of flesh cut off here and there. I saw terrible cases which still make me shudder. I saw prisoners crucified and castrated and torches put to all part of their bodies.'

Nada's astute family's connections spared him from death inside the military concentration camp but his stories of what went on make you want to turn deaf, to press your hands to your ears. In the prison clinic where he was taken it was discovered there was an extra portion of food, someone had died. He was told: 'Youssef, take it to cell thirteen.' He did. It was dark.

A voice said: 'Take it next door. He needs it more than me...' He found the source of the words on the floor. He could just make out the red eyes and mouth on the man's body which was burned all over, charred beyond recognition. 'He needs it more than me...' He took the food to the next cell. There were parts of a man there. Everything between his legs had been eaten by starved attack dogs.

That barbarism became part of the way of life in Egypt after Colonel Nasser emerged as the power of the nation following the 1952 revolution. He feared losing control, losing the hearts and minds of the Egyptians, to the popular Muslim Brotherhood: his reaction was to get them out of sight, and so more than 300,000 Brotherhood followers were imprisoned in Nasser's early years.

'Before the coup d'état, Nasser said he was going to put Islam in the society and not contradict the Sharia law, but when he took power he started to hammer the Muslim Brothers. He established a dictatorship. The clash began. The Muslim Brotherhood were strong. To eradicate them he had to find a reason, and he did.'

Youssef Nada was blessed with caring parents and their ability to prevent him becoming a total victim of the new Egypt. While still in captivity he was in great pain from appendicitis, and through their connections his family had him moved to the military hospital. Still, the security, with the prison paranoia, was immense. 'Our guards included a team from the military prison, a Ministry of Defence group who were monitoring them, another from the Intelligence Service and yet one more from the Presidential Security Force. We were isolated from the main prison and there were a lot of people from military families coming to visit patients in the hospital. Sometimes you could talk with them and they'd call your family and give them news of you.

'A terribly troubled Brother arrived and I tried to calm him down. I said the doctors would care for him and he'd be able to contact his family. He was surprised: "My father and my wife and her father? Can I see them?" I said he could and asked him: "Is it better to have them one by one, or all together?"

'He looked at me and then down at himself and said: "All together, I prefer." I thought he'd want to meet with his wife on his own, to see and talk with his family individually but he looked me in the eyes and said: "I am not a man anymore." The torturers had cut him all away. He felt he had to divorce. Everything was gone – because he was opposing the dictator. I've never forgotten this case. If what happened in that prison happened to the poorest, dying animals I couldn't forget.'

Youssef Nada's life was never to be normal after that. How could it be? It was to be extraordinary. He watched – and heard – men tortured to a point where there was nothing left to confess. Nothing left of their dignity, of their soul. The boy, they say, is the father of the man. Yet, so were the antecedents of his decency through his family and experience.

While Nada was in jail, the security police imprisoned the renowned scholar Muhammad Al-Qaraxi who was aged 80 and in poor health. Al-Qaraxi had to wear high prescription spectacles to see a little and even then it was hazy. The cruel guards played games with him. They would whip him and asked if he could see who had done it. No matter what he answered they beat him again. Throughout the daily ordeals he would pray for the man wielding the whip and say: 'Allah grant you health, my son.'

Angered by this treatment, the young Youssef Nada suggested that the soldier with the whip should have his hand paralysed or broken. He balanced on that always fine line of submission and rebellion. The tormented Muhammad Al-Qaraxi gazed at him through his milk-bottle lenses and said: 'Youssef, my son, what benefit will I gain if his hand is paralysed? Have you forgotten the verses of the Koran about pardoning and forgiveness.'

Years later, as he tells the story, Youssef Nada has tears in his eyes: 'He was smiling as he said to me: "Oh Youssef, are you a fool? Are you crazy? What will I gain if his hands are clasped shut. What will I gain if his head will be broken? Maybe God will make him good and he will be converted and he will see the others and mix something good for the humanity and for Islam."

'I stared at him. Either I was mad, or he was mad. With all that was done to him, it didn't change him. He still wanted good for others. He was more pure than me. It was an unforgettable lesson.'

Incarcerated with Nada and other political prisoners were some of the country's most vicious, hardened criminals: 'The prison was sectioned, one for general prisoners and one for high security prisoners who'd been sentenced to 100 years by military courts and had nothing to lose. Once a week we were all taken into the yard to wash our clothes in a long, communal basin with many taps. There was very little time and lots of pushing and shoving.

'I was not used to it and very wary – even the soldiers were afraid of these men who had been locked away forever. Somebody kicked me with his shoe and said: "You are not fit for such a job. Leave it and I will do it for you. It's not your job." He was laughing. I was frightened. He said to me: "You don't know me, but I know you very well. You are Youssef!"

'How did he know who I was? Was he there to assassinate me? I didn't answer. He explained to me: "I worked for your father; I was fed by your father. Your mother was always sending food to us, to our families."

'He protected and helped me. He'd remembered the kindness of my parents when he saw me – just like the soldier handcuffed to me on the train. My mother had sent food to him too and he asked me for my father's phone number and alerted my family to where I was. We have a proverb: "Make the good, and throw it in the sea/One day it will come to you."'

THE WORLD VIEW: NEWS REPORTS

NEW YORK TIMES

CAIRO, 3 JANUARY 2012
'With the Muslim Brotherhood pulling within reach of an outright majority in Egypt's new Parliament, the Obama administration has begun to reverse decades of mistrust and hostility as it seeks to forge closer ties with an organisation once viewed as irreconcilably opposed to United States interests.

'The administration's overtures – including high-level meetings in recent weeks – constitute a historic shift in a foreign policy held by successive American administrations that steadfastly supported the autocratic government of President Hosni Mubarak in part out of concern for the Brotherhood's Islamist ideology and historic ties to militants.

'The shift is, on one level, an acknowledgment of the new political reality here, and indeed around the region, as Islamist groups come to power. Having won nearly half the seats contested in the first two rounds of the country's legislative elections, the Brotherhood on Tuesday entered the third and final round with a chance to extend its lead to a clear majority as the vote moved into districts long considered strongholds.

'The reversal also reflects the administration's growing acceptance of the Brotherhood's repeated assurances that its lawmakers want to build a modern democracy that will respect individual freedoms, free markets and international commitments, including Egypt's treaty with Israel.'

THE EGYPTIAN INDEPENDENT

CAIRO, WEDNESDAY 18 JANUARY 2012

'In a meeting with Muslim Brotherhood Supreme Guide Mohamed Badie, US Ambassador to Egypt Anne Patterson congratulated the Brotherhood-affiliated Freedom and Justice Party for winning a majority of seats in the People's Assembly, the lower house of parliament, according to a statement released by the Brotherhood. It said she assured Badie that the US looks forward to cooperating with the government the Egyptian people have selected. Badie said that consecutive US administrations have judged nations based on the actions of dictators, and that the US has propped up some dictators, causing its popularity to decrease among citizens of nations under dictatorial rule. He urged the US to take action to restore its credibility, especially with regard to the Israeli–Palestinian conflict. Patterson admitted that the US has made "some mistakes" and called for learning from them so they would not be repeated in the future.'

MAP OF EGYPT

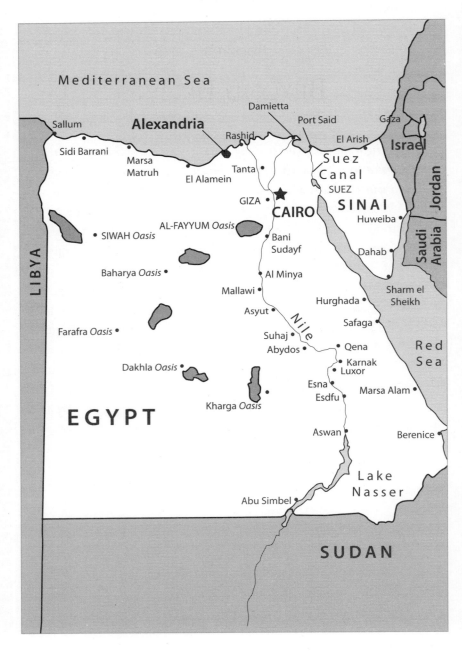

BOOK ONE

BEYOND BELIEF

'If I am right the Germans will say I was a German and the French will say I was a Jew; if I am wrong the Germans will say I was a Jew and the French will say I was a German'.

Albert Einstein, 1922

CHAPTER ONE

BIRTH OF
A BROTHER

'I returned, and saw under the sun, that the race is not to the swift, nor the battle to the strong, neither yet bread to the wise, nor yet riches to men of understanding, nor yet favour to men of skill; but fame and chance happeneth to them all.'

Ecclesiastes, 9:11

ALEXANDRIA 1948

Like most trouble, it began in a small way with two youngsters arguing with each other and then their friends taking sides. The voices became raised and angry. Quickly, the fists and the fighting began as 17-year-old Youssef Nada emerged at the corner of the street near his family home.

Knives appeared and flashed in the sun and the fighting became deadly. How could he help? He wanted to, but was fearful as the rival factions inflamed the ferocious actions. The battle closed in on him but he couldn't move; he was rooted to the spot by that sometimes dangerous desire, curiosity. Now, more than 40 people from neighbourhood families were involved.

1

The teenager thought the police would arrive at any moment. There was no sign, no sound of sirens. The battle went on until a group of young people ran into the middle of the antagonists. They pulled them apart, hugged some, deflected raised fists, and slowly, slowly, with pacifying words and actions, brought calm to the warring crowd. Nada was mesmerised. To him, it was some sort of miracle. One moment this crowd were trying to kill each other and now they were talking.

The mediators were from the Muslim Brotherhood. Looking back on that day, Nada recalls: 'They started to talk, saying that they were neighbours, they were families, and about morals and mixing all these things through religion with some phrases from the Koran, from the words of the prophets, and things calmed down. The quarrelling people were asked what would happen to their children if they were killed: "Who will support your family without you?" They said that most times the "fire", the trouble, started with a spark. This was repeated several times in front of me. The trick was to avoid the spark – or contend with the fire.

'I knew of the Brotherhood through their centre being near our house, and on religious occasions they had activities. But we were of a different life. The general atmosphere of all the Egyptians was that religion should be respected. That day we heard the invitation for prayers that happens in every mosque, and you hear it five times. All the people started to make lines and the Imam came in front of us and started to pray. He chose the phrases of brotherhood and mercy, and good behaviour with others, and avoiding fighting between Muslims.

'When Muslims fight each other you must intervene and support the one who has the rights. It is about fairness, always about justice. The angry crowd who'd been fighting picked up what he was saying, the lesson he was delivering. He asked everyone who loved his religion and Allah to apologise to him and embrace his opponent. They did this. They had tea together and everyone was happy.

'For me, it was as a hymn. I'd witnessed a working philosophy and I wondered: "Who are those people?" That was the start. I went to the centre where two or three Brothers talked to me. They said everyone was welcome and on Tuesday one of their leaders, Farid Abdul Khalek from Cairo, would speak. I went along, and he was very intelligent and emotional.

'One of their respected members asked me to help, as the father of one my classmates, Mahmoud, had been paralysed in an accident. The mother had been working to support the family but she had also become ill and there was no income. He asked me to take money to the family but not to say where it had come from. I got a practical lesson in how to assist silently without hurting a person's pride. My life in the Muslim Brotherhood began as easily as that. I talked to my family about it, but they never encouraged me, and they never discouraged me.'

Nada's parents, Mustafa Ali Nada and Nemat Abu Saud, were well regarded in their community and raised a large family. Youssef was born the fourth of eleven children in Alexandria on 17 May 1931. Mustafa Ali Nada owned a farm and a dairy products factory, and his son would help there. His father provided, but his mother, who was to die tragically young, led the family's attitude and thinking: it was always about doing the right thing. She had to truly trust her judgment when Nasser's security men used her husband and a younger student son, Sobhi, to trap Youssef, who was a thinker.

Youssef Nada's schooldays began at the Al-Ramliah Elementary School and he stayed in that system through to high school. His hobby was to attend the city's law courts. He was fascinated by the lawyers and their arguments – as one would say one thing and the other would counter it, and the judge would quiz them on points of law. 'It taught me how to negotiate, how to bring new ideas to the table,' he said. 'Also, to understand what another person was getting at before they offered their conclusion. I was just twelve when I started going to court and I kept going while my friends would play football or go to the cinema after any demonstration against the British occupation. My interest was in the legal world.

'There were two courts: one for the Egyptians and one for the foreigners. During the occupation the British didn't accept that one of their nationals would go to an Egyptian court if he broke the law. I visited the Egyptian court – the other was the court of the enemies! There was a double standard.

'When I try to analyse myself now, to turn the film back, I wonder how it started. Did it come from the school, or from the family? I believe it came from seeing injustice in the courts.'

Yet, Nada and his siblings did have some freedom in their lives: 'We had freedom in the way we were brought up. We got advice to do one thing and not another. We were told someone was good because they acted in a certain way. My father was very busy and my mother taught us the way to lead our lives.

'My father had a big dairy farm and a team of about fifty workers to process our milk and collect the milk from other farms. As children we went with the workers to faraway farms and saw how they milked the cows and the buffalos. We were with these men all day and knew how they were thinking and behaving. It gave me an understanding of how other people lived and ate and thought. I was not brought up in a vacuum.' It gave the young Youssef Nada a bond with his fellow men.

The Muslim Brotherhood began in Egypt in 1928 as a social and cultural movement; it was founded by schoolteacher Hassan Al-Banna along with half-a-dozen employees of the Suez Canal Company. The intention was based on altruistic Islamic principles, but instantly the organisation was branded as sinister.

The Brothers were targets for imprisonment, torture and death. This intimidation made them, by necessity, secretive while they quietly grew in number and influence. When Youssef Nada joined the Muslim Brotherhood they existed in a complex environment in which the Cold War was getting icier by the day.

During their residency, the occupying British were blinkered by events, focused on the communist threat to the Middle East and to the control of the Suez Canal. King Farouk was getting fatter, and in his oversized shadow the Wafd Party was the recognised political power in the country. American and Russian interests were served by the CIA and the KGB, employing their black arts to much effect, whispering cryptic contagion that the king was totally in control of the imperial, exploitative British. It was all very uneasy and myopic.

The incorrigibly political Gamal Abdel Nasser served as an infantry commander when King Farouk sent his troops into Palestine, ending in what Nasser judged a humiliating treaty. In October 1948 he made contact with the Muslim Brotherhood with a view to forming an allegiance with them. Compatibility was never assured, as, indeed, it wasn't with the British. The Brotherhood were at odds with the ruling government Wafd party, who didn't want the Brotherhood's popularity to increase. Neither, of course, did the British, the colonial power which held the reins of the Wafd.

Youssef Nada had the attitude and strong views of a young and confident man, speaking out without inviting favour. It stood him well at university where he went to study agriculture, about a 30-minute bus ride along the long-gone landscaped streets from his home. He was a member of the Students' Union and once, during a meeting with the Dean, Shafiq Alkeshen, he made a point, strongly opposing the Dean's view.

The Dean gave a rude reply and his student responded: 'Don't be angry doctor. I have great respect for you. You are my teacher. Why are you angry with me? I'll resign.' Nada said that he's never forgotten the Dean's answer: 'You would leave me with only those who say "Yes sir". You are needed here.' The other students didn't question the Dean and obeyed him without saying what *they* believed and thought. 'I felt I was respected,' said Nada, 'because I offered my opinion – even though he didn't agree with it.'

When he was 20, Nada was conscripted into action. 'It was 1951 and Egypt was asking for the withdrawal of the British military. There were demonstrations and violent clashes between the police and the British army. The trouble was ugly and flared up in all the universities. On the campuses they started Egyptian army training camps for the students. I did full military training in the use of weapons at Alexandria University and most of us being taught were Muslim Brothers.

'When the militia heard that the Jews were arriving from everywhere in the world to settle in Palestine, which was the country of Muslims and Arabs, all those in the area mobilised on the side of the Palestinians. The Muslim Brotherhood joined the insurgents against the invasion. All the people's hearts were with the Palestinians, even members of the Egyptian government. They were against the settlement but weren't prepared to take the road of trouble; they wanted peace. They wanted to live calmly. They didn't want problems with the British but their hearts and minds were with the Palestinians.'

Strong post-war world diplomacy was needed, but instead arrangements under the guise of political necessity brought the rule of arrogant self-interest. With long spoons, Washington and Moscow stirred the Egyptian melting pot into 1951 and through into 1952. Nasser was plotting and had joined the Free Officers Movement aimed at restoring the dignity of Egypt. This organisation was headed by a more senior officer, Mahmoud Labib, who was a member of the Muslim Brotherhood. When Labib died, Nasser swiftly took his place.

There was a fearsome reprisal incident in January 1952 when British forces guarding the Suez Canal attacked a police headquarters in Ismailia, injuring more than 100 and killing 49 Egyptian officers, provoking riots. Demonstrations, encouraged by the Free Officers and several thousand strong, marched through Cairo, putting in danger any building or business or person linked to the British. It resulted in 80 deaths, including nine British nationals. Fires burned, King Farouk fumed, and politicians failed to stop that winter of deadly discontent.

The 'Cairo Fires' of world headlines raged on metaphorically until the July 1952 military coup led by General Muhammad Naguib – soon to be overtaken in power and position by Nasser. It was at this time that the now military-trained Youssef Nada was called up. 'Nasser promised the Brotherhood that he would personally not allow anything to be done against the religion, against Islam. Because of that he had all our support.

'We had been pre-warned the coup d'état was happening. We were told to protect the foreign embassies, the banks, and the Government buildings, as they were sabotage targets. I got a tough one: they appointed me to help guard the British Consulate in Alexandria – a prime target. It was only months since Cairo was burned up, so there was great concern. The Brotherhood were afraid it could happen anywhere in Egypt, with property ruined and people killed.

'The Brothers in the jails were released following the coup. They were in the streets, involved in the preparation for a new beginning. Our voice was very loud at this time and the support of the people was enthusiastic. Gamal Abdul Nasser and his crew had to keep them happy – he was a Brother and had lived among a group of the Muslim Brotherhood, and they considered him very faithful. But he turned on them.

'He wanted to be the only power in the country. The Brotherhood leaders were rigid when they negotiated with him. They were sincere and they believed sincerity is the only factor. In politics, sincerity is not the only factor. The message was one of strong nationalism which was grabbing the emotions of the people: the British had to go! We must evict them, we must be free! We must not be occupied by the British forever. Egypt was everything. The British must go! That was the mood and it was ferocious.

'After the coup d'état the negotiations between Nasser and the British began. A man called Evans, who was doing the talking with Nasser, asked to meet the Brotherhood, but they didn't want to make any secret moves, to deal behind the new government's back. So they told Nasser that Evans wanted to meet them.' Nasser advised the Brotherhood to go ahead on the grounds that 'the British will know the total position with us, and that will support our position in the negotiations.

'The Muslim Brotherhood met Evans, but later when Nasser betrayed them, he said the Brothers were spying and in contact with British secret agents. He said the Muslim Brotherhood were nothing but traitors. It was staggering to be accused of working with the British – Egyptians had suffered so much under the occupation.'

Youssef Nada had personal experience of the suffering when his elder sister was getting married:' The bridegroom supplies the house, and the bride's family is responsible for furnishing it. My mother was everywhere, buzzing about, and bought everything for the marital home and supervised it being loaded onto delivery lorries.

'Two British military trucks hit the lorries, and the furniture broke free spilling on to the street. The drivers were drunk but nobody could touch them. The authorities protected them, not only from our family but from the people in the street who saw what happened and were very angry. The British Military Police came and took the drivers away in cars. There was no justice in that.

'The British occupation was hard for our people – we all believed we should be free; we had to fight for our freedom, fight the occupation by weapons. I cannot deny it. Anyone who battles against the occupier of his country is a hero. When de Gaulle fought the Nazis he was a hero. But they didn't want to consider me a hero when I fought the occupation of my country. Every loyal citizen in the world must defend his country when it is occupied, or you don't deserve to be a citizen of it. I would be a traitor if I didn't protect my country.'

Yet, with his membership of the Muslim Brotherhood, Youssef Nada had a more immediate enemy in the revolutionary Colonel Gamal Nasser, who very much wanted to be his own man. At that time America was keen to keep Nasser on its side against the Soviets in what became known as the 'Game of Nations'. Then there was one of those intriguing happenstances of history when in 1910 Teddy Roosevelt, shortly after declining to run for another term as President of the United States, spoke at what would become Cairo University. Roosevelt angered Egyptian nationalists by backing the British occupation and arguing that Egyptians weren't prepared for independence or, for that matter, democracy.

More than 40 years later America – and another Roosevelt – was still meddling in Egyptian politics. Then, when President Eisenhower and America were trying to persuade Nasser to be 'their man', Kermit 'Kim' Roosevelt Jr, a senior CIA official and President Roosevelt's grandson, arranged for US$3million in cash stacked in two suitcases for a clandestine delivery to Nasser. (Some reports put the cash at four times that, but in 2011 CIA officials with access to files from the time insisted it was 'only three million dollars'.) Nasser didn't stash the money but put it to work creating the free-standing concrete Cairo Tower on Gezira Island on the Nile. The structure, taller than the pyramids, near to the downtown district and across from the US Embassy, remains a city landmark. Nasser intended the Cairo Tower as an elaborate display of disdain to the American diplomatic mission, Kim Roosevelt and the other CIA spooks. His aides knew it – politely – as 'Roosevelt's folly'.

A man big in personality and stature, Nasser wanted to be the boss and have 'no partners' in his administration. The Muslim Brotherhood were influential – and irritating. He couldn't get on with his own policies and plans without considering those of the Brotherhood. He used Egypt's recent history, and the tormented and turbulent times, as his weapon of choice to silence the Brothers. In November 1948 the Egyptian Prime Minister, Mahmoud Fahmy Nokrashy Pasha, began a clampdown on the Muslim Brotherhood whom he accused of political violence, of bombing and attempted assassinations. After police investigations, it was announced that sufficient explosives to blow up half of Cairo had been discovered, along with plans for bombing foreign and Egyptian institutions in the city and Alexandria on the coast. The authorities said that in one Jeep alone they found 'large amounts of explosive materials, fuses, dozens of various kinds of mines, time-bomb detonators, a machine gun, a large number of revolvers and tommy guns, daggers, ammunition, a mask, leaflets, and secret instructions and documents referring to previous explosions as well as others in preparation'.

The Prime Minister's office said the houses raided and the Jeep belonged to Muslim Brotherhood members. The Brotherhood were also accused of being responsible for an explosion outside the house of Mustapha el-Nahhas (the popular president of the Wafd); the attempted bombing of the Sudan Agency; the bombings of department stores of Ades, Ben Zion, Gettegno, the Delta Land Company and the Société Orientale de Publicité; and for machine gun attacks on politicians.

The Brotherhood issued denials, arguing that there had been 'a frame-up'. In turn, two weeks later, Premier Nokrashy Pasha, in his role as Military Governor of Egypt (and with the strong encouragement of British advisers) ordered the dissolution of the Muslim Brotherhood. They were to be no more.

The Government – officially for the first time – accused the Brothers of 'aiming at seizing power and overthrowing established order in the country'. The Prime Minister announced a 'state of emergency throughout Egypt', and with that the Brotherhood headquarters in Cairo was taken over by police. The government said the Brothers were targeting everyone from students to city officials with their propaganda. Members were forbidden to continue any form of activity, to hold elections, or establish other similar organisations.

Abdel Rahman Ammar Bey, Under Secretary of State for Security in the Ministry of Interior, said the Brotherhood had been founded as a religious and social organisation without political purpose. But when they won huge popularity the leaders 'went beyond legitimate political purposes to other aims prohibited by the Constitution and the country's laws, and aimed at changing the basic system of society by force and terrorism'. As if to prove that correct, Nokrashy Pasha was assassinated 20 days after the pronouncement and after he had banned the Brotherhood from existing.

The assassination took place on the morning of 28 December 1948 when a young man in the uniform of a police first lieutenant sat in the lobby of Cairo's Ministry of Interior as the prime minister walked toward the elevators. The uniformed man got up and saluted. His arm dropped and he pulled a high-powered revolver from his trouser pocket and fired six bullets. Five rounds hit Mahmoud Fahmy El Nokrashy Pasha, killing him. The assassin then pointed the revolver at his own head but was overpowered by guards. He was identified as 21-year-old veterinary student Abdel Meguid Ahmed Hassan, a member of the Brotherhood. Government minister Ibrahim Dessouki Abaza Pasha said Hassan had claimed he murdered the Prime Minister 'because he caused Egypt to lose the Sudan, surrendered Palestine to the Jews, and dissolved the Muslim Brotherhood, which had been the only organisation reviving Islam in the last twenty years'.

Immediately Hassan Albana, the head and founder of the Muslim Brotherhood, condemned the assassination, declaring that terror was not an acceptable way in Islam. Even so, several thousand arrests were made following the killing and several internment camps were opened to imprison Brotherhood members. Many were sent to Abu Za'abal, Fayoum, the Citadel, and Kharga and Hykstep which were concentration camps in all but name. The government said that an inner circle of the Brotherhood had recognised Hassan el Banna as Caliph, which was as good as naming him political chief of the Islamic world. This group were accused as conspirators who carried out acts of terror by lottery. Youssef Nada joined the Brotherhood leaders in condemning the charges as inventions.

The tit-for-tat actions and the vendetta bloodshed continued. On 12 February 1949, the Brotherhood leader Hassan Al-Banna was murdered – shot five times as he left the Jamiyyah al-Shubban al-Muslimeen headquarters in Cairo. He was there to talk with the government's Zaki Ali Basha but Ali Basha did not turn up for their meeting.

Hassan Al-Banna was waiting for a taxi outside the offices when gunfire from a group of youths in a car blasted him and his brother-in-law Abdul Kerim Mohammed, who was wounded in the arms and legs. The Muslim Brotherhood did not end because of the death of their founder – the one-time school teacher in Ismailia on the Suez Canal, and a man who cited the Koran as support for all his arguments. Rather, although shaken by events, the Brotherhood all but began again. They entered the 1950s with a readjustment of the organisation in a new world: the world of military rule.

CHAPTER TWO

JAILHOUSE SCHOLARS

'He who binds to himself joy
Does the winged life destroy;
But he who kisses the joy as it flies
Lives in eternity's sun rise.'
William Blake, 1792

G unfire changed history and the life of Youssef Nada. Eight bullets from a pistol on 26 October 1954 did not end the life and rule of Gamal Abdel Nasser but it conveniently provided him with the ammunition to turn on his rivals for popularity.

Nasser was delivering a speech in Alexandria's Manshieh Square, marking the agreement for a British evacuation from Egypt, when the shots were fired. He was not hit but there were screams and shouts, a cacophony of fearful wailing, which drowned out anyone trying to make statements.

Nasser stole the moment and appealed for calm: *'If Abdel Nasser dies then every one of you is Abdel Nasser. Each of you is Gamal Abdel Nasser. Gamal Abdel Nasser is of you and from you and he is willing to sacrifice his life for the nation.'*

He brought his hands up by his head, triumphantly waving them backwards and forward in an empowering *Baladi* movement. It was a vote winner, if votes had mattered: a huge moment in Egyptian history.

But it was a set-up. Hassan al-Tuhami, a CIA contact for many years and Chief of Intelligence during Nasser's rule, revealed (when he was Egypt's Deputy Prime Minister under Anwar Sadat), that it 'was all an act'. This was something that had been argued from the moment of the 'assassination attempt' by Mohamed Abdel Latif which began the nation's biggest political repression and reign of terror − officially endorsed terror. Latif was branded a Brotherhood assassin, and when he returned to Cairo, the confident and ebullient Nasser had his passport for repression.

Youssef Nada isn't convinced by the Brotherhood's denials over the violence of the late 1940s, but he has no doubts the Alexandria incident was a pre-meditated ploy to compromise the Brotherhood. 'Nasser had promised the Brothers much, but when he came to power he started to attack and exclude them,' said Nada. 'He said he could press a button and all Egyptians did what he wanted − except the Brotherhood. He told his people: "I have to kick the Brotherhood out of my way."

'He played on the desperate incidents of the past, and from them developed the plan to crush the Brotherhood by accusing them of trying to kill him. When there was any trouble the Brothers were accused of using violence to pursue their politics.

'Yes, there was violence in the 1940s and I don't fully accept the Brothers' explanation for the death of Prime Minister Mahmoud Fahmy El Nokrashy Pasha and of a judge. The Brothers said that those who did it were not Brothers and what they did was against Islam. Even Hassan Al-Banna said they were not Brothers as he did not know that they were Brothers. He was an honest man and none of the Brothers informed him that they were members. It is not expected from a leader of such huge organisation to know all the members but he could not believe that any member would defy his teaching. But indeed they had been members. The prime minster received instruction from the

British Occupation to disband the Brothers and this maverick group from the Brotherhood killed him. The judge handed out harsh sentences to some Brothers for crimes they didn't commit; the judgment was not correct and politically dictated, but that doesn't mean you go and kill him.

'There were other stories: one that the Brothers arranged groups against the British during the British occupation. Another that in Palestine in 1947 – when the Zionists movement started to prepare for the declaration of Israel – that groups from a lot of Muslim countries went to assist the Palestinians to defend their homes. It is true the Brotherhood sent groups to help the Palestinians. But that is it – there are no other stories. If you go to their history which is written by their opponents you will find violence and more violence. It was all contrived.

'There has not been violence by the Muslim Brotherhood since that time in 1948. Rulers have said that agitators like the people of Osama Bin Laden had come out of the Brothers, that they were in the Brotherhood and they left to form other factions. It was individuals who did it; not all the group did it; not all the society did it; just one or two among hundreds of thousands. You cannot condemn the countless others for the mistakes of a few.

'The Brotherhood was coming of age. It started to appear in the universities and among more educated people. It had grown into this society, like a person growing: during the time of adolescence, the teenaged years, you can expect mistakes from the child. The Brotherhood was strong, and to get them off his back Nasser had to offer a reason. He had to show them as violent, as killers, as his potential assassins. Hassan al-Tuhami orchestrated it for him. After Nasser died, Hassan al-Tuhami admitted the plot to "kill Nasser in Alexandria" was fabricated by him with Nasser's consent.

'But it was in too many people's interests to accept this explanation. They wanted the Brotherhood to stay branded as terrorists – even when the testimony came from the man who had arranged it, and facts supported him. It was good propaganda – there were about 100,000 people there. The police said that they had caught one of the Brothers among the crowd and he was the shooter. In prison they hanged him by his legs with his head down and whipped him to get him to confess and name those who had supposedly told him what to do. 'But the pistol didn't have the range to hit never mind kill Nasser. They said the gunman was well trained and that was why he was chosen. To use a pistol with a range of about 400 metres doesn't sound like an expert marksman. They can torture people to say anything.'

Nasser began to imprison the Brothers wherever they could be found, and Youssef Nada was one of them – one of many thousands. Nasser showed no humanity with the Brotherhood or any other perceived foes or political threats. The 26 October events were branded a 'crime against the revolution'. Mamdouh Muhammad Salem, a future Egyptian prime minister, was in charge of security in Alexandria and enthusiastically pursued his orders.

A 'People's Court' was established and the guillotine-minded Gamal Salem, one of Nasser's 'Iron Guard', appointed as president. Anwar El Sadat and Husain El Shafie were the other two judges. Gamal Salem had eighteenth-century revolutionary zeal, saying: 'A head like Farouk's only interests me when it has fallen.'

King Farouk retained his head, yet several Brotherhood members were given the death sentence. Seven of them were hanged. The group's Supreme Guide, Hassan Hodeibi and the thinker Sayyid Qutub, had their lives spared. Countless others were charged with a vast range of conspiracies. Many of them were sent to military prisons or concentration camps without being charged or convicted of any crime and remained there until three years after Nasser's death. (Four of them became Supreme Guides of the Muslim Brotherhood one after the other starting from 1972. The last was Mahdi Akef who in 2011 insisted that the organisation must elect someone from the younger generation. Mohammed Badie was chosen.)

It took them time to capture Youssef Nada. He was at home in

Alexandria when a friend who had been arrested called and asked him to tell the boy's parents of his plight. He hung up the phone. 'I thought how stupid he was to call me from the police station for now they will know me and where I am,' said Nada. 'After about half-an-hour the doorbell rang. I was in the hall near the entrance. One of the servants went to open the door and I stopped her. My mother went instead. There was an officer with three guards. My mother said I wasn't there.

'The officer knew my mother and out of respect called her "Aunt". He said: "Aunt, we need Youssef to sign a declaration that he will not contact the Brotherhood anymore. Where can I find him, with his father?" My mother just answered "Maybe".

'They went but left six guards at the house. I had to go. I went up over the roof to our neighbour's building and I escaped. When my father and brother Sobhi returned at 10pm they were arrested and taken away. My mother was distraught but still she was able to deal with the situation. She called one of her cousins, a high ranking police officer. She asked about the arrests of my father and brother and he told her: "If Youssef surrenders, we will release them."

'It was a dreadful thing for my mother, a horror of a choice: give up a son for a husband and son? What could she do? When I called her at 2am she told me all that had happened. I said I would give myself up – but if I surrendered they might keep all three of us. She asked her relative and he assured her that wouldn't happen.

'There was no choice for me. I couldn't leave my father to be arrested in my name. I asked my mother to arrange my surrender. I knew that if I was picked up on the streets I'd be tortured. Her cousin said he would meet me and personally take me to the prison. When that was done they released my father and brother immediately and I was not tortured when they arrested me. But they didn't tell my family where I was going.

'Then, there was to be another bounty from my mother the miracle worker! The guard who was handcuffed to me contacted my father. When the train stopped at Seedi Gaber station I found my father looking in every window of the train. My mother had once given the guard food and been kind to him when he was on duty near our home; he remembered that and phoned my father to say I was being taken to military prison.'

Nada entered the jail with an inflamed appendix. Again his mother and her relatives used every influence and managed to get him moved to the prison clinic – a series of 13 cells on each side of a corridor. 'It was meagre,' Nada recalled. 'There was an office for a doctor and a nurse, a bathroom and a toilet. I had been crushed in a cell with others at the prison but when they locked the door on me in the clinic I was alone. I started to pray and recite what I remembered from the Koran. There was nothing I could do but wait for another miracle.

'They gave me nothing to eat but in the morning they opened the cell for me to go to the toilet; the guards took me. One by one the cell doors were opened for prisoners to go with the guards. I said to one man: "You have Koran?"

'"Yes."

'"Can you give me some pages from it? I don't have anything to read."

'"I cannot tear the Koran."

'You cannot believe what I felt when he said that to me. The stupidity that some pages cannot be taken from the Koran to be read. I was sick and weak and I fell to the floor. They bundled me back to my cell. The next time the door opened they threw food ate me and slammed the door.

'When I went to the toilet in the evening I discovered a prisoner they said had tried to kill Nasser. He was cut, his arms were dangling down, one hand broken, one arm paralysed. He was accused of being the head of the Brotherhood's "secret apparatus" and was called Youssef Talat. I said: "God help you brother Youssef."

'He looked at me: "I am not Youssef, I am Salah Shadi."

'I knew him as a high-ranking police officer and close personal friend to Nasser. He was one of the Muslim Brothers. He had instructed the Brothers everywhere on 23 July, the day of the coup, to go and protect the banks and the embassies and the main buildings and the courts. That was when I went to defend the British Consulate. The instructions came from Salah Shadi. Despite his connections to Nasser, when Nasser went after the Brothers he was imprisoned and tortured and spent 20 years moving from prison to prison until Nasser died and Sadat released him 1972. I remind you that Sadat was one of the three judges who sentenced seven of the brother to death and they were executed. Although Salah Shadi was also sentenced by the same judges to death but they were kind!!! And converted the sentence to life imprisonment.

'From the beginning, Nasser promised the Brothers that he would completely change the law and the constitution and make a good and moral society. But he went to war with the Brothers and Salah Shadi suffered. Nasser showed him no mercy. He was tortured; they did despicable things to him. He was bent over at 90 degrees and they filled him with air, blown up with pumps. It ruined his spine and he could never stand straight; he remained in prison for twenty years until Sadat released him. Sadat was one of three judges who sentenced him to death and then reduced it to life time imprisonment.'

Nada returned to his cell in a miserable condition. As well as the mental turmoil over what he'd just seen, there was the constant pain of his grumbling appendix. By proxy, the goodness of his mother, Nemat Abu Saud, helped again. She was the glue which kept all strands of the family connected, especially during the ongoing upheaval in society.

She counselled the dying, attended the ill and those relatives who were simply confused and alone. One distant relation was the brutal Anwar Ahmed who had a justifiably cruel reputation in the Nasser regime as the head of the military police. Nemat didn't care about that when it came to her son's well being – and Anwar Ahmed was a relative.

Nemat told him that her son needed urgent surgery and he ordered treatment. Youssef Nada only discovered his mother's intervention when his cell door swung open and a nurse came in and questioned him about his illness and the whereabouts of his family. 'This quiz went on like a game of ping pong and the corruption charade began,' Nada recalled.

Dr Mohamed Shafik Safwat visited his prospective patient but did nothing. A week went on and after complaining that he was still in pain, the doctor visited Nada again. His 'prescription' was for the crippled-up young man to carry a 50kg weight and run in the sun for two hours – every day.

An hour later the nurse appeared again with a message: if Nada's family could be contacted and 'an arrangement made' then treatment would be forthcoming. The nurse wanted something in writing but Youssef Nada was wise to that, knowing such evidence could result in years in jail. Still, the deal was done. At 2am he heard his name over a loudspeaker: 'Youssef! Moustafa! Nada!' He banged an answer on his cell door. When it opened a smiling Dr Mohamed Shafik Safwat, the nurse, and a supervising prison officer were there.

The acting began with the doctor's beside manner: 'Why is your face pale. What is wrong with you? Are you sick?' The doctor went through a cursory examination and announced that his new patient should be swiftly treated and he was soon at the military hospital outside the prison in Cairo.

'When I opened my eyes I found four other Brothers in beds next me also having had treatment,' said Nada. 'It was a new atmosphere with different levels of guards. It was twenty-four hours after my surgery and I was weak and couldn't speak when the military commander Anwar Ahmed appeared with an entourage. He told Dr Safwat: "See how many days he will be here, because after that we are going to send him back." He left. The doctor was used to taking bribes to treat prisoners.

'He had his own protector – his brother Ali Shafik Safwat was the manager of the office of Major Abdel Hakim Amer who was an important figure in the coup d'état and became Egypt's Chief of Staff and Minister of Defence. It was a chain of corrupted people. [Major Abdel Hakim Amer was poisoned by Nasser and Sadat after his failure in the Six Day War.] Anwar Ahmed came to satisfy himself that I had been operated on – and, more importantly, that his family obligation to my mother was completed.'

Nada stayed in the hospital for three months. Each month he had to pay the doctor 50 Egyptian pounds which at the time was the salary of Deputy Government Minister. Every patient had to pay the same. It was a goldmine.

'There were riches for me too,' said Nada. 'I met the man who helped shape my personality. After my surgery I was exhausted and even when I woke I couldn't move; I was still under the anaesthetic. I opened my eyes to find a lady, a stranger, sitting by a bed near mine where another patient was sleeping. She said to me words in Arabic which mean: "Thank God that you are good. What is your name?" I told her who I was and that I was from Alexandria and a student at the university. She asked which faculty and I told her agriculture and she exclaimed: "You know Shafiq Alkeshen?"

'"That was the Dean of my college.

'"I'm his wife. This is my brother in the other bed. Give me the telephone number of your family? My brother is Haroon Almujadidi"

'She was Tahra Almujadidi. Her name reflected her soul and mind: Tahra in Arabic means virtue and moral excellence and she was all of that. The situation was very political. The Dean of the Faculty had been chosen by Nasser to be the Deputy Head of Parliament which was headed by Anwar Sadat. He wanted Dr Shafiq Alkeshen to be a power buffer against Sadat. He played them as favourites against each other. Because of his political position, his wife was able to send her brother, who was a Muslim Brotherhood member, to the hospital to remove his gall bladder.

'She had a very good heart. Her younger brother, Haroon Almujadidi, was in a worse condition than me and couldn't speak but in time we became friends. He was about fifteen years older than me and he treated me as his son and I started to learn from him. Haroon and Tahra were the children of Sadik Almujadidi who was the Afghani Ambassador in Egypt during the time of the King Farouk. He was very friendly with the palace and held high religious authority in the Muslim world.

'He was a close friend of Sheik Almaraghi who held the title of Sheik Al Azha as the leader of Al Azhar, which is the oldest Sunni theology, established more than 1,000 years ago. Haroon was Chargé d'Affaires, a senior ambassador at the Afghan Embassy, and was a member of the Muslim Brotherhood.

'While King Farouk was still in power he was one of the group which kept secret contact between the Brotherhood and Nasser and the other military officers. Before the coup, Nasser stole weapons from an army depot and told Haroon Almujadidi that he needed his car with diplomatic plates without telling him why. Because they were good friends and Haroon had good heart he gave Nasser the car. It was a Jeep and they made several trips to transport the weapons and explosives.

'Another Brother was a famous lawyer called Hassan Al-Ishmawi and Nasser and he and Haroon worked with others who were very deep in the Brotherhood, high up in the system. Nasser asked Hassan Al-Ishmawi to use his farm to hide the weapons to be used against the British occupation, and with three other army officers they built an underground store for them. Hassan Al-Ishmawi trusted them not to make anything "bad" from it for him.

'And then came the burning of Cairo. Who did it? Still, today, no one knows. And then curfew, and the coup. No one investigated but the fire led to the military being in charge and then unknown officers challenged the king and the government – and then came Nasser's coup. The new rulers brought some outrageous cases of corruption and presented them to the courts. Yet no one asked who burned Cairo. They kept silent. How can history interpret it? Everything was a means to an end: needs must.

'When Nasser ordered the crushing of the Brotherhood he told his security to go to the farm of his friend Hassan Al Ishmawi and find the guns he himself had helped place there. Nasser then accused the Brotherhood of keeping weapons to topple his regime.

'In the Middle East nothing is ever as it seems: promises and pledges are made in private, contracts are agreed, but they are in secret so no one ever knows what motivates men or the events which they created to pursue or break the promises or pledges. It is the mystery and the enigma of the Middle East.

'In hospital we were all paying our fifty pounds each. The doctor had a tame patient, a "collections officer", but he was sent back to prison. The doctor tried to enlist me to collect from the Brothers. That way I could stay in hospital but I told him: "Excuse me doctor. I am responsible for myself, but I cannot do it."

'The next day I was sent back to military prison. Bribery! I am ready to pay myself to save my life, but assisting bribery is a big sin. It's wrong. The price was very high for me in prison. I did not like being part of the bribery. After that, when I recognised any corrupt person, I had to cut them from my life immediately.

'If I do recognise something or someone as being corrupt, then I have to find another way to do my business. If there is no one, I have to drop the business rather than deal with anyone corrupt. It would be wrong for my life because it would harm my honour and my character, which is coming from my religion. You take the rights of the others when you bribe.

'Nasser tried to bribe Sayyid Qutb who was in prison with me after the Alexandria shooting. Before the coup d'état, Nasser had secretly created the Free Officers unit and courted Sayyid Qutb. At the same time, he was dealing covertly with the Brotherhood.

'Sayyid Qutb didn't suspect Nasser's plot and met him for many hours a day to discuss the form the Egyptian government would take after King Farouk was gone. When he understood what Nasser was up to and realised that Nasser was setting him up, he walked away. Nasser pleaded with him and tried all manner of bribery, every job in the country – except the throne, the job of king. Sayyid Qutb rejected it all. He was his own man. Later, others tried to use him, just as Nasser had, to give their enterprises some authority. Osama Bin Laden and others adopted him as their inspiration. The Americans called him "the father of terror".

'Nasser was clever to try to recruit Sayyid Qutb because he was a knowledgeable man. I witnessed it when he joined the Brotherhood in 1952 after the coup d'état and he had clashed with Nasser about the dictatorship.

'When he was in the prison he was in a cell next to me. He was a weak man and he suffered terribly by the torture. He was a philosopher and he was very knowledgeable about Islam, and at the same time he was a poet. He put the three things together: philosophy, Islam and poetry, into twenty-four highly regarded books.

'It was clear from his books that he understood the effects of injustice which he had observed and which had happened to him. He was living a clean life himself, and he was angered by the corruption in the country – which he believed was ruining the new generation – and he started to attack it in his writing while opposing the dictatorship. He criticised the society which accepted corruption morally, clerically and politically.

'He was sincere in himself and in what he said, but he began to go too far and started to say things which, although we respected him and his knowledge, the Brothers and I could not accept. The direction of his theory to put a wall between pure Islamism and society and to judge others as evil went too far. He attacked Nasser and the dictatorship and the military and for that they finally hanged him in 1966 along with six other Brotherhood members. He was sincere but he did not influence me.

'But Haroon Almujadidi was someone who had the greatest impact on me as a person. I had great respect for him as a man of ethics, protocol, and the highest standard of personality. I learned much from him including supreme ethics. When I came out of prison I became closer to Haroon and it became a family connection.'

When Nada was released after two years, without charge or any convictions, he discovered that Nasser's security team had issued orders for him to be kicked out of university, and his registration was cancelled.

'I told Haroon's sister, Tahra Almujadidi, that I had to find a job in business or try another faculty, but "security" would probably block that too. She said to leave it to her. The Dean [her husband, Dr Shafik Al Keshin] with his high political connections got permission for me to return. I was a student again. But I was changed, especially by Haroon's influence on my behaviour and in all my way of thinking of how to treat others.

'Haroon had an outlandish Cadillac limousine, a long car no one could miss. One day he said to me: "If you're free tomorrow let's go visit a family." We drove about 180km along muddy streets and bumpy little roads and through tiny villages until we reached the house he was looking for. A boy came out followed by other children. Haroon had some presents with him, and he asked the children to call their mother. When she came he didn't look at her face, he just prayed. He said words of encouragement and prayers and we left.

'It transpired that her husband, Saleh Abu Ruqiek, was one of the Brotherhood leaders who had been one of Nasser's inner circle, and he had been one of the creators of the Arab League in 1945. After the Free Officers' coup he was sentenced to death but that was commuted to a life in prison. His family were under surveillance by the secret police day and night to watch who might contact them. Haroon knew this, and he understood that accusations of conspiracy plots could be conjured. And he knew what reprisals could be – torture and death.'

Nada and Haroon drove to see the family once a month. 'It was not about politics but about humanity,' said Nada. 'The Muslim Brotherhood is not a club, it is an organisation based on the ethics of the Islamic religion. It's about trying to help people comply with the ethics in their life, with teaching them until they, themselves, implement it in their life socially and economically and morally, with their soul and mind.

'The Prophet says that you are responsible not only for your neighbour but up to and including your seventh neighbour, no matter what his class, creed or colour. They are the same as your family. If they need anything and you can assist, you give it – during the good and bad times. If they have anyone sick, you have to try and help, whether medically or at least emotionally. If anyone dies, if anyone marries, has a problem with social life, you have to be helpful. If you are a doctor or a teacher, you have to help the sick and the students. If you are an engineer, you have to try and train the workers in their work.

'That is all charity. You don't take money for it. That is the reason the Brotherhood doesn't need to have much money. Anyone who can do arithmetic can understand that with more than 100 million members of the Muslim Brotherhood around the world, if every member subscribed one dollar a month then the income would be $100million.

'Mubarak and his lieutenants failed in arithmetic. They made a plan against the Muslim Brotherhood in 2005 with three dimensions. One: to try to stem the finance resources. Two: to take to court the known activists and paralyse them through imprisonment. Three: to please his mentors and protectors (the US administration). Mubarak decided to choose forty members of the Muslim Brotherhood, including me in absentia, to the criminal court in Cairo.

'The court dismissed the case – saying there was none to answer. The case was sent to yet another court with the same result. And then it was sent to another court and rejected yet again. The majority of Egyptian judges are not corrupt but the rest are the Government's people and always ready to do what the Government wants. President Mubarak didn't give up. He used another means – the military court, which is not restricted in the terms proscribed by criminal law. They, of course, said "Guilty, Guilty, Guilty". The accusation was financing the Egyptian Muslim Brotherhood.'

Nada found the outcome 'strange, amusing if not so distressing' and went on: 'The whole world knew that since 2001 until September 2009 all my assets and bank accounts all over the world were blocked by the order of the UN Security Council. Although my assets and money were frozen I was supposed to have financed the Muslim Brotherhood with one billion American dollars!

'I was sentenced in absentia to ten years in prison. In June 2012 that sentence still stood. If I went to Egypt right this moment they could arrest me. That was not the first time: in 1966 Nasser's Special Court sentenced me in absentia also to ten years, again for supposedly financing the Brotherhood.

'In 2005 two of the three judges of the military court were members of the military junta which was ruling Egypt early in 2012. Their ruling was signed by Hasan Al Rueni a member of the present Supreme Council of the Armed Forces (SCAF) to which Mubarak ceded his authority following the Arab Spring. In Tunisia in 1993 Ben Ali, who was forced out as President in 2011, sentenced me in absentia to three years imprisionment. But up to July 2012, none of them succeeded in putting me back in jail.

'The Brotherhood are banned in many places. In some places we don't exist legally but we are there. In Egypt, in all the years we were outlawed we were in the streets, in the parliament, hospitals, schools and universities, in the factories and in the fields.

'When the Brothers were being herded into jails, others tried to help their families with food and money. If you gave five pounds to a starving family you were given, not sentenced by a court, but *given* five years in prison. If the charity had been ten pounds – that was ten years in prison. And so on.'

When the Arab Spring demonstrations began in Cairo on 25 January 2011, the Muslim Brotherhood were criticised for not taking part, but as Nada points out, there is always another side to the story: its members would have been threatened with jail if they had demonstrated representing the Brotherhood. Ten of their leaders were arrested on 22 January but escaped when the guards deserted the prison.

'Given the history of torture and punishment, it was wise to be careful. All the members were told that they should be part of the demonstrations, but as individuals. That way they could help express the feelings of the people without being thrown into jail and forgotten. I joined the Brotherhood when I was 17. I was jailed when I was 23. You could call where I was a concentration camp, you could call it a jail. But I had never been prosecuted, never interrogated. You can call it what you want to call it, but it was wrong. I stayed there for about two years.

'I was only asked for the names and addresses of my family. They never asked me about any crime. How could they? After two years they released me with no explanation. It was into another a world of intrigue and more danger.'

He is a devoted Muslim but Youssef Nada wryly points out: 'I am a Muslim but also human. My mother gave birth to a baby boy – not a Muslim. I shared humanity with her before being a Muslim. Your religion doesn't mean you are cut off from your origin.

'I never killed anyone. I never used a weapon, although I was trained, yes. Even if it is justified to defend your country from invaders, how would you feel if you killed another person? Once, I hit a cat with my car. I swear I trembled for half-an-hour afterwards – and the American intelligence agencies accuse me of paying for violence, paying for people to be killed! Never. I will never forget what I saw in the military prison.'

About two years after he left the prison, Nada was visited by one of the soldier-guards who had tortured the prisoners. 'He had left the army and was looking for work,' said Nada. 'I'd watched him kill people – three in front of me. One was a thirteen-year-old boy from the Brotherhood. He'd been caught distributing Brotherhood pamphlets and they brought him in and sliced him up. He was called Abd El-Hadi. I never knew all his name, but his face – I remember his face. And his wounds – his chest all covered in blood. When I tried to help him he said: "Brother Youssef, there is no need to trouble, it's all over now."

'The man who killed him was called A'oud. When he came to me the killing rolled before my eyes as if it had just happened. My mind played it to me again and again. I could see it so clearly. It frightened me, for I hated that man so much. I looked at him and put my hand in my pocket and pushed a bunch of cash at him and said: "May Allah be pleased with you but please… please, don't come here again."

'I could not seek revenge, because of my belief. This doesn't mean that all the Brotherhood are the same, but we are taught to try to keep within the pure limits consigned by God and his messenger. I can't say I that the Muslims don't make mistakes, or that all the Brotherhood are perfect – like society, there are good and bad. The hope is everyone is trying to be good, which is a wonderful thing.

'The last statistics, which were computed in 2009 from all over the world, showed those who are committed to the way of thinking and the principles of the Brotherhood are more than 100 million. There is no official registration – a Brother is one who adopts our way. And they are people working with political parties in all countries – in the schools, in the mosques, hospitals, universities; students and professors and peasants in the farms and workers in factories; parents trying to make their families inherit their way of thinking. It's everywhere in society, throughout all standards of living.'

Of course, not all the world has a benign view of the Muslim Brotherhood, but to claims that the Brotherhood want world domination by lethal force, by atrocity, Nada has a quiet answer: 'If more than one hundred million people attacked today could they be stopped? We want to talk, to educate, to negotiate. I have done that all my life.

'When it comes to tyranny, we are glad to be humble. When we are confronted by muscles we are glad to respond by wisdom. We are the students of Muhammad Al-Qaraxi who asked me what would be gained by violence. Nothing is the answer – the very thought of taking another life is repugnant to me.'

Yet, in 2001 George W Bush accused Youssef Nada of financing atrocities and ordered the Security Council to list him as a banker of terrorism. 'I continue to deal with another severe case of injustice not by a military junta and not by totalitarian regime but by the biggest democratic country in the world as well as the small but most civilised country in the West: the United States of America and Switzerland.'

CHAPTER THREE

FASTEN YOUR SEATBELTS

'The robbed that smiles steals something from the thief.'

Shakespeare, *Othello*

Throughout his university career, other than that time rudely interrupted by his imprisonment, Youssef Nada ran a dairy business with an export office. By the time he graduated from the Agriculture College of the University of Alexandria in 1959, he was hugely successful, but filled with disquiet. He says he felt he was living in a police state.

The regime employed hundreds of Stasi-style spies. 'Everyone was guilty until proved innocent, not innocent till proved guilty,' said Nada. 'Everyone was under suspicion. It was a chilling and claustrophobic environment in which to live.'

His dairy complex supplied one-third of the milk drunk each day in his home city. He also supplied a Swiss company pasteurising milk in Egypt and he was contracted by an Austrian company to produce a white cheese, what we now call feta cheese, for export. It helped him make a critical decision – that contract was to be Nada's passport to a new but even more tumultuous life. He had played everything quietly when he left prison. Yet, censorship and control dominated everybody: 'I couldn't bear the way they were running our lives. We were all the pawns of a dictator.'

Nada was under constant surveillance by Nasser's so-called Intelligence Service and at one point the authorities tried to involve him in a conspiracy. They took him in for questioning and interrogated him.

'What car are you driving?'

'A small Ford.'

'No, you drive a blue Chevrolet.'

'No.'

'Do you know a lady called Fathia Barakat?'

'No.'

'Write a list of the officers you know.'

Before going to the university some of Nada's friends went to military academy or the air force. He wrote down six names.

'No. That is not enough.'

'I don't remember any more.'

'You have to remember. You know but won't say.'

'No.'

'Okay. We'll give you a chance. Go home and come back tomorrow. Think more – if you don't you know what will happen! Think where you were before. You know where you have been, and you know where you will go again.'

Nada went home feeling really depressed and thinking that a catastrophe was coming. 'Then a man called asking for my younger brother, Sobhi,' said Nada. 'When Sobhi completed his engineering studies he went on to the Air Force Academy. He was well connected to the regime and had flown major government officials, including Nasser's second-in- command.

'The caller said he was Alae Barakat. The security people had asked me about a woman called Barakat. The caller was a pilot colleague of my brother. His mother was Fathia Barakat and her son and my brother had been in her blue car. They'd been followed back to our house where my brother was staying while on leave. Then I immediately understood: they were being monitored and the spies thought it was me who had the military and air force contacts and I must be plotting a coup d'état! I called the security: "The foolish man who you sent to follow me mixed me up with my brother. My brother is an officer and he has contacts everywhere. They're not my contacts."

'Then they went after for me because I did not vote in the presidential referendum. Nasser was the only candidate and you had to say "Yes" or "No". To say no was a problem. I didn't want to accept to say yes. What could I do? I simply didn't go. After two weeks they called me. They said: "Why didn't you go to the poll?"

'I said I was very busy and I had no time to go. They said: "You either accept the regime, or you are against it – not to vote means you won't admit what you think." What could anyone do? There was no way for me to live in that atmosphere of suspicion and hate. Some people were obliged to. I knew that I could leave for a better life. I wanted to be a citizen with rights. I decided to emigrate. I was not married. I could still have contact with my sisters and brothers. My father was at home and they were living well. They didn't need me, and I knew how to look after myself. I had contacts everywhere.'

With his contract to produce feta cheese for export, Nada applied for an exit visa which was granted. His dairy machines went to Haj Abbas Al-Sissi, who had a cheese factory in Rashid. He left Egypt in1960 with full government permission on a work permit and a visa. And a remarkable metamorphosis began.

Youssef Nada became an internationalist and an industrialist of high merit. He set up offices in Vienna, Tripoli, Riyadh, Glasgow and Liechtenstein, and commuted between Europe and the Middle East as he worked on business arrangements throughout the Middle East and Africa. With electrifying energy he developed as many businesses as he had those famous contacts. He moved commodities like a carousel: corn, oil, barley, iron, wheat and cement, flour, copper, and aluminium and fertilisers. His trade in cement and accompanying construction materials were the most profitable of all.

Such was the level of his enterprises that his discussions involved the leaders of nations and businesses. He's always enjoyed an instinct for finding the true decision makers in industry and politics – and all were told of his membership and pride in the Muslim Brotherhood. Among them were President Habib Bourguiba of Tunisia and independent Libya's canny King Idris Al-Sanoosi who had remained allied with the British and the Americans. Both countries were involved in the establishment of his kingdom after World War Two despite the Suez Canal crisis in 1956. The king's international relations upset Arab nationalists like Nasser.

In 1962, Youssef Nada met and became friendly with King Idris through Fathy Alkhoja his Chief of Ceremony who the young businessman recognised as an honest and devoted Muslim. The young Nada told him of his incarceration and treatment in Egypt. He also had contact with officials like Dr Mahmoud Abu-Saud an international economist and Brotherhood member who was with him in the Nasser military concentration camp in 1954. King Idris appointed Dr Abu-Saud to be financial adviser to the Libyan Central Bank as well as the Ministry of Economy. In Tripoli, Saad Al-Jazairi the grandson of Prince Abd El-Qadir Al-Jazairi was also a close friend.

However, it was the powerful President Habib Bourguiba of Tunisia who gave Nada the precious freedom of movement: he gifted him with Tunisian nationality and with it came the passport which opened world travel for him. And in Libya he had high-level support from the king.

Youssef Nada could handle the complexities of high commerce. Domestic issues were another matter. A bachelor, he was living between homes in Vienna and Tripoli in between visits to Saudi Arabia where he preferred not to spend too much time. Haroon Almujadidi visited him in Libya and spent about one year in his house. His father, Sadek Pasha Almujadidi, came to Nada's house several times when he visited

King Idris, as they were very close friends, and with him came his daughter, Tahra Almujadidi.

'When she came I was overloaded with work and she treated me as if she was my mother.' recalled Nada. 'All the pots and pans and utensils for the kitchen were still in boxes. I had no time for domestic matters. She got an Italian couple to look after me and they stayed with me in Tripoli and Vienna and Campione until they retired. I spent my time with work and following my religion. This turned out to be a watershed in my life.'

The construction business was a goldmine in Libya, the Gulf, Nigeria and East, West and North Africa. Youssef Nada's companies became the chief supplier of cement. In collaboration with the biggest Italian cement company, Cementir, he developed the world's first floating cement terminal in Cantieri, the biggest Italian shipyard at that time. He became known across Europe and the Middle East as 'The King of Cement'.

Nada had his own business fiefdom in Libya. He was young, confident and successful – possibly too confident. Watching the commodity markets he predicted that the price of steel was only going up. In the early part of 1969 he bought 100,000 tons of steel for US$20million at US$200 a ton. He was to take delivery of it in October that year. As the price of steel rose, supplies of it ran out.

One of his business competitors in Libya was Vittorio Haddad, an astute industrialist. 'One day I was walking in Tripoli when a hand touched my shoulder,' said Nada. 'It was Haddad whom I did not know. I told him I knew of him and his reputation. He asked if I would sell half of my steel consignment to him. By then the price was US$450 a ton – the steel was worth another US$25million. I saw no reason to sell to him – the price was still going up.

'Haddad looked at me and said: "Will you take some advice from a Jew?"

'"It will be difficult but go ahead."

'"Sell half and play with half."

'I didn't listen to him. I didn't sell.'

By 1 September1969, the day Colonel Muammar Gaddafi took control of Libya, Youssef Nada's kingdom was thriving. He had his fleet of 36 ships at sea, bringing riches to Libya – oil and iron, and barley and wheat and some of the cement which helped build huge portions of the modern Middle East. And also US$45million-worth of steel which he owned outright.

It was 7am when Youssef Nada got the news of the coup by phone from Saad Al-Jazairi. And when he turned on the radio at his home in Tripoli the news was echoed by artillery fire in the city. He knew instantly that Gaddafi's action would have the support of Nasser. Libya was no longer safe for him.

With the coup came the curfew. To walk out on the streets would invite a bullet, unless that is you were essential – like Youssef Nada's friend Dr Singh: 'He was a Sikh from India,' said Nada. 'We were both bachelors and he was always coming to my house for dinner and to listen to music and talk and read in my library when I was busy. We were good friends and he was allowed to move around: doctors were given special permission during the curfew and the first thing he did was come to visit me. He told me the situation. All the rebels were praising Nasser as if he were their God. Gaddafi and the rest saw Nasser as a hero – and that was bad for me.

'I was well-known as being against Nasser – on his death list – and a friend of King Idris. They would be after me. I had ships in port but they had not been unloaded. Into this came my neighbour Victorio Bagani who was the agent of Volkswagen in Tripoli. He was Jewish and very frightened about what would happen to him. He said: "I am alone. My family left to Rome two days ago to celebrate Yom Kippur and I was planning to follow them tomorrow but now I am alone and very afraid. Can I stay with you?"

'I said to him: "The house is here, the music is here, the library is here, the kitchen is here, the freezer is here. The cooker is here, the bedrooms are here and they are for you to use. Do what you want to do." I had to concentrate myself on how to stay alive. He called his secretary to the house and she eventually arranged his escape to Canada from Tripoli via Malta. I too escaped, but only just. I took a cement cargo ship to freedom.

'For the first few days a 24-hour curfew was enforced but because of necessity, for food and essentials, it was lifted for a couple of hours and then four hours a day. All of 9,700 tons of freight was unloaded from one of my ships but there were still about 300 tons on board. The captain was in Tripoli, the owner of the ship was in Greece and I was paying the bills from Vienna.

'The captain was demanding money, communications were interrupted. But if I sent any cable to Vienna even from the ship I'd be accused of smuggling money and a crime against the new regime.

'The captain told me: "Mr Nada the owner says he will be bankrupted and it is better that you talk to him from the ship's system." I had a plan and agreed to do it from the ship the next day. There was a shortage of food and those who had it in port could go there but with a permit. It was my chance. When you go on a pilgrimage to Mecca you go not with your passport but with a *hajj* travel document which is a special visa for Saudi Arabia.

'I went to the port with the *hajj* document, two passports, my cheque book and money in my shoe. I had a plastic handgun. Nothing more than that: no clothes, no razor. The *hajj* document worked as an ID to get to the harbour and past the guards. On the ship I told the captain we had to leave. He was in a panic, wanting money for the owner, wanting me to sail with him for support but frightened for his own safety. I told him to get permission from the port authority to sail.

'They told him: "Wait. The guards will come for an inspection."

'And they did, by a speed-gunboat. There were about a dozen of them in uniform and carrying machine guns. When they boarded the ship the captain lost his nerve, saying, "Mr Nada, you have to get out. Mr Nada you have to leave the ship."

'I replied, are you mad? You said to me to stay here, and he pleaded, "Mr Nada I have children." "Yes, you have children. You want them to live without you or with you? If I am to be killed, you will be killed before me." I had no choice but to threaten him with the plastic gun, which looked like the real thing. It was life or death. There was a big refrigerator in his cabin-office and he said I could hide behind it.

'His desk was across the room and I told him: "You sit at that desk where I can see you. If you move from there I will shoot you." It was tense and it was hot. The guards appeared before the captain: "Anyone stowed away?" I was watching him from behind the fridge and he was sweating. The guards took an inspection. Of course, they found nothing and we were given permission to leave Libya.

'I stayed behind the fridge for seven hours until we left territorial waters, leaving behind my home and Libya and my business involving tens of millions of dollars. When I emerged from my hiding place the captain had to carry me – my circulation had stopped. My body wouldn't move on its own, the plastic gun was locked in my hand.

'My eyes were on the captain all the time. He was a frightened man and that is always a dangerous man. I didn't know what he'd do. From Libya we went to Tunis, for which I had a Tunisian passport. The captain begged me to stay with him until Greece because he feared the crew would say I had paid him to take me, a fugitive, out of Libya and that he was a communist. I was his only witness to what had really happened.

'I was between two minds: I was already safe but if I stayed with the ship I would pass through the territorial waters of Libya again, and they could catch me. On the other hand, I thought: "If he will be a victim and I will be saved. How can I live after that?" I had an internal struggle about if I could live after that with the feeling that I'd dumped somebody who was instrumental, no matter how reluctantly, in my freedom.

'I said that I would take the risk and stay with him. When the security came to the ship in Tunis they said that because of my passport I could disembark but we sailed on and passed the Libyan territorial waters. I went to the ship's tower to use the radio telephone to talk to the bank in Vienna. I had tipped the radio operator quite handsomely with cash and he said: "Mr Nada, take care of yourself. The captain asked me to send three cables to Piraeus to the security and the harbourmaster and the president and it is very dangerous for you."

When he learned I'd been in the radio room the captain looked distraught; I took it seriously. I stopped eating and drinking anything that wasn't sealed because he might poison me. I stayed in a cabin until we arrived in Greece. Three gunboats surrounded us guiding the vessel to a berth. They had information that there was a fugitive, a stowaway, from Libya on board. The ship's owner, who was my friend, arrived and started to quarrel loudly with the captain in a very loud voice in Greek, and tried to hit him.

'Next the police arrived and asked for my passport and demanded to know where I had come from. Angrily I replied: "Tunisia. I have a passport. I don't need a visa. I'm entering your country from a port which is allowed for anyone to enter. I have a valid passport."

'Another official saw the steam from my ears and came forward: "Mr Nada, don't be upset. I understand your case. Where is your passport?" He looked at the passport and he said to me: "We have a problem Mr Nada. Your case is not in our hands. It is in the hands of the president. Cables arrived to us and to the president. Today is Friday, nobody can contact the president. Tomorrow and Sunday nobody can contact him. Can we ask you to stay on board until Monday morning?"

'I had no choice: stay there or go on land to prison for the weekend. I asked the ship owner to arrange a lawyer and to call Ghaleb Himmat, a contact I trusted, to join me from Munich as soon as he could. On the Monday, the Civil Security Service people arrived and my lawyer asked where we were going. The leader replied: "I'm not allowed to say to you."

'They told my lawyer to stay behind and took me the office of the president, Georgios Papadopoulos, who'd taken over the government with a military coup two years earlier. I hadn't met him before. "Mr President," I said. "Is there anything I have done wrong?" "No, no, no.

There is not a problem. If you want asylum we can give to you. I told them to stamp your passport for one year and if you want more there is no problem. You are the only one who has come out of Libya. All the news which we hear about Libya is from the BBC. I want to know the reality. Libya is very important for us. The king is here in Greece. If we do not treat him well and he returns we will lose Libya. If we treat him well and he doesn't return and Gaddafi stays we will lose Libya. I need to know."

'The king had been in Turkey for medical treatment when Gaddafi took over. He had sailed from there to the village of Kamena Vourla on the Marmaris Sea. Georgios Papadopoulos asked me if the king was popular. I said he was and he was loved. He asked me if I thought the king would return to Libya. I said he wouldn't and he quizzed me about that contradiction. I said it was true his people like him but King Idris's people, those with power around him, are all corrupt and cowards.

'I told him that the people were fed up with the corrupt people, the gangsters in the government and that they will welcome Gaddafi and the new officers. Nasser's propaganda is there for them to build on. Gaddafi and his people were praising Nasser as I left Libya. He looked at me and said: "That means the king will not return."

'I agreed with him and he made arrangements that I was to have any help I needed from his offices. I asked if I could visit the king?' "Mr Nada, I didn't hear anything." He repeated it two times. I thanked him very much. I left and after meeting with the lawyers and the shipping people, Ghaleb Himmat and I rented a car and went to visit King Idris.

'It was very sad. He was old and very weak. I kissed his hand and said to him: "Your Majesty. I am at your disposal if I can assist." He said: "I believe I have to spend the rest of my life in Egypt." He couldn't stay in Greece. If they treated him as a refugee he would not accept it. If he was treated as royalty the Gaddafi and the Opposition would be angry: it was a fine line. He was a righteous man who was surrounded by bad people.

'After this meeting nobody heard about the king being in Greece.

He stayed about ten days or so, and then he left for Egypt. Mr Himmat and I took the first plane to Vienna. By then I was very ill. I had no strength at all, even to stand up.'

But Nada was aware enough to hear about Nasser's list of 80 dangerous enemies to be extradited to Cairo from Libya, a list Nasser personally had sent to his acolyte Gadaffi who harboured his own ambitions to replace the Egyptian dictator as the leader of the Arab world.

Youssef Nada left Tripoli on 9 September 1969, once more hiding behind the ship's master's fridge. The following day the 'most wanted' list arrived from Cairo. At the top of the execution list was Dr Mahmoud Abu-Saud and after him, at number two for extradition, was Youssef Nada.

Dr Mahmoud Abu-Saud, chief adviser for the Central Bank and Economic Ministry during the rule of King Idris, was on holiday when the coup happened. He went on to help organise the Muslim Brotherhood in America and was involved with the Muslim Society in the United States (MAS). Youssef Nada was still in hiding behind a fridge, at sea, when the order arrived in Tripoli. The others were extradited and were imprisoned without trial for many years until Nasser died and Sadat released them. Some vanished.

Nada had lost millions including his consignment of steel ('From that day I have always split my business in half and heeded Vittoria Haddad's advice', he said ruefully). Yet, through pure determination he re-established himself, principally in Europe taking up residence in the municipality of Campione d'Italia which rests quietly inside the Swiss canton Ticino, separated from the rest of Italy by Lake Lugano and the magnificent mountains which surround it. From there he set up offices as far apart as Indianapolis in America and Glasgow in Scotland and many others in between, including Riyadh in Saudi Arabia, Liechtenstein and Lagos.

The 24 hours in a day were not enough for him to follow the stream of business orders. He was the front runner, business hunter, nucleus of public relations, alert elastic negotiator, managing a complicated net of contacts in business, politics, religion and social activities. His relations with his staff and employees was formal and businesslike. He needed someone he trusted not only in business but also in the other lines.

That person must be known to him, a committed Muslim, trustworthy, polite and able to act as a 'shock absorber'. He believed Ali Ghaleb Himmat was equipped with all those specifications: 'He is a very peace-loving man: between man and man, and man or woman, not only between nations or factions. It was said once that if somebody pulled at his jacket, he'd take it off and give it to him.'

Youssef Nada had first met Himmat in Munich ten years before in a Muslim camp during the Christmas holidays. 'I called him to Vienna and surprised him with my offer to join me as a partner. He said he didn't have money or experience or knowledge. I said he didn't need money, I would train him, and the experience would come in time. I told him: "Your duty will be the back office whether I am present or absent, and you can travel to where I am not able to travel. I take you as my younger brother not a business partner."

'I offered 50 per cent of the profits and he had no chance to refuse and I had no time to negotiate. Nothing was written and the agreement was implemented and lasted 40 years until our names were delisted by the UN Security Council black list. We each took 50 per cent from the joint business assets residuals and though the business partnership ended we are still one family and he is still my younger brother and his family is mine. Mr Himmat was the silent motor who I supplied with the fuel of ideas. Before he finished one job I'd have another for him as important as the previous one. He is a sealed box — he'll never reveal to anyone what he knows. This does not mean that he is an angel without drawbacks. He is a human but a good human. I never tolerate neglection of duty or postponing jobs or slow speed and he coped with that. He treated me as his father and I wanted my sons to be as him.'

From Vienna, Youssef Nada gathered his resources and rose once again and business boomed. Saudi Arabia, Kuwait, North Africa and Nigeria, all rich in petrol dollars, were building by the moment, and with his cement silos and a fleet of vessels, he easily moved building materials from Europe to the Middle East and Africa – no one could compete with Youssef Nada who retained his crown as the Mediterranean 'King of Cement'. He was able to deliver in bags and also in bulk as the market might need. With the floating terminal, bulk carriers and bagged cement from Greece, Yugoslavia, Bulgaria, Romania, Russia, Italy, Spain Turkey and even Germany, he dominated the market.

Within three years of his escape from Libya he was trading seven million tons of cement a year and shipping equally impressive amounts of iron. He'd lost tens of millions of dollars with Gaddafi's takeover of Libya but he'd returned even more powerful and higher in international industry. In 1974 he established Nada International in Riyadh in Saudi Arabia, where some years later he had contact with King Fahd and his advisers.

Until his silos went into operation the cement so urgently required for the construction bonanza was being discharged by helicopters in the port of Jeddah. His business deals and his fortune multiplied and diversified – and so did his roles for the Nasser-outlawed Muslim Brotherhood, although he played his politics in the shadows.

With Nasser's death from a heart attack in 1970 the man he'd treated as his poodle, his deputy Anwar Sadat, was installed as president. The powerful military group around Nasser believed they would manipulate Sadat to their will. 'Sadat was very loyal to Nasser but he was weak and just looking after his own interests, watching out for himself,' said Nada. 'The other officers took the power and installed him and thought they could contain him. He was more intelligent than them. He put all of them in the prison. Now, he had to cover his back.

'Although Sadat had persecuted the Brotherhood by order of his boss Nasser, he ordered the Brothers to be released from prisons. He said those exiled could return and would not be hurt again. Many

Brothers returned; the majority were in the Arab countries, Islamic countries. Though I had offices in many of them including Cairo I was not living in any Arab country. I refused to return.'

By 1977, Youssef Nada had moved up the vertigo-inducing twist of a road which takes you out of Campione d'Italia proper and into the hills. He established himself in the splendid mountainside Villa Nada with spectacular views over the lakes. He was also recently married to Amal Chichakli from Hama in Syria where her father was an army commander and politician. Following a coup, her uncle, Adib Chichakli, became President of Syria in 1953. It was a short run into 1955 when he himself was overthrown by an Iraqi-backed coup involving the Bathists, Syrian communists and the Druze Party (Ahl al Tawhid).

Adib Chichakli had huge army and government support but to avoid blood flowing in the streets of Damascus when his power was challenged he avoided a confrontation and exiled himself to Switzerland for four years. There, he was warned his assassination had been decreed and he left for Brazil where he bought a farm. He worked the land but it was no escape – on 27 September 1964 he was murdered in Ceres, Brazil, by the Syrian Druze member Nawaf Ghazaleh.

Youssef Nada's bride was no stranger to turbulent politics, but first there was the delicate subject of the hospitality of diplomacy to deal with. They had been in their Campione home for only one week when her husband announced there would be some guests for dinner. How many? Probably about 120.

Amal Chichakli, although an engaging, strong and confident woman, was not used to such big numbers. Her husband had a team of servants and a cook and assistants at the house and the nearby five-star Hotel Olivella in the village of Morcote, supplied extra food and staff for the catering. The event was hosted by Youssef Nada to welcome many Muslim thinkers from around the world, including Youssef al-Qaradawi, Ismail Faruqi, Mahmoud Abu Sauod, Mohamed Al Mubarak, Kurshid Ahmad, Ahmad El Asal, Abdelhamid Abusuliman and three directors of Nada International Riyadh (Hisham Altalib, Jamal Barazanji and Mohamed Shamma), and many others.

For many years it has been widely reported that their purpose was to establish the International Institute of Islamic Thought (IIIT) but Nada, the conference host, insists differently: 'This meeting was not to create the Triple IT. It was to have a group committed to Islam to be united in ideology, to try to bring the Muslim understanding together. You cannot spread religion with war. In the beginning of Islam wars were not to dictate Islam or against those who did not accept it, but were fought against those who tried to stop their mission.

'You must reach people's minds to convince them of your ideas, of what you want. It is true that those that attended the meeting at my home were from different countries, from different ways of thinking but all of them were connected one way or another with the Muslim Brotherhood ideology: they didn't want to fight, to go the way of violence.

'The Muslim Brotherhood began in Egypt and until now every government which came to power in Egypt had targeted the Brotherhood: jail them, imprison them, stop them, stop their activity. Everything to stop them was done. As an organisation they accepted all the problems which were put on their shoulders without fighting back. It is true that one or two, or as many as ten, went out of line and used violence, but it was not the organisation, it was individuals who ran out of the line and acted independently.

'The man who was Osama Bin Laden's number two, Ayman Mohammed Rabie al-Zawahiri, was a member of the Brotherhood, but when he tried to convince others that violence was the way forward they put a wall between them and him. In turn, Ayman Mohammed Rabie al-Zawahiri attacked the Brotherhood and considered them infidels.

45

'He defected and started his own violent group. But he was never able to convince the Brotherhood to join him. He was considered immature. He went alone and did what he wanted with others he recruited. The Brotherhood couldn't stop him, the Government could not prevent him, so how could we?

'Even before Bin Laden was killed the so-called Al Qaeda was only al-Zawahiri and a few people around him, that is all. In my opinion in 2012 Al Qaeda doesn't number more than around 100 persons. They are nothing, and they can make nothing. Only shadows. But there is fear in the shadows.

'America created a ghost and talked it up so much that the fear of it heightened too. Terrorism has been in the world since the two sons of Adam. All life must be changed because of a few mad people?'

Yet, it is and was a violent world and Youssef Nada knew to take precautions. He was on the move constantly. When he travelled, Ghaleb Himmat and the team knew his movements and they would check on him. Often he would use a visa separate from his passport which would not be stamped and later compromise him.

'We had a check and re-check system when I went anywhere. I would phone, they would call back to make sure the call was not made under threat and that I was where I said I was. And then, every few hours, they would check on me again. I always did this, for often I was with people who were targets for bombs or bullets or both. I might have been innocent collateral damage and not the intended victim.'

But when he moved through the Middle East in the 1970s he said he discovered an extraordinarily honest society: 'I was going to my company in Riyadh and the offices there asked me to bring half a million dollars for payments. It was normal and not prohibited to carry cash. I had the cash in a bag and went to the office. About four hours later they asked me about the money. I didn't have it. I thought I'd left it at the reception area of the hotel. I called and was told that a taxi driver had brought a bag full of money and he said it was my bag and I'd left it in the taxi.

'The taxi driver knew it was a great deal of money and he brought it back. He gave it to the desk in the hotel and they knew it was much money. Nobody touched it. I went and I opened it, and not one dollar was missing. Then I found the taxi driver to reward him but he would take nothing. He said to me: "I cannot take money to prove that I am trustworthy. I don't take money which is not mine. That is my duty to give it to its owner otherwise I am a thief." I tried, and no way would he take anything.

'At the end of the 1980s in Riyadh I had a ready-mix factory for cement in Saudi Arabia and it had a safe built in with concrete in the wall. The staff came in one day and it had gone! The change in society was happening.'

In the mid-1970s, Egypt's Minister of Housing and Construction, Hasballah Al-Kafrawi, visited Youssef Nada to try to convince him to help his country. Cement was being sold for ten times its commercial value on the black market and the government wanted a solution. The prime minister was Mamdouh Salem who as the security commander had overseen the arrest of the young Youssef Nada in Alexandria. Hasballah Al-Kafrawi assured him there would be no trouble returning to his homeland: 'All the Brotherhood members have returned home from all over the world.'

Youssef Nada was not convinced, but kept his counsel. He knew that unless all arrangements went smoothly he would not be engaged with any project. He asked for a berth in Suez harbour for one of his floating cement terminals and permission to move 100 railway wagons there from his Swiss fleet. The port berth was given to an Israeli national named Ben Natan. No explanation was given. At the same time he was approached by Prince Mohammad Al-Faisal, the son of the recently assassinated King Faisal of Saudi Arabia, who wanted to establish a bank in Egypt.

'He had good relations with Sadat and he got the licence for the Faisal Islamic Bank,' said Nada. 'There were a lot of influences. The head of Saudi intelligence, Kamal Adham, was a brother-in-law of the king and was well connected to the American administration and the CIA. The Egyptian Ministry of Awqaf [the nation's religious endowment government department] proposed that the Islamic bank licence was written so that 50 per cent would be Egyptian and 50 per cent from the other Muslim countries.

'Mohammed Faisal said to me: "I don't want the others to dictate to me something against the Islamic rules. I need with me, within the Egyptian portion of the bank shares, somebody from the private sector who I can trust and who is committed to the principles of Islam in the country. I need you to be there. You have to participate and take some shares."

'I said I wouldn't go to Egypt and that in 1966 they had sentenced me to ten years in jail in absentia. I was innocent – but a target. He said: "Now, there is no problem, and we have good relations with Sadat. We can arrange it."

'I refused. He insisted. He said the meeting for the allocation of the shares had to be in Egypt. Without alerting anyone I went to Cairo at the end of 1977. Mr Himmat and my office were to monitor my movements. I took my Tunisian passport, not Egyptian. I arrived at 8pm. They held me at the airport until 2am in the morning. An officer came in from time-to-time and then disappeared. My passport went to police intelligence and then military intelligence and eventually a high ranking officer in the airport turned up and said: "Mr Nada, you have to sort it out with the higher authority. We are servants. We were executing orders."

'They allowed me into the country and I went to the hotel in the early hours of the morning. I called Hasballah Al-Kafrawi and told him I was leaving that day. I told him what happened. He said to wait for him. Within half-an-hour, he called me. God bless him, he was kind to me; he was very polite with me.

'After fifteen minutes the Minister of Interior, Nabawi Ismail, who was also the Deputy Prime Minister called me: "Youssef, I have heard this story, it is impossible. The country is not as before. It is open and we need our sons. We need the Egyptians from everywhere. It was a mistake. It might have been military intelligence. We have to meet."

'I told him: "I'm sorry Your Excellency. Whether it is small officers or big officers, it happened. That means that there is something wrong. I have to leave today." He arrived in thirty minutes and I told him: "I know that you have done a lot of good things to the country. You are offering your best to the others and to me. I appreciate it, but what can I say? When it happened to me? I understand and I believe you, but there must be other motives involved, other parties playing in this game.

'He said: "Maybe it came from Almahi [the chief of military intelligence]. If I wanted to arrest you now, I couldn't." I said: "Of course you can. This is very clear to me." He said: "I would not be telling you this, unless it is true. Also it is your mistake for one in your position must announce his arrival in order to be received in the VIP lounge." I said: "No, I believe you, but what happens from your side or from any other side is the real issue for me. I wanted to see the reality."

'The same day, Hasballah Al-Kafrawi arranged a lunch with Nabawi Ismail and four of the biggest businessmen at the time: Osman Ahmed Othman, his brother Hussein Othman, Haj Hilmi Abdul Majid, and Abdul Azeem Luqmeh, who were also friends of mine. They all told me that everything in the country had changed radically; it was another period, but they all wanted me to stay. I wondered about that and I said: "Thank you very much." I stayed for one week.'

The next time Nada went to Egypt was with his wife, to choose members of the Board of the Faisal Islamic Bank. The Ministry of Awqaf had to have the larger portion of the Egyptian share and Nada had the next biggest shareholding and was elected as a member of the first board of directors.

The visit was disquieting: 'My wife and I had each been given a car and driver and while I was at a meeting she returned to the hotel and asked for the key to the room. It wasn't there. She thought I must be, but when she went up to the room she met three men coming out. Later, I was told the men might have been military intelligence, or some other agency. I said: "Where they're from doesn't matter. The result is the same. If they did it, they can do it again."'

Nada attended the first board meeting of the Faisal Islamic Bank in Egypt with Prince Mohammed but then resigned as a member of the board whilst retaining his shares: 'I had many friends inside the bank as well as the chairman and the founder, and because it was an Islamic Bank there were people working inside from the Muslim Brotherhood.

'But as for Egypt – I left and I have never been back. I cannot forget what happened to me – I can't wipe it away like a pencil mark with a rubber. After the suffering in the military prison, I'd never risk being locked up in jail.'

But that didn't stop him putting himself in peril.

CHAPTER FOUR

THE SHAH'S LAST RIDE

'They seek him here,
They seek him there,
Is he in Heaven,
Is he in Hell,
The damn'd elusive Pimpernel?'
            The Scarlet Pimpernel, Baroness Emmuska Orczy, 1903

An early mission as an emissary–diplomat and negotiator for the Muslim Brotherhood embroiled Youssef Nada in one of the landmark events of the 20th century: the Iranian revolution, the return of Ayatollah Sayyid Ruhollah Mousavi Khomeini, and a resurgence of the West's wider fascination and fear of all aspects of Islam, its politics and its spirituality.

Before the arrival Ayatollah Khomeini, the casual Western observer might have viewed the Islamic world as 'all about oil and terrorists' and the ongoing problems in Palestine. Few could tell their Sunni from their Shia – the two branches of the Muslim belief were much the same to most people in the West.

But Nada maintains the question over the two factions has been a tool of divide and rule for colonial interests for centuries. Each has different interpretations of the legacy of the prophet Mohammed – just as scholars and theologians find alternative meanings in the teachings of Islam. And as we so often see, some twist the words to promote their own brand of idealism or politics. It's not just beauty that is in the eye of the beholder: piety can be manipulated too.

While Mohammed was dying in the year 632, the leadership of Islam was in question. He without male heirs. His three sons died as babies, and without naming a successor he was intestate, and that is always trouble.

The Sunnis (followers of the *sunna*, which were Mohammed's acts during his life) say that the close companions of Mohammed voted his respected father-in-law Abu Bakr to be the *khalifa*, the caliph, the leader of Muslims. Meanwhile the Shias (deriving from Shiat Ali, the supporters of Ali) maintain that Ali was not present when the voting took place. They claim the prophet mentioned Ali who was his first cousin and son-in-law as his successor.

It was the Sunnis who took over and the Shia became distinct from mainstream Muslims. The Imams (community or spiritual leaders) are integral to the Shia, for although they cannot change the Koran's 'divine revelation' they can interpret it because of their own special divine endowment. Ali himself never accepted the division and continued to work and cooperate with the first three khlaifas (Abu Bakr and Omar and Osman) and he became the fourth. His supporters continued to believe that his descendants are sacred.

Ayatollah (chief priest) Khomeini was a Shia and as such part of the majority of Iran. The Iranians regarded their doctrine as religious and political, allowing them to stand apart from the Sunna majority.

While exiled in Turkey and later Iraq the Ayatollah's denunciations of the bouffant-haired Mohammad Rez Sh h Pahlavi – the Shah of Iran, the Shah of Persia – became more blistering in the 1970s. In sizzling diatribes the Shah was 'the servant of the dollar'.

Only the British intelligence agencies – superbly up to speed at this time in the Middle East – saw the simmering problems. The American CIA thought the Shah was safely 'in the hip pocket' and that Ayatollah Khomeini was a 'Bugs Bunny', a Looney Tune, who could be ignored. The British Foreign Office and their spooks correctly regarded the Ayatollah Khomeini as a potentially world-changing figure and not the raving madman which Washington had defined. Iraq kicked out Ayatollah Khomeini in 1978. Kuwait didn't want him but France, after the Shah gave his approval to President Giscard d'Estaing, allowed him freehold entry.

It was before the advent of pre-social networks electronic communications, but the proliferation of recording cassettes at the time helped to bring about the Iranian revolution. Instead of lying low in France, the Ayatollah Khomeini was in direct dial contact by telephone with Tehran: he dictated his sermons directly into the country and they were put on cassette tapes and distributed everywhere. Western newspapers published profiles of him and reported his words as did the BBC. His PR was splendid.

To many, Ayatollah Khomeini was a distinguished man, while the Shah was seen to be an arrogant – and corrupt – leader who was destined to be the last ruler in 2,500 years of continuous monarchy. A secular Muslim, the Shah's modernisation programmes – and also his regal behaviour – increased the disenchantment of the Shia clergy. The Shah's prisons were packed with political prisoners. The unrest, the almighty upheaval in his country, finally forced the Shah into exile in January 1979. The spin doctors said he'd gone on holiday. He never returned.

The Muslim Brotherhood were monitoring every signal in the evolving Iranian revolution. The Ayatollah was staying in Neufchatel-sur-Aisne in France at the village home of his fervent supporter Abolhassan Banisdar who was associated with activists like Ebrahim Yazdi who was exiled in America and had worked with the Muslim

Brotherhood community. Similar thinkers included the scientist Mostafa Chamran, the great intellectual Ali Shariati, and Khomeini's then trusted aide Sadegh Qotbzadeh had also kept contact with the Brotherhood and Youssef Nada.

'This group were in many Islamic countries,' explained Nada. 'They were in contact with us and our Brothers in American and European universities during the time of Shah. We regarded the Shah as against Islam. The Brothers helped when there were demonstrations against the Shah who was selling the country and the oil to the West. The Shah was in a very critical position and Khomeini was preparing to return. The media everywhere were talking about what was going to happen. All Iran seemed to be on the Tehran streets [estimates put it at 6million] and some army units stripped off their uniforms and joined them. It was all in the name of Islam. The Brotherhood expected a Muslim country would emerge to replace the Shah; that Islam would be in control.'

As the time for Khomeini's return it drew closer, Nada arranged a Brotherhood team to go and congratulate him at the chateaux in Neufchatel. He welcomed them and they praised him, together with Brothers from many other countries who had been in contact with Khomeini for many years.

When Khomeini flew back in February1979, the Brothers arranged to greet him in Tehran with representatives of the Islamic movements in Indonesia, Pakistan, Egypt, Jordan, Saudi Arabia, Iraq and Turkey, Malaysia and Syria. 'We believed we were doing God's work by supporting the revolution. Any movement in the world that can lift injustice off the Muslims is our movement.'

By March 1979 Iran was an Islamic Republic and by November Khomeini was the Supreme Leader, and the former outlaw and exile Abolhassan Banisdar became the first President of Iran.

America maintained diplomatic relations with the new order in Iran – but not for long. On 4 November 1979, radical Iranian students were angered at the Shah being allowed into America for cancer treatment. They believed this was President Jimmy Carter's opening move in returning the Shah to power and they seized the US Embassy complex in Tehran. The crisis which ensued created a near state of war, ruined Jimmy Carter's presidency, and began ongoing hostility – which escalated to a sizzling hot nuclear level by 2012 – between America and Iran.

The subliminal reason for these events lies in America's long support for the Shah government. Reza Pahlavi had ruled Iran from 1941 to 1979, with a brief period of exile in 1953 when he fled to Italy due to a power struggle with Prime Minister Mohammed Mossadegh. Because Mossadegh's policies and announcements created concern over access to Iranian oil, fuel prices, and possible Soviet influence in Iran, the United States and British intelligence services worked with Iranian military officers to overthrow the Prime Minister. On his return to the throne, the Shah established a gloved alliance with the United States which supplied weapons, training, and technical knowledge for the 'modernising' of Iran.

However, the Shah ruled as a dictator, using SAVAK, his spooky secret police, to terrorise his political enemies. He was opposed by both the Marxist Tudeh Party, and by fundamentalist Islamic leaders who believed his policies and his reliance on the Americans were corrupting Iranian society.

After the Shah's entry into America in 1979 – using the pseudonym David D Newsom – for his medical treatment, the Ayatollah Khomeini called for anti-American street demonstrations, and on 4 November that year, one demonstration developed into the takeover of the US Embassy. Students scaled the walls of the compound and took 63 Americans hostage. Three more US citizens were taken prisoner at the Iranian Foreign Ministry.

Within three weeks a group of women and African-Americans were freed and the remaining 52 hostages were held for 444 days while the world looked on in horror, wondering where it might all end. The hostages were paraded in front of television cameras, often blindfolded or hooded. Though the hostage-takers were not members of the Iranian government or military, their public loyalty to Khomeini and the Islamic government created an international crisis.

The American Government enlisted the assistance of the Muslim Brotherhood, and Youssef Nada was also asked to help: 'The Americans visited the Supreme Guide [Omar Al Telmesamy] in Cairo and made an official request that the Brotherhood intervene to help free the hostages, saying, "You are head of an Islamic Organisation and Iran is considered to be an Islamic state and you know their language and you can intervene. Will you help?"

'Al Telmesamy knew the Brotherhood would not accept the taking of hostages. It is forbidden in Islam except in war. He didn't promise the American representative anything other than to study the problem and how to tackle it. Any discussion in Iran would be with Imam Khomeini and in Washington contact had to be with President Jimmy Carter, and he was given a direct number for Carter in the White House.

'Then Al Telmesamy came to Campione and instructed me to begin discussions. I was young but I said we had to verify the request with higher American authorities – and know what they were prepared to offer the Iranians. We had to be careful not to be a bridge to deceive the Iranians. If there was a chance of peace, and to avoid destruction of a Muslim country, then we had to try, but otherwise we must not be involved.

'The Supreme Guide agreed. He didn't want a repeat of what had happened with us and Evans, the Political Secretary of the British Embassy in Cairo in 1954, when Nasser played the double game. We had to discuss it directly with the White House.

'He was with me when I called the White House and said, "I am calling in the name of the Muslim Brotherhood in Egypt. The Supreme Guide is here, he was asked by the Embassy to assist and we want to hear that request personally from the president – then we are ready to move."' The person who took the call told Nada that they couldn't put him through but that someone would call him back. 'I gave them my telephone details and asked them to call urgently as we had to move quickly. They never called me.'

Meanwhile, America reacted to the crisis by halting oil exports from Iran, expelling many Iranians living in the US, and freezing Iranian government assets and investments. Many Americans called for military action to free the hostages, but the situation became much more complicated when the Soviet Union invaded Iran's neighbour, Afghanistan, in order to crush an Islamic-based rebellion against that nation's Marxist Government.

There has never been an explanation why Jimmy Carter – or someone in authority who could have responded for him – didn't take that phone call from Youssef Nada and the Muslim Brotherhood which might have short-circuited a solution. Instead, Carter was in a face-off with oil-rich, but hostile, Iran, a rekindled Cold War with Moscow, and an America angered by his leadership.

The result was President Carter launching Operation Eagle Claw to display his strength and to liberate the hostages: it was to fail disastrously. On 24 April 1980, units of the rescue force landed in the Iranian desert to refuel their aircraft. Faulty equipment and a desert sandstorm forced the cancellation of the mission. In retreat, a transport plane and a helicopter collided and eight of the rescue team died. Tehran branded the abortive enterprise as an 'American invasion of Iran' and claimed it was 'support from God who conquered the invaders'.

The Shah died on 27 July 1980, and two months later President Saddam Hussein of Iraq invaded Iran. These two events spurred the Iranian government to enter into negotiations with America, with Algeria as a mediator.

The one-year anniversary of the start of the hostage crisis fell on 4 November 1980 – pivotally just as America went to the polls to elect a new president. Ronald Reagan had an overwhelming majority by 5pm California time, even before much of the west of the nation had voted. The incumbent Jimmy Carter hadn't had a hope: he was the biggest presidential loser in nearly 50 years. As the celebrations went on, one of the Reagan aides stood at a stairwell off the lobby of the hotel and said: 'We're going to rewrite the Iran story. Bring them home.'

When Ronald Reagan officially became President Reagan on 20 January 1981, the hostages were allowed to fly out of Iran. At the same time $8billion of confiscated Iranian assets were released.

For Youssef Nada and the Muslim Brotherhood it was not a time for celebration. They regarded the end of the hostage crisis as a victory for all Muslims and were shocked when the Shia claimed the honour of it – rather than helping the unity of the Sunni and the Shia it stretched the division between them. 'We should all be pouring our belief into one ocean,' said Nada. 'We are exporters of Islam, not exporters of revolution.'

The Middle East was boiling, with the Iran-Iraq war splitting loyalties and factions, and the Muslim Brotherhood somewhere in the middle. It was a riddle: to Iran the Brotherhood were agents acting for Iraq or Saudi Arabia or the United Arab Emirates (UAE) or for their own avaricious interests... and vice versa several times over. Saudi Arabia, the Gulf states, Iraq, the USA and, above all, the Egyptian government considered the Brotherhood as raising the same flag as Iran.

Nada controlled links between the Brotherhood and the Iranian revolution but he had to keep his meetings and negotiations secret because of the paranoia about the intentions of the new Iran. In Saudi Arabia, Iraq and the Gulf, any person or organisation having contact with Iran could be arrested and jailed.

Yet, he managed to quietly arrange many meetings inside Iran and abroad with important leaders, senior government ministers, ambassadors, the clergy and Pasdaran chiefs – those of the Revolutionary Guard created to enforce Islamic codes and the new power. He was invited to Tehran several times and met the controlling clergy.

An American-instigated shipping embargo had left Iran painfully short of food and other essentials. The Minister of Commerce, Reza Sadr, asked Youssef Nada for help. He was, after all, 'the king of the seas', the Poseidon who could move all commodities. Against the odds, and the embargo, he did – and lost $5million in the process.

He transported 100 thousand tons of steel and 450 thousand tons of wheat into Iran. The goods went by rail – the steel required 3,300 railway carriages – from Hamburg by train to Kotka in Finland and then east over Russia to the Caspian Sea and on to Julfa in Iran. This enterprise was in defiance of the embargo. 'I used all my skill and contacts and means to do it legally,' said Nada. 'No one can find a hole in the process to say that I did it outside the law. The embargo rules excluded contracts which were signed and confirmed before the date of the embargo resolution.

'I did it for God, for an Islamic country. I make a difference between commerce and profits and relationships and assistance. They are two different things. I lost a great deal of money because the Iranians disputed the amount of goods which were shipped with what was delivered in different warehouses inside the country. In foreign trade the exporter should be paid according to the bill of lading and delivery in the harbour, not in warehouses inside the country. Within the inland transportation process some trucks could be stolen. They said that although they were certain I was correct, there was a revolution going on! And if I was given government money they could be accused of corruption – as I would be too. I accepted the loss.

'I have met with people I can never speak of or name as it would betray confidences. These names and these situations will go to the grave with me. Bad men could cut me into a thousand pieces and I would not give the names. It is that trust which gives me my name and the Brotherhood its veracity as an honest broker in conflicts.

'With the Kurds, in Iraq and Iran and Saudi Arabia and Yemen and

Malaysia, Turkey, Syria, Lebanon, Algeria, Afghanistan, Pakistan, Russian, China [East Turkestan], and others we have acted in many roles and have often had success. When it has not been 100 per cent success at least we have mellowed some difficult situations, prevented violence and deaths. Nothing can be more important than trying to achieve a solution in such circumstances.'

In the difficult days following the Iranian revolution, and hard on the heels of the Iran-Iraq war, Youssef Nada met with the majority of the Iranian leadership, including the conservative Ayatollah Seyed Ali Hoseyni Kh mene'i who succeeded Ayatollah Khomeini as Supreme Leader of Iran. He visited him at his home together with Mohammed Souri who built the National Iranian Tanker Company (NITC), the biggest tanker company in the world.

He was also close to Grand Ayatollah Hussein-Ali Montazeri Najafabadi, who at one time was Khomeini's designated successor but fell out with him over the direction of post-revolution Iran. A hugely respected Islamic scholar, Hussein-Ali Montazeri supported women's rights and civil liberties which he believed were being infringed by the new leaders.

He and Youssef Nada had long, enjoyable talks. Hussein-Ali Montazeri, who had worked on the new constitution for Iran, presented his friend with the book of his theory, ideas and plans. It is inscribed with the Persian year and has a place of pride in Nada's extensive library (with a copy of Hussein-Ali Montazeri's Persian dated – 1409H – obituary carefully tucked into the pages).

From their meeting in France, Nada always remained in touch with Iran's new president, Abolhassan Banisdar, through Muzafar Bartooma. They developed a close relationship and they met in Tehran after the revolution: 'There was a revolt in Kurdistan that was divided into warring factions.

The president wanted us to intervene to settle the dispute – the Revolutionary Guards shouldn't have been fighting people who helped the revolution. One communist group was linked to the Soviet Union from the north and the other with the Brothers. They were Sunni, not Shia, but Khomeini didn't grant them their freedom to teach the Sunni version of Islam or allow them to have a Sunni mosque in Tehran. Or use Kurdistan oil income in their own territory.

'Some of them were killed. The leader who I knew, a Kurdish Iranian called Ahmad Moftizadeh, from Kermanshah, went into hiding. Abolhassan Banisdar had a Kurdish adviser, Muzafar Partooma – a Brotherhood member who'd been living in America but returned after the revolution – and he contacted us. He asked us to make peace between the government and the Kurdish people. Mr Himmat and I went to the war zone.

'Although Ahmad Moftizadeh was a fugitive, our assignment to seek him out was approved by Abolhassan Banisdar. He knew any contact between Muslims was good. Governments may have more resources than the Muslim Brotherhood but we sometimes achieve what they cannot. We know our limitations and we stay within our boundaries, but personal contacts always help us. We took precautions – there were communists within the revolutionary Islamic government who were moving in the name of Islam and dividing from inside, and they could have followed us – as the government could – to locate Ahmad Moftizadeh. His problem was that he helped the revolution, and the Kurdish nationalists, like the communists, didn't like that. They were after him, as were the Iranian revolutionaries. He was a most wanted man. He disappeared.

'Mr Himmat and I flew from Tehran to Kermanshah. We both went on this mission as it was absolutely necessary that one should cover the other; both of us were ready to die. Ahmad Moftizadeh's people were waiting. We met his cousin and then two cars escorted us to the house where he was protected.

'Ahmad Moftizadeh was very angry with the Ayatollah. He said again and again how his group had supported Khomeini and the Iranian Revolution: in return they had been promised increased influence within the new government. Instead, he complained that his Kurdish faction had been abandoned to the Soviets, who were killing them "every hour of the day". We told Ahmad Moftizadeh the killing had to stop. Anyone dividing Muslims was wrong, anyone dividing Iranians was wrong. We wanted union and tolerance for all the mistakes which had been made.

'We talked of the benefit of the country for all Muslims together and not just for racial actions. Because he was a Kurd he wanted the proceeds of Kurdistan, the rich revenues of the oil in the region, to go directly to those people and not to central government.

'He complained that in Tehran there was no mosque for the minority Sunni. The mosques there were all for Shia. In the West they might regard a mosque as a mosque, but for example the Sunni cannot smoke cigarettes in the mosque; the Shia can. Also, in prayers, there are differences. The Shia pray three times a day and the Sunni five times. They complained the mosque was not open for them to pray five times and therefore they must have their own mosques.

'I said to Ahmad Moftizadeh that from the Islamic point-of-view we cannot be racist and we cannot discuss the race. He complained they'd been sent Shia teachers to teach their children. In some demands he was right and we had to carry his message.'

By the time they finished talking it was late night and some of Zadeh's guards took them to their hotel near the airport. It was agreed the guards would collect them 90 minutes before their plane left. They had just checked in to their room when there was a knock on the door. When Nada opened the door he was faced by a dozen men there holding machine guns. 'Brother, you have to go with us now,' one of them said. 'You can't sleep here, if you do, you will be killed here.'

Nada recognised one of the leaders, and they went with them. 'He said there was a plot to kill us. Ahmad Moftizadeh had sent them to protect us and they'd been ordered to stay with us and march us to the plane. Somebody wanted myself and Mr Himmat dead, and there was plenty of choice about whom – from communists to the revolutionaries and all the factions in between. We had a guard until we reached the plane and returned safely to Tehran.'

The Islamic Revolution was spinning with a carousel of politicians in and out of favour. President Abolhassan Banisdar was no longer there: he'd fled back to France after falling out with Ayatollah Khomeini who had signed impeachment papers against him in June 1981. The Revolutionary Guard had taken over the Presidential Palace and executed some of Banisdar's friends and several of Nada's contacts in the government.

What friends Ahmad Moftizadeh had in the Revolutionary government soon vanished altogether and in 1982 he was captured in his mountain lair and charged as a threat to national security. The exact notion of his wrongdoings was never spelled out but he was jailed for a decade.

With happenstance, the two men who had tried to help him all the years earlier, Nada and Ghaleb Himmat were in Tehran for a meeting with the Foreign Ministry two weeks after his release in 1993. When he learned he was freed the concerned Nada asked if he could see him. They said they didn't know where he was, but using a Brotherhood contact, Himmat was taken to the house where he was living. He was shocked when Ahmad Moftizadeh came out, a physical wreck, looking like a skeleton. He told Himmat: 'I was going to leave yesterday but I was too weak to go. I didn't know why, but now I do. I was waiting to see you.'

'They'd held him in a cell one-and-a-half metres high and he couldn't stand up straight,' said Nada. 'All the bones had been broken again and again. His body was ruined. He died two weeks after that meeting. After he died some of his associates were sought out by the Iranian authorities and murdered. They didn't want them gathering around the memory – the martyrdom – of Ahmad Moftizadeh. I had made good my promise and found him, but there was no satisfaction in that with the discovery of the wreck of a man.

'He was another victim of the manufactured war between the Shia and the Sunni. The differences between the Sunni and the Shia have been manipulated for the purpose of divide and rule over the decades:

first by the British and then the Americans. The Saudis conjure up this dispute on behalf of the Americans all the time. The great fear of the West has always been that all the Arab nations would be united, and the game has always been to play one against another. In 1907, at a conference in London, the British Prime Minister Campbell Bannerman said: "In the Middle East the people have the same religion, the same language, the same feeling: we have to divide them."

'During the 1950s in the Middle East an anti-American movement was guided by Nasser as the leader of the Arab nationalist movement. Although the Americans had backed Nasser he whipped anti-American feeling as part of Arab nationalism. In my opinion, the main reason for that was the case of Israel. For me, the existence of Israel in the area is not for the Jewish. Israel was created to have an entity to police whenever any troublesome neighbour raised his head. Israel was made to bring down upstarts, and to look after the interests of others.'

(In February 2012, Baroness Tonge, a senior Liberal Democrat, was expelled from the UK political party for saying: 'One day, the United States of America will get sick of giving £70billion a year to Israel to support what I call America's aircraft carrier in the Middle East.')

'When Nasser got the emotions of the Arabs with him the Americans decided to use the Shah of Iran as a buffer against him. The Shah happily did their bidding. He boasted that Persians came before the Arabs and were imperial when Arabs were sitting in tents in the desert. It was one nationalism against another – Persia versus Arabia – all created for American interests. It wasn't a war by weapons: every side was trying to get the emotions of the people. The Shah said "Persian Gulf" and the Arabs called it the "Arabian Gulf".

'When the Americans turned the Shah against Nasser, they had to divide the Arab bloc to stop it becoming too strong. They convinced Saudi Arabia to co-operate with the Shah against Nasser's nationalism and that divided the Arab side too. That way the Americans were able to protect their huge commercial and political interests in the area. They pushed King Faisal and then Fahd and Saudi Arabia to be against

Arab nationalism and against Nasser. They made two fronts and Arabism became much bigger: not only strong but dominating the areas of American interest. Iran was a part of that interest – the oil is there, the gas is there and the Soviet Union is very close by.

'When the Six Day War ended in 1967 with the failure of Arab Nationalism, the Americans sought to find another flag and another issue to continue dividing and ruling the area while sucking its wealth and oil and the energy.

'After Nasser became weak and needed to rebuild his army he cosied up to King Faisal of Saudi Arabia. Faisal, for his interests, did not want to deal with Israel alone and to revive Nasser he financed a new Egyptian army. In a very short time Nasser died and King Faisal teamed up with his successor Anwar Sadatand and kept the cash rolling into Egypt.

'The Shah was impotent without America, which wanted to keep him very strong because of the Soviet Union on his border: he was definitely stronger than Israel. These were the players and the Americans moved them like chess pieces to defend and attack for self-protection. King Faisal and the Shah got on but the power game changed. The Shah was strong and arrogant. He started to discriminate against the Saudis and they started to fear him.

'When Nasser died, Sadat was the choice of the system – the army and the Military Intelligence, the power then and today – to take his place. The clique who'd been around Nasser regarded Sadat as weak and totally controllable. That changed. They quickly started to be afraid of him. He wasn't a glove puppet after all. Sadat claimed they were about to mount a coup d'état and arrested all those who'd been the real governors in Egypt, the circle with which Nasser controlled the army, intelligence, police, and the ministries. When he had total control of the country he concluded a secret deal with Israel. Sadat was backed by the Americans.

'Although Saudi Arabia made the link for him with America, when he came into power the White House took him alone. When he negotiated the Peace Treaty [it was signed in Washington by Sadat and Israeli Prime Minister Menachem Begin on 26 March 1979, following the Camp David Accords a year earlier presided over by President Jimmy Carter] the Arab League accused him of betraying them. They transferred the Arab League from Cairo to Tunisia. Sadat, and so Egypt, were no longer the champions of the Arabs. And so came the time of Saddam Hussein as the hero of the Arab world.

'History repeats like tough meat.

'Even the Arabs as well as the Americans assisted Saddam Hussein against Iran. They believed in the likes of Saddam Hussein? Saddam was against all of them. In his newspapers, in his speeches and on the radio he attacked all of the Arab leaders. He considered all of them traitors for the Arab case. Yet, when the Americans wanted to stop Khomeini and pushed Saddam to war with Iran he asked all the Arabs to back him, and they did.

'Since the 1930s, after the international economic crisis, America tactically reconciled with Islam. It inherited its colonial behaviour from the British, French, Italian, Spanish, Dutch and Portuguese imperialists. Its economic interests in oil, along with political and military considerations, were mainly settled in the Middle East during the fight against communism, given that Islam is the fieriest enemy of atheism which is the main pillar of the communist system. If America finds that its interests require reconciliation with the Muslim Brotherhood it will do it. [The first formal meeting was in Cairo on 10 January 2012, almost 14 months on from this remark being made by Nada.]

'From the Sharia side, the stories in the Koran teach us that dialogue is a civilised way of life accepted by Allah, messengers, believers, and wise men. US actions are the product of policies which may be tactical and change according to reality for serving the strategic and stable long-term interests. As for democracy, human rights, allies, friends, moderates and treaties – they are just cosmetics according to who or what is the US administration.

'Yet, like past empires they can't beautify ugly and deformed imperial goals. In the contemporary world, Noriega the monster in Panama, was one of the best US allies in Central America. When America turned against him, it ended his political, moral and human life. It threw him in prison for tens of years and then sent him to French prisons and then back to Panama to jail again. This is their friend. The same with Mobutu in the Congo – he was their big African ally but died from cancer in exile in a dirty, diseased hospital in Morocco.

'Ferdinand Marcos, who excelled in serving America in South-east Asia, had the same fate as Mobutu. Even the Shah, who acted as a US policeman in the Gulf and maintained American strategies against the Soviet Union and was the sole supporter of Israel in the Middle East, was not cosseted. His end was the same as Mobutu and Marcos. Saddam Hussein was used by America to paralyse the Iranian revolution in a bloody war, causing poverty in the region and giving the oil to America at prices lower than the cost of water in the oil producing nations.

'The lesson is that America is serving American's interests. The money America takes from the oil producing countries in the Middle East is enough to make the Middle East paradise. When a *gallon* of petrol in the United States sold for $1, the price for *just a litre* in all the Middle East countries, in Egypt and North Africa, was $5.5. It makes no sense. But the Americans have in their pocket the rulers of the Gulf countries who have the oil – rulers who, because their great-grandfathers conquered some tribes in the desert consider themselves the owners of the oil; and the owner of the country. King Saud, for instance, who named a country and its population with his name – Saudi Arabia.

'What if America was run by "King George Washington"? Or Britain by "King Winston Churchill"? And their family were in charge in perpetuity, and all the others are their slaves? I am trying to clarify the events. I am not against this or that nationality.

'The Brotherhood and I believe that although the British left the area a long time ago, their influence and their intelligence until now is stronger than the CIA. Quietly and silently, the British still have all the keys, even in Iran. They know better than the Americans. Even during the time of Saddam in Iraq, they knew more. It's built into Britain's history, their empire, and is systematic and silent. The British buried themselves into the nations which they controlled. So much goes on which no one ever knows about. There are so many secrets in the past and will be in the future.

'As my wife said to me: *"The most important factor which makes everyone correct is that he has his policeman inside him. God sees him wherever he is. God follows him whatever he do. When nobody sees you is when evil is made."'*

CHAPTER FIVE

STORM IN
THE SANDS

'All treaties between great states cease to be binding when they come in conflict with the struggle for existence.'

Otto von Bismarck, 1872

E vil is no stranger to Youssef Nada. He has confronted it face-to-face and fought it all his life. With his life's mission to bring some sanity into a world of disputes and death he has encountered all manifestations of what we can do to each other. What he especially abhors is the constant manoeuvring to keep the Sunni and the Shia at odds with each other: what he calls a false war.

This self-interest tactic has balanced kingdoms and changed history. Nada offers an interesting solution: 'The Sunni have four schools of religious rules: the Malki, the Shafei, the Hanafi, and the Hambali. It would be better to say that the *Muslims*, not the *Sunni*, have five schools by adding the Shia Jafari, which represent the majority and most moderate Shia followers. By accepting the difference, all could be reconciled.

'The Shia, since Ali the cousin of the Prophet co-operated and worked alongside Sunni caliphs, should not use his name to condone what he never did – reject the other three caliphate. They are dead and gone and there is surely no point in their descendants fighting in their name for 1,500 years preventing the unity of one religion. All the five religious schools believe in the same God and Prophet and pay *zakat* [compulsory giving] and accepted the same Koran and said the same prayers. Those who betrayed and divided Muslim generations for fifteen centuries must not dream to go to paradise.'

Al-Azhar University, a thousand-year-old mosque in Cairo, is the premier Islamic centre of thinking and learning in the world (the equivalent of Oxbridge of all the four Sunni schools of scholarship) and has missions everywhere. It lost much of its prestige when Nasser placed its mosques and colleges under strict state control. (Later, with the end of Mubarak in 2011, it began to try and re-establish itself as a force in Egyptian politics and society and in Sunni Muslim thinking – just as the fall of Saddam Hussein eight years earlier opened up a different world for Shia theologians.)

Nevertheless it has always had power as controller of the Justice Ministry which issues religious legal rulings – *fatwas*. But not all follow the ways of Al-Azhar. It is the conflicting thinking and interpretation of Islam which has led to so much strife. Youssef Nada believes some ideology, some way of looking at and understanding the Muslim religion, was developed to put down one side or another: an unholy union of politics and religion.

'When Fahd became King of Saudi Arabia in 1982 he opened universities in Saudi Arabia to teach Islam, and not be reliant on what was being taught in Egypt. The Saudi universities are supported by monies and scholarships and they created their strict way of interpreting Islam. It was used as a weapon against Nasser. When his call for Arab nationalism started to echo from Morocco to Iraq and from Syria until Yemen, the rulers of Saudi Arabia were in trouble. Nasser in one speech said: "We are going to topple them even if they enter Mecca." (Mecca is sacred and no one, certainly no Muslim, is allowed to fight there.)

'The guardian of Mecca is Saudi Arabia and they started to spread their version of understanding Islam. They said it was forbidden for Muslims to support nationalism because all people under God are the same. Nationalism was not allowed in Islam. That is not the Muslim teaching. That is politics. The Saudis extracted from the religion anything to support what they said.

'The Shia were discriminated against because Saudi Arabia's version of Islam stretched throughout the Gulf. To them, the Shia's faith was a deviation from true Islam. Nasser, and his nationalism, has long gone. So has the Shah – but in 2012 the discrimination is still going on, and being manipulated. It's not a mistake of Saudi Arabia or the Shia or the Sunni. They have to defend themselves, but self-interested groups and nations will always pour oil on the fire. Mad people will conjure up craziness in the name of religion and use it to justify wrongdoing. It is a tinderbox: the ongoing challenge is to stop it bursting into flames.

'When Khomeini returned to Iran, the Brotherhood encouraged the regime to revive talks between the Shia and Sunni clergy and everyone agreed. It fell apart almost immediately. Iran was accused of "exporting revolution" and wanting to destabilise the Arab countries. It was decreed that any talks between Shia and Sunni were dangerous for security. The talks were frozen.

'The Ayatollah Khomeini arranged a committee to conciliate between the factions and asked the Brotherhood to be involved. The Supreme Guide gave me the mandate but I could not put forward a theological case. I had to put the political case. It was clear: the head of the clergy could not be told what to do or say by the head of government. The head of the clergy must say what Islam wants. He must be elected by the people and not by the State.

'The clergy and the State must be completely separate entities: religious independence from the power. If the head of state said to the Pope on the pain of death "declare that it is forbidden to deal with Arabs" you get what the State wants, not the religion. This is how it is

71

in Saudi Arabia. All the time there is much to consider: politics, sometimes religion, sometimes self-interest.'

And, people striking out at those who want to help. Under Nada's
watchful eye the Muslim Brotherhood were very much involved in
Afghanistan when the Soviets were there. 'There were mujahideen
[strugglers in the path of God] but there were also thieves and killers
too and wild, insane groups who were fighting each other while being
at war with the Soviets.

'Whether they were Sunni or Shia they were bandits; they robbed
and pillaged, and some of the stories were like storybook nightmares.
A group of doctors from the Brotherhood were sent there by Dr
Ahmed Al Malt to help save lives, but they were kidnapped by a group
of Shia fighters. The Brothers contacted me to ask if I could help.

'I believed that the best solution was for Iran to intervene. In Tehran
I met the authorities and they said they would talk to the chief of the
kidnappers, named Mansouri, who told them. They said: "The
Brotherhood are rich and they have to pay a ransom." I exploded. That
made me so angry. Which Islam is saying that? Iran says it is a Muslim
state and yet they send a message that if we want the doctors to be safe,
we must pay a ransom.

'It was outrageous. They should have gone after the kidnappers,
kicked them out! It was one of the lowest points between me and the
Iranians, after we had co-operated in a lot of things in the past. But that
is the way of politics. Then the solution came from God: a sandstorm
blew in and the kidnappers fled for shelter leaving the doctors, and the
Brothers were able to escape. It was a miracle that they came out.'

During the Brotherhood's involvement in Afghanistan, Youssef Nada
was in touch with leaders like Burhanuddin Rabbani who visited him
in Campione – a meeting that caused problems for Nada. Rabbani was
the President of the Islamic State of Afghanistan for four years from
1992, and was assassinated by a suicide bomber at his home in Kabul in
September 2011. He visited Nada with one of his aides and they

discussed the cooperation between the main factions fighting the Soviets: Rabbani himself, Gulbuddin Hekmatyar, Abdul Rasul Sayyaf and Mohamed Nabi. It was a friendly meeting.

'The next day his aide sent me a letter thanking me and saying they considered themselves part of the Muslim Brotherhood. They also asked me to help them get military advisers, guns and missiles, uniforms, radios... and even shoes. The letter was signed by them both.

'Despite all my contact with them, and others like them, I never put myself in that grey zone – of being involved in weaponry. I am a politician, not a rebel or fighter. I never forgot the Cairo Abbasia military prison and how the people were tortured. My conviction is that I must never be involved in violence even if it is justified. I did not answer the letter.'

The most important person in the Afghan problem was Gulbuddin Hekmatyar – the strongest player and the leader of Hezb-e-Islami, a paramilitary and political group on the Pakistani border fighting the Soviets. They were, said Nada, 'supplied with a great deal of money and war materials'.

'If anyone wanted to make peace in Afghanistan – to get to a situation of anything but war – he had to do it with the Pashtun, the Taliban or Hezb-e-Islami who were parts of the Pashtun tribes. The Taliban were in their early stages of formation and were very tough to talk with. Hezb-e-Islami weren't tolerant but they were easier to deal with; Gulbuddin Hekmatyar was comparatively open-minded. It was a complex tribal situation with the factions and their loyalties to the Taliban and Hezb-e-Islami, the Uzbeks, and, of course, to themselves.

'This time the Brothers said to me, "Do what you can. This war must end – every day there are Muslims being killed by the hand of Muslims." I was flying solo. They gave me the signal and I started to work. No one told me what to do. I contacted Gulbuddin Hekmatyar and went to Pakistan. I was met in Peshawar by a member of Hezb-e-Islami.

'I was handed around like a bag of laundry, taken to one place and then another and finally delivered at a group of buildings that were alive with spotlights to identify anyone coming close. I was escorted to an office-like room, the door was opened and in he came, Gulbuddin Hekmatyar – the big warrior with a big smile. He knew me; I had met him several times.

'We immediately started to speak. I had no time to lose. He knew the Brothers couldn't condemn him battling the invaders of his country, but I was able to show his strong negotiating position. I explained that the best way for them to take their rights was by being strong and negotiating. I went on: "Let us assume the Soviets leave next week. When you are in charge of the country you will find dying people, no hospitals, no schools, no food, no roads, no houses. Even the fields where the people go to cultivate their food are full of mines. You are stuck. If you talk now, when the Soviets want out, you should ask them to clear the mines and to make reparations."

'I explained that when you are weak, the other party will dictate to you. When you are strong, go and negotiate. You take what you want, but without any sacrifice, without damage. The Soviets wanted to leave – and didn't want their men to be killed during their retreat. They also wanted to have a good relationship with the new regime and not have an enemy on their borders. I asked him what was better – to take charge of a country that had not been totally destroyed, or play the hero shooting missiles in the air?

'I told him: "You will take over a barren land. If the Americans or the Pakistanis are helping you today [aid was around $600million from America and Saudi Arabia by proxy via the Pakistani Secret Service] the issue for you after that is that you will have nothing. Help will stop." I said that everyone considered the Soviet Union to be the great Devil. They had destroyed all before them but they were weak. I returned to the same rule: when you are strong, you negotiate, and the cheapest and easiest way to win any war is to avoid it.'

Nada explained to Gulbuddin Hekmatyar that if he talked immediately with the Russians he could demand reparations, not charity. He told him to demand that all the landmines be cleared, and compensation paid for the roads, schools and hospitals and all the facilities they destroyed.

He tried to make Gulbuddin Hekmatyar understand it was not a betrayal to deal with the Soviets, it was to protect the interests of the people and the country: 'Every situation has its requirements. Feelings are one thing and the reality is another and you must deal with the reality.'

The two men talked for about six hours, then Hekmatyar told Nada: 'I believe we can go in this direction, but I don't have the means. I don't have any contact with them. On the contrary, I am fighting them. How can I talk to them?'

Nada's plan was for the Iranians to act as intermediaries and talk to the Soviets about some reasonable solution to try and save Afghanistan from certain ruin.

He asked Hekmatyar to give him a chance to work it out: 'Let me try to see whether the Iranians are prepared to mediate. The Iranians don't want the Soviet and the Americans against them. If they help the Soviets they will ask their support against the Americans.' Hekmatyar told Nada: 'I authorise you to do this, but let me follow step by step.'

It was well-known throughout the Middle East that Nada had contact with the Iranians – 'with everyone. I hear everyone. I don't close my door'. The Iranians said they had no objections and agreed to meet Hekmatyar.

'From then on I asked Ghaleb Himmat to travel with Gulbuddin Hekmatyar so that he would be treated properly in the negotiations,' said Nada. 'The relationship between him and the Iranians was evil, very bad. Mr Himmat was able to support him, to protect him from condescension, from being dismissed as a mountain warlord.

'It was arranged for him to fly to meet the Iranians, together with Mr Himmat. Three hours before their flight left the Americans intervened. Prince Turki bin Faisal Al Saud, who was head of the Saudi Intelligence Service and worked with the CIA and Pakistan against the Soviets in Afghanistan, went to see Gulbuddin Hekmatyar. Just before Hekmatyar was to leave for Tehran, the Americans took him to Riyadh and everything we'd worked for collapsed.

'The killing in Afghanistan did not stop. The Americans wanted the war to continue: they wanted the Soviet Union to bleed as much as possible, they didn't want them to retreat safely. And they got what they wanted. Gulbuddin Hekmatyar continued the aggression: he bombarded Kabul and tens of thousands died.

'The tribal leaders fought with themselves over who would be the saviour of Kabul, who will be the hero. Then they started to kill each other and more tens of thousands died. Such things are troubling but you cannot be frustrated or sidetracked from the good intentions. When you have done all you can to prevent horror, you must not be diverted from your purpose if you cannot do it. You try again and hope for success the next time, like your Robert the Bruce.

All I ever wanted was to stop violence, it was the purpose of the Brothers and why we acted and worked with every faction.

'When Mir-Hossein Mousavi Khameneh, who was President of Iran [from 1981 to 1989] and is now an Opposition leader, wanted to meet with Gulbuddin Hekmatyar and the others he found it hard to make connections. We made arrangements for him. I supplied him with telephone numbers and places to be in Peshawar. We were in contact with him in Islamabad and when he was established pulled away and allowed him to make his mission.'

Youssef Nada's unbending beliefs did, and do, support him through dashed hopes. Yet, he is human and there is a sadness in his eyes at the stumbling of efforts which could have accomplished so much in saving lives and protecting countries.

The complexity of the parallel importance of religion and politics in so many of his negotiations as a statesman for the Muslim Brotherhood has enforced on him the need for a swiftness of mind; problems are to be solved and not dismissed as beyond resolve. He often looks to the past for guidance, if not total answers, but his starting point is always that all people, all individuals, are equal.

'There is much talk that the Muslim Brotherhood want to make the *khalifa* [the caliph], the head of state,' he said. 'It was historically but can never exist again because of changes in the world and Muslim history and reality, also because of the way Muslims were ruled after the first four *khalifas* whom the Prophet asked the Muslims to follow after him.

'After them there were several Muslim empires, not Muslim Ummah [a commonwealth of believers]. It was like a nation ruled by a family dynasty; there were Muslim and Turkish empires headed by strong men and their families or tribe. The head man gave himself the title khalifa.

'During the time of the first four khalifas, the khalifa was an arbitrator and the ultimate decision maker. There is a story well-known in Egypt: the second khalifa, Umar ibn al-Khattab, appointed the head of the Muslims in Egypt. The son of a Christian priest was walking with the son of the head of the state who turned and slapped the priest's boy. His father went to Mecca and met the khalifa and told him about the incident.

'The khalifa summoned the boy who had slapped, and his father, to come to Mecca. He told the Christian boy: "Return the slap." He did. Head of State's son? Christian priest's son? Everyone is equal irrespective of class or religion. That was justice.

'But after the first four khalifas, the tyrants from *banu umayya* [the first Islamic dynasty] ruled every Muslim community and state. The past is packed with tyrants who created empires: the Romans, Greeks, the Arabs and the Turks. They carved their names in history and were able to rule huge expanses of the planet. I've studied most of them and none of them compare with the first four khalifas of Islam in justice, devotion and respect for human dignity.

'After centuries of exploitation, people developed several systems to prevent mankind from tyrannies. I believe the best are democracies. I don't see any conflict between Islam and democracy. Islam is a religion but democracy is a tool. Islam requires every Muslim to implement rules which allow freedom and justice. With all the defects and deficiencies of democracy, it is built on dividing and separating the powers to reach justice. No one person can have the decisive power – be a tyrant.

'After the first four devoted khalifas, the system of khalifa went wrong and couldn't compare to what went before. Today, the khalifa system doesn't work and could not implement the highest value in Islam which is justice. I cannot find in the Koran or the Sunna any obligation for the Muslims to be ruled by a khalifa. I found that the highest values in Islam are justice and equality, and any system which can secure that is accepted by Islam.

'Throughout the world today you find Muslims – in Pakistan and Afghanistan, Indonesia, the United States, in Britain in the Middle East, China – from everywhere. Wherever a person is they like to preserve their traditions and not just religion: the family life, the relationship between the people.

'The difference is that they have an individual style from their own society which everyone has to respect. You can't complain that Muslims won't become a mirror of us. You can't expect them to give up their history and personal and private sentiments. Even among the Muslims there are differences, just as there are in every Western community. The Italian mentality is open, for instance, whereas the Swiss are conservative.

'The selfish and arrogant attitude, the smugness that we must be like another, is not just and will never work. There is controversy about the mosques in the West and people are praying in the streets. But what if they have nowhere else to pray? If they are part of the society, you should assist them to have their own privacy and their own prayer rooms and places. If you prohibit them you create a feeling of discrimination. In European history the Protestants in France had to go in the small back streets to pray. It is the same thing: no respect for others.

'Muslims are accused of wanting to change the West but they want to be judged as people looking to respect others, who want to be equal with others. When you provoke someone, they act out of character.

Some of them might give their bad word to you, some might hit you. If you provoke, then you have to expect them to respond.

'All those who are denying the others the liberty to meet in their beliefs and to be able to think with freedom – why deny them? Some accept to live without liberty, but you should expect that others don't accept that? This will create the hate, the hate will create the revolt, and the revolt will create crimes.

'You must not blind your eyes to the difference between fighting ideology and fighting religion. If you look into history, see how the Romans tried to fight the Christianity and the Roman Empire vanished and the Christianity continued. If you try to fight religion with power and force, you don't have a chance. You need distraction from both sides – to try to find a way that this religion can accept you, and you accept it without adopting it. You cannot force those who believe in it to adopt your way.

'The biggest wars in humanity were the First and Second World Wars – these were not Muslims' wars. They were Christian wars, and tens of millions were killed. Consult history about the following atrocities:

- the Crusaders who went to Palestine and filled the streets of Jerusalem with floods of Muslim blood;
- the Andalusia in Spain and all types of crimes against the humanity which was done to the Muslims;
- about what was done to the Jews in Europe 1932 until 1944;
- about one million Afghani and another million Iraqi civilians killed at the beginning of the 21st century, and the residual of two million widows and five millions orphans;
- about what was done in the Chinese opium war and the wars in Cambodia, Laos and Vietnam;
- about the shipping of humans from Africa to enslave them on the other side of the Atlantic;
- about Hiroshima and Nagasaki.

'History does not forget or forgive. It will tell you that they were not Muslims who did these things; they were not Muslim terrorists; they were not coming from the Middle East or Asia or Africa. This cannot be justified religiously – unless you corrupt the message of God, or intentionally misinterpret and twist it. Those who carried out such atrocities were wild and savage creatures. This wasn't God's work. It was people who did it and people make mistakes. And politics and religion collide.'

Youssef Nada became involved in that sort of conflict following a violent disturbance between the Shia of Iran and the Sunni of Saudi Arabia during a most holy moment for them all. With the Iran–Iraq war in its seventh year, a group of Iranian pilgrims were caught up in a riot with Saudi security forces during the *hajj* [pilgrimage] to Mecca in 1987. The death count remains disputed but most reports put the toll at 402 people: 275 Iranian pilgrims, 85 Saudi police, and 42 others. What is not in dispute is they were all Muslims.

News of the death of the Shia Iranians and the involvement of the Sunni Saudi security led to disturbances in Teheran, with the Saudi and Kuwaiti embassies being attacked. In Mecca, there were street battles beside the Grand Mosque – fighting which is completely forbidden in Islam. They were on the eve of the hajj: one of the five pillars of Islam, and the high point of the Islamic year.

Iranian pilgrims had held an annual demonstration against Israel and the United States for half a dozen years, but in 1987 a cordon of Saudi police and the National Guard had sealed off part of the planned protest route. That provoked the confrontation. It was a difficult moment for the world – the West was wary of what it saw as growing Islamic fundamentalism, and there was tension over American efforts to escort Kuwaiti oil tankers through the Persian Gulf.

Underlying the unsettling mix of torn interests was the prospect of an all-out Sunni versus Shia War: what Youssef Nada regards as the policy of divide and rule. The violent demonstrations began when

80

Iranian pilgrims massed after Friday's midday prayers for a political demonstration, which had been forbidden by the Saudi authorities. The pilgrims chanted 'Death to America! Death to the Soviet Union! Death to Israel!' and brandished portraits of their leader, Ayatollah Khomeini. Iran claimed that the Saudi riot police shot at 'innocent demonstrators'.

Before the start of the next pilgrimage season, the Middle Eastern leaders wanted to prevent future trouble in Islam's holiest city. Youssef Nada was approached to mediate. For once he changed world events without leaving his home in Campione. The dispute was resolved in his sitting room overlooking Lake Lugano. At the meeting was a representative of King Fahd of Saudi Arabia (Ali Ben Musalem with other two junior aides), another representative from Ali Akbar Hashemi Rafsanjani, the Iranian President (Moustafa Fumani), together with two Iranian ambassadors (Husain Malaek the ambassador to Switzerland and Javad Turkabadi, the ambassador to Bahrain).

The animosity at the meeting chilled the room: 'The dispute was flaring and war was a great possibility. Preparations were being made for the next pilgrimage. King Fahd arranged a large extension for the place of worship in Mecca but there still wasn't enough room for all the pilgrims. The Saudis gave a quota but it reduced the number allowed from Iran.

'Old pilgrims wanted to make the journey before they died. The Saudis calculated the quota according to the population of every Muslim country. The Iranians had waiting lists shifted from year to year. When the negotiations nearly stalled as everyone merely repeated their respective positions, I said to the Saudi: "They want 120,000 and you say the maximum you can give is 80,000. The difference is 40,000. Why not give the 40,000 visas during the [Hurum] four months which the Shia consider a semi-pilgrimage to Mecca?"

'I asked the Iranians to consider going to Mecca during the months of Hurum and to regard it as a proper and full pilgrimage. If they did that, the Saudi would be obliged to issue them visas for that time. In the beginning, when I gave the proposal, both of them had stopped talking as if they were paralysed: no answer. Then they asked to use the telephone. The Saudi went to my bedroom. The others went to another room. One called King Fahd and the others Rafsanjani.

'And it was settled. But earlier, every party was preparing for a fight during the next pilgrimage. Saudi Arabia wanted to show the whole world they were in control of their country and that Khomeini could do nothing. If there had been no agreement many thousands and thousands of people would have been at risk.'

Nada's dealings with the Ayatollah Khomeini were always delicate. Because of his sensibilities he could be manipulated, as in the case of author Salman Rushdie whose Booker prize-winning novel *Midnight's Children* in 1981 was not a landmark event in Iran. However, the publication of his *The Satanic Verses* in 1988 was.

When the novel and its author were accused of blasphemy and mocking Islam, the Supreme Leader of Iran issued a *fatwa* calling for Rushdie to be executed. 'I tell you frankly, Khomeini was mistaken,' said Nada. 'The Rushdie affair was a petty matter and the Islamic movement shouldn't have been caught up in such a thing – the Ayatollah was egged on. It was not good for the Muslim world to announce that someone was going to be killed on the streets.'

Nada maintains the Rushdie issue helped others to play up the Ayatollah's 'madness' in the eyes of the West. 'It became nothing but headlines when the Ayatollah issued his *fatwa*. From the Islamic point-of-view this misguided man couldn't say more than what you find in every book in Europe, so to make an issue of the words he wrote was wrong. And to ask people to go and kill him was disgusting. It is not acceptable, but it became politically guided from both sides.

'The British remain hugely influential in the Middle East including Iran and have the intelligence – MI6, not the CIA. There are many contradictions in our lives. What we see is not always what is there. You can only attempt to do good amid all the complex relationships.'

CHAPTER SIX

WARLORDS

'If you don't prove the link between war and its precedent politics then you will not understand anything in this war.'

Vladimir Lenin

G oodness was never associated with Saddam Hussein. He never
indulged in it. The rivers Tigris and Euphrates flow through Iraq
but, surrounded by Syria, Jordan, Kuwait, Turkey, Iran and Saudi Arabia,
so does trouble. With Saddam Hussein it was also deplorable evil.

This was brutally illustrated by Saddam Hussein's bloody singled-
minded climb to power. He had tribal loyalties – that byzantine web of
links and rivalries which bedevil the Arab world – but joined the Arab
Socialist Baath Party which he used as a vehicle to drive himself to
power with his cousin Ahmed al-Bakr. They'd been involved in coups,
torture and attempted assassinations, much of it with the co-operation
of Iraq intelligence chief Colonel al-Nayif.

After al-Bakr took over and ruled with Saddam Hussein doing
the dirty work, Colonel al-Nayif was banished from Iraq. He
was personally escorted out of the country by Saddam but then
shot dead in London: an afterthought to ensure no problems; the

former Minister of Defence General al-Tikriti went the same way in Kuwait.

Ten years later, Saddam 'encouraged' his cousin to resign as president and allow him to take over in 1979 – just as Ayatollah Khomeini was changing the politics of Iran. Both countries had Shia majorities; Saddam was a Sunni Muslim but not a man who lost sleep for his prayers, or over the victims of his ambition and his wars.

The Iraq-Iran War, which he engaged in shortly after becoming President of Iraq (as defender of the Arab world, the replacement Nasser) was one long slaughter. The price in life was incalculable, with at least half a million people killed. The cost was high in other ways: in billions of dollars and in international chicanery. The CIA worked with Iraq and America revived diplomatic relations with Baghdad. The Soviets and France were with Saddam. Israel, sensing Saddam as the greater enemy, sided with Iran. In the twilight world of international diplomatic happenstance, the British sold Iran spare parts for their armaments, and America – in the infamous Iran-Contra Affair – sold arms to Iran through Israeli intermediaries, with the approval of President Reagan and Vice-President George Bush Senior.

By the end of the fighting and the settlement talking it was 1990 and the disastrous enterprise had resulted in no positive outcome. Saddam's bill for it all – billions of dollars – was owed to his neighbours, including Saudi Arabia and Kuwait, the small sheikdom which, like Iraq itself, had been created by British imperialism. The Arab Cooperation Council refused to write off Saddam's debts or indulge in his plan to push up the price of oil. He considered he'd fought to defend them as well as Iraq – and Iraq had paid in blood as well as the money they should write off.

Youssef Nada was given the inside story by someone who was present during the crucial events: 'The Alrumailah oil field is on the border line of Iraq and Kuwait. During the war, the Kuwaitis were pumping from this well as if it belonged only to them. After the war, when they asked Saddam to repay the war debts, he asked to swap it with his share of what they'd pumped from the shared oil well.'

Saddam had a huge army and he used it to attempt to intimidate Kuwait into helping him. He accused the oil rich country with all manner of malfeasance. He deployed tens of thousands of troops to the Kuwait border. They thought he was bluffing, but the international interests looking on were not so sure.

At the very end of July 1990, the Saudi government arranged talks between the two countries. Youssef Nada has the details: 'He sent his deputy Azat Ibrahim to negotiate in Taif [Saudi Arabia] with Sheik Saad Alsabah, the then Crown Prince of Kuwait. The arrogant Crown Prince threatened that if he picked up the telephone he could call 100,000 American marines to protect Kuwait. He said that 'we are going to starve the Iraqi until Iraqi women can be bought with ten dinar'. Saddam was incensed when the remark was repeated to him. He acted as he so often had – irrationally. He ordered Azat Ibrahim: 'Get back to Bagdad.'

On 2 August 1990, his troops and a couple of thousand tanks went into Kuwait. It only took a matter of hours for Saddam to be in control and half-a-dozen days before he annexed Kuwait as an Iraq province. All overseas workers and visitors were held hostage while many people of Kuwait were brutalised or killed.

Many Americans had never heard of the country but their masters had. Kuwait was overflowing with oil. It was also Saddam's path, a bridgehead, to Saudi Arabia which sat on another huge lake of the world's oil. Britain's Prime Minister, Margaret Thatcher, in the final days of her political life, knew her country had made guarantees to Kuwait three decades earlier and was determined to enforce them.

She engaged with President George Bush Senior in defying Saddam but international action takes time. In September 1990, an Islamic delegation visited Saddam and vainly tried to persuade him to pull back from Kuwait. Following that failure, the Muslim Brotherhood leadership contacted Youssef Nada and instructed him to find a way to move Saddam out of the oil state, and as fast as possible.

It was not a long conversation: they knew their international special agent had the capability and the contacts. Within hours he was talking to associates in Baghdad, and in 24 hours Saddam's brother, Barzan El Tekritin, invited him to a meeting in Geneva. Nada was not impressed with Barzan El Tekritin (who was later executed with his brother) or his cultural and political knowledge. He gave no hint of his assignment and instead relied on his own Iraqi contacts. They quickly came good, with an invitation to take the once-a-week flight from Amman to Baghdad – Nada was on his way to see Saddam but emphasised he only had 48 hours available.

On arriving in Amman it immediately became clear from Saddam's agents that his meeting with the dictator was not fixed within his 48-hour parameters. Nada told them he would return when a time was finalised. Five days later he was invited back to Baghdad under his conditions. A chief of Saddam's personal security police, a man who did not give his name, accompanied him on the flight to Baghdad's Saddam International Airport where he by-passed passport control and all other formalities. His entry into Iraq was not official. He was escorted to the Al Mansour Hotel by an army officer who told him, ominously: 'You are in the hands of the president's guards.'

At 10 am the next day he was invited down to the hotel lobby. When he left his room there were armed guards posted at each end of the corridor. The lobby was empty other than president's men. 'I never saw a signal,' said Nada, 'but they moved as if they were choreographed. Soon we were off to meet Saddam in a fleet of cars on a route that turned and turned and turned again. There were curtains in the car and I could hear the sound of a machine or wireless or telephone in the back of the car. We left the city and stopped again and again at barriers. When they opened we sped on until we came to a villa.

'It wasn't huge and we went inside to a sitting room that was modest, not luxury. Tea arrived and then came the police, then Saddam in his army uniform. There were preliminary introductions and official photographs. All the time, armed guards watching. I could feel their eyes constantly frisking me, watching the room as if I was going attempt an escape.

'We moved to another room where I sat down with Saddam. There was a guard behind him, two other people and a Minister and the man responsible for the media. I had to be aware of restrictions on what could be said. Saddam might not accept certain things being said in front of his people. There is a technique of how to deal with Heads of States – and how to deal with dictators.

'But I had made my preparations. My plan included the involvement of Iran, and I had already negotiated that with Iran's National Guard. Saddam had no prior knowledge of that arrangement, which I'd made in Switzerland. I knew what I was doing. I knew I was going to meet a dictator – that I would meet somebody who would kill his own people and those from other countries, and who would kill me without a thought. I knew that he was a tyrant.

'When I go on such a mission I must expect anything and everything – the possibility of being jailed or executed. Or Saddam's rivals might kill me. Or he might be assassinated. If someone I met for political talks was hurt or killed what would happen? Would I be held responsible? I was frightened of this, but above all, I put my trust in God, and since I had good intentions I knew God would help me.'

When Youssef Nada started talking to Saddam Hussein he quickly realised that the tyrant was not used to being spoken to in a direct way. 'People either obeyed him or vanished.' said Nada. 'He had clamped down on the Brothers in Iraq and it was vital that he knew who I was and whom and what I represented. Thankfully, I got a chance to say what I wanted.

'He knew I was from the Muslim Brotherhood. He was also very aware that some members of the Brotherhood had met in Amman and condemned his invasion, while at the same time condemning the

American invasion. He was angry because of the Brothers' views on his invasion of Kuwait but that was not political, that was a fundamental point on right or wrong.

'In politics there is no right or wrong. There is what is possible, and as they say the expression about politics, it is the art of possible. It is an art: of what is possible and not what is right. You are right to be half wrong but you can be half right. The most important subject of my mission was to present a plan which would stop the killing and the destruction of a country.

'There was one aim – to get him to pull out of Kuwait. My message to him was how staying in Kuwait was dangerous for the area and the Iraqis, all the region. I had to engage with something in common with him and not as if I was opposing him. It is political negotiation. It is not a matter of "I am your enemy. You made a mistake, you are the Devil."

'It is "You are the president. You have a justified case and the problem with you is the family and the Emir of Kuwait." The touchy point for the Iraqis was the Crown Prince's remark about "selling their women for a few dinar". This offends their honour, especially the tribes, and they have to defend their honour.

'I said to him: "We understand that the problem is the ruling family in Kuwait. You say that the Kuwaitis don't like them and your army is there because this family is imposing itself on the Kuwaiti. The Kuwaiti must rule themselves. It could be that because the Iraqi army are in Kuwait the Americans will come and destroy all the area and Iraq."

'The plan had to be attractive to him. He'd declared that the ruling family in Kuwait were his enemy, not the Kuwaiti people. He said to me: "I want to save the Kuwaiti from this family which sucks them dry." He is a killer and a dictator but for him it's the other family that are dictators, but not him! He considered Kuwait as part of Iraq, and that was historically true. But the Muslim Brotherhood didn't want to encourage him to spread his influence in other places. I had to divide my approach:

'Number 1: How to get in the subject when I talk to him. I am talking to a dictator, to a president of a country who is self-confident and conceited. I must not offend him and end the talking before it starts.

'Number 2: You must get his attention by talking about what he wants to hear, go in the line of his way of thinking to a certain extent, then give him new ideas to think that he is mistaken – but not in so many words. The words must be: "You can do something else."

'Number 3: To talk about the subject you want – your target – and not be bullied or sidetracked away from it.

'To mix all that together you must have a solution to work on. I started with what he was proud of: that he won a war with Iran. And I presented my thesis: "Mr President, thank God you won the war with Iran and you came out of the war with triumph. But you didn't invest this victory up to now. You won the war and chose to end it. That means that you are convinced that the war must not be repeated. To avoid the repetition of the war, there must be interaction which benefits both countries. There must be compromise to avoid new wars every five or ten, or fifteen or twenty years. The Americans are charging into the area with destruction and it will be everywhere. Even, if you win a war the country will be destroyed. There must be another way.

'"The solution is to allow the Kuwaiti to choose their Government. If they want this family, I don't believe that you have the right to refuse them. If they don't want them, then the family have to leave. To make this happen you have to get out of Kuwait. But you fear if you get out of Kuwait the Americans will come. The answer is to form an army from different Muslim countries to monitor an election and who wins, wins. The Americans want to reinstall the Government because it profits them. Don't leave the Americans to hold the election; a third party must take control of the election and replace the Iraqi military in Kuwait."

'I quickly gave him the alternative: "It is well known that you don't accept Saudi Arabia and you don't accept Egypt. Let us exclude them and also come back to the point that you didn't invest your victory in the war with Iran.

'"If we engage Iran in the problem it is in their interests to calm down their neighbours and talk with them. If units from the Iranian Army and from Sudan, Malaysia and Indonesia – who have never been your enemy – replace the Iraqi military in Kuwait it will bring peace. If you accept that and there are elections then you avoid the destruction which is coming to all of the area, not only to Iraq.

'"Whatever you can take by negotiation, why use your energy and take it by force? If the Iranians are a part of a Muslim unit, which will arrange the election in Kuwait and you pull out of Kuwait, this will lead to interaction between you. If you are both attacked by the Americans you can go for it together to solve the problem of the Americans. The problem is invading Kuwait. This problem will disappear."

'His reply was: "Who can say how the Iranians will react? Will they accept this?" 'I told him: "Mr President, before coming to you I discussed this problem with the Iranians, and it is so." I had talked for two-and-a-half hours before he even asked that question. He had taken off his gun belt and laid it aside, but his eyes never left my eyes.

'Eventually he said to me: "You have been talking logic, but there is an important factor you neglected in your way of thinking: that is the honour. We are ready to die with honour rather than live with dishonour." A dictator talking about honour! What do you say to him? He's most certainly not a democratic person but he's talking about honour. He accepted everything I said and then talked about honour.

'He went on: "It's true the Americans are the stronger. But be sure, we are ready to sacrifice the 200,000 to 300,000 to die with the first battle. But if we kill 5,000 American they will pull out. We will fight on to keep our dignity and existence, our fortune and future. We are ready for the sacrifice. If the majority of the Iraqi people will die defending their honour, the rest will live with honour."

'The Muslim Brotherhood insisted we'd never approve of foreign forces going in, or the continued occupation of Kuwait by Iraq. We said that the invasion was wrong. The Brothers knew that there was a great catastrophe coming. Saddam knew what we thought. I had not expected to be able to speak so freely or so long to Saddam. With many leaders you don't get such an opportunity, but he was a listener, any governor who listens must be interested. Saddam let me speak my mind.

'At the end, I wanted to take a note from my jacket pocket and for the first time my eyes left his. When I looked around those with him had startled looks on their faces. They were surprised, astonished I think that I had spoken so strongly and been so forthright. I was concerned that my tone would spoil my case and I turned back to Saddam and asked him to forgive me for being aggressive. He had listened to all I said but although he told me he admired my enthusiasm, he felt my solution offered more disadvantages than he could accept.'

Youssef Nada's initiative in meeting with Saddam resulted in some consternation among the Kuwaiti Brotherhood, but he has always worked with a need-to-know policy kept within the inner circle of the Brotherhood. 'The Kuwait Brotherhood had nothing to do with it. There was no room for them to know. I was pursuing the interests of the people of Kuwait and Iraq. I didn't care about Saddam as a ruler or the Kuwait governing family.

'If you enter into an international process the entire world is unable to solve you must have a project to talk about, to present. The Brotherhood considered the attack by the Iraqi army on Kuwait as unlawful under any context, one which no sane person in the region would accept. It was unacceptable and rejected from the point of view of Arab nationalism and Islam.

'We were not talking about the past but what was in front of us. If Saddam did not leave, the foreign armies would arrive. There was a chance to get the Iraq army out. If foreign forces entered we wouldn't have a way to get them out. History tells us they stay around.'

CHAPTER SEVEN

REVOLUTION AND RESOLUTION

'Two things fill the mind with ever new and increasing wonder and awe, the more often and the more seriously reflection concentrates upon them: the starry heaven above me and the moral law within me.'

Immanuel Kant, 1788, *The Critique of Practical Reason*

Youssef Nada is a tidy man. It is his care and precision and strict attention to the rules and detail which have often kept him alive and most certainly saved him from late life incarceration and torturous interrogation. He is on talking terms with mortality, for he knows too well we all only get a certain run at life.

He often says with an impish grin that some things must be said before he dies but other information must stay with him until after he's gone. He has a gift of being able to place parts of his knowledge and his life in separate compartments of his mind: it enables him to focus on the most important issue of the moment without being influenced or distracted by anything other than what is required to find a solution.

Being organised is part of his neatness of character. His suitcase is always carefully packed to anticipate any type of weather, or intrusive

93

customs officials messing up his indexed documents. The library at his home in Campione is a treasure trove of learning and pleasure; his sitting room is a muted showcase of blue Persian silk carpets linked into pastels of blues and pink and grey all overlooked by a ceiling emblazoned with a gold frieze of prayers and verses from the Koran. All around are gifts and purchases which heighten his memories of Egypt – his home nation of which he is a most reluctant exile. Yet needs must.

Nada has been portrayed, especially in America, as a sinister being masterminding the Muslim world from his mountainside lair, a little like Ian Fleming's Dr No, but in reality he has a better sense of humour than any megalomaniac leader, fictional or otherwise –which is why he is amused by absurdity.

All his life he has worked towards harmony, to one world, not a Muslim world or a Christian world or an atheist world, but what he calls a human world. Religion, he most fervently believes, is for the people, belongs to them, and not for the use and misuse of governments or tyrants. A human world is one in which, simply, people help rather than kill each other. It sounds trite, like a television soundbite, a moment on the evening news. Yet, essentially, that is the message. It's just there are so many political hoops to jump through and greater national and personal egos to manoeuvre around. Nada has his own ego, as he must. All his life he has dealt with world and business leaders, and in often heated and delicate negotiations both sides must trust the sincerity and intelligence of the other – and their ability to deliver, which so often depends on the range and value of their contacts.

On Youssef Nada's desk you could find the private telephone numbers and other connections to almost everyone who matters in his world – and most other people's too. One book has more than 15,000 names and numbers. As we talk on his balcony overlooking Lake Lugano he is matter of fact, not boastful, about his ability to intercede.

'I can make any contact anywhere – now. If I wanted to make

contact with my biggest enemy while I'm sitting with you here, I can do it. The connections are there. A contact may be dormant, but when it is needed I use it. But there are a lot of things that must die with me, like how my network operates. There is no way I can reveal some things about the Brotherhood. We don't move in a classic way for solving disputes, of making contacts and reaching the goal.

'A condition for what I was doing in politics was that no one knew about it. Nobody could be interrogated about it. If it was thought I could not keep the secrets there'd be no trust and I couldn't do my job. Politics in the Middle East is all secrets, but the Muslim Brotherhood are everywhere in the world. It is not a membership, it is a way of thinking.

'We are a society that a lot of powers in the world would rather didn't want to exist. Our means are not and cannot be classical in trying to mediate to solve problems between Muslim countries or Muslim societies. To reach this goal your connections must be trusted in the places where you want to move. But it must not be known that they are from the Brotherhood otherwise they will not be accepted in some areas where you want to intervene.

'For decades in Egypt, with Mubarak or the elite that were around him, anyone connected to the Brothers had to be cut off. They would be imprisoned or hanged. We kept contacts but they were shadows, "moles" who stayed below the radar. But when they were needed the connections would be made live. It was the same everywhere the Brothers were considered outlaws. We knew these men accepted us and thought like us and hopefully would do what was expected when they were asked.

'Sometimes we failed by overestimating a person – not because of his sincerity but his courage. Not all will risk their lives and I cannot blame them. If our contact doesn't work then we have another channel, and another. It is not known what channels belong to us, to the Muslim Brotherhood.'

An example of the power of the Muslim Brotherhood web of contacts happened during the final months of Hosni Mubarak being in power in Egypt. Nada had a Swiss friend, a businessman who was well connected to Mubarak's son, who asked him why he continued to oppose Mubarak. He told Nada: 'Why don't you find a way to persuade him to bring in policies which are the for the benefit of the country and he can slowly implement them?' He would do that if he had your public support.

Nada explains: 'The biggest problem in Mubarak dealing with us was his relationship with the foreign powers, including his neighbour Israel. I told my friend: "You are ready for that, but he doesn't want to hear us. He doesn't want anyone, whether they are Americans or Europeans, to know that he has any contact with the Muslim Brotherhood. He is living on the slogan that he is the first enemy of the Brotherhood. The other nations support him for this reason."'

Nada's friend then asked him why he didn't see Mubarak's son, Gamal, 'if it wouldn't ruin your relationship with the Brotherhood'. Nada happily told him: 'I am sure of myself and the Brothers are sure of me. If he accepts to come he will be welcome.' The friend said: 'Give me two weeks.'

'I never heard from him again,' said Nada. 'He went to Egypt; he never came back. He never visited me or called me after that. He could talk to them about politics and the economy but when he talked to them about the Brotherhood it became controversial for him. It stopped. They didn't want dialogue – they didn't want to let others to have any hint that we might be in contact.'

Nada said that when it was suggested that Gamal Mubarak might put himself forward to be elected President of Egypt he had no objection, but only if Gamal went into the election the same as any Egyptian – not as the son of the president. 'He is an Egyptian, he has the right to go to the election the same as anyone else. I cannot say that he doesn't have the right, but he does not have the right to use the influence and the machinery of the Government to get himself into his father's seat.

The Brotherhood has a network of connections around the world, including people like Nada's Swiss businessman friend. 'We have also been close to the kings of Saudi Arabia from the time of King Faisal in the 1970s,' said Nada. 'One of the Brothers was a skilful doctor who became King Faisal's personal physician. Our link was there, directly to the ear of the king if we needed the contact. The security services check the backgrounds for all those close to their leaders so we had no open contact with the doctor or he with us. But the connection was there.

'We would not deal with anyone in such a place if he was involved with corruption or opposed our way of thinking; he would be kicked out of the Brotherhood. He must be clean in soul and mind. That is all. We could not ask for deception. We cannot ask that a Brother prays in church as a Christian. It is not accepted in Islam that anyone deny that he is a Muslim – whatever the motivation. If you are a Muslim you must declare it.

'Which was why all the fuss in America about President Obama truly being a Muslim was a nonsense. Obama declared he is Christian. He cannot be a Muslim and go to pray and follow another religion and not Islam; it cannot be. The name is one thing and the declaration is another. I see many people from other religions adopting Islam. And they change their name. That is not obligatory. You can be "Hector Thompson" and be a Muslim. You don't have to be Mohamed or Youssef to be a Muslim. Sometimes it's just fashionable when people change their names – it doesn't mean that you are not a Muslim if you don't. That is part of the interpretation of the religion by the Muslim Brotherhood.

'The majority of Muslims who work to understand their religion, to read about it and investigate it, to talk to people about it, will find in the end, the correct interpretation is the Brotherhood one. Those who do that will be convinced to be with them. We have to work at it, for nobody can deny the power of the media to make white into black and vice versa.'

This explains why Youssef Nada so often worked alone or with the trusted Ghalab Himmat on his missions. And why, later, he became known as the Shadow Statesman of the Muslim Brotherhood. He is most certainly a statesman and his learning and diplomacy go before him, as does his prescience, although sometimes what he says can make uneasy listening: 'Revolutions? We always say there have been only three in the world: the Bolshevik Revolution, the French Revolution and the Iranian Revolution. All the others were coup d'états, not revolutions.

'The coup d'état is a military takeover – revolution comes from the population. During the French Revolution, the Bolshevik and the Iranian revolutions, the nations mobilised and all the people came out on the streets. It was not a military takeover, like Nasser in Egypt or Gaddafi in Libya.

'There are other places ready for the next coup d'état, but the next revolution will probably be in Saudi Arabia and the Gulf. Those countries are vulnerable. When a revolution happens there, the Americans in turn will arrange a coup d'état – they are preparing for it, either through a member of the ruling family or from the army or security services. They want their own person on the throne, in control.

'The royal families became too big and not all of them are organised, and not all have the same advantage. Some of them have more leverage than others. It is very complex. The Americans will use that to divide and be in charge again. During the time of King Fahd, my connection with him succeeded in stopping the war between Saudi Arabia and Yemen. I mended the position between Saudi Arabia and Iran. Also, I worked with the Yemeni for their war with Eritrea, because it was for the island [Greater Hanish] involved in the dispute. I also worked on assignments in Indonesia and in Malaysia and Turkey.

'You need the means to go to the decision maker. I never went on any mission without the permission of the Supreme Guide of the Muslim Brotherhood. I never talked to any king or president without them knowing that I am a member of the Muslim Brotherhood. Inside their country they are against the Muslim Brotherhood, yet the majority of the heads of the states with whom I discussed politics knew I had spent all my life in the Brotherhood.

'Anyone known to be in the Brotherhood in Iraq will either be sent to prison for life or executed. In Saudi Arabia it's forbidden to be in the Muslim Brotherhood. In Yemen, the Brothers are in politics. In Malaysia the Brotherhood is banned but exists in another guise. In Indonesia, they are in power, inside the government, and they have a political party, but not in the name of the Brotherhood. In Morocco, they are the official party but not with the name of the Brotherhood. But they have to teach each other to be tolerant to the Brothers and the regime. For certain things they cooperate, but everyone knows that the other one is not his close friend.'

Recalling the Hama Massacre in Syria in February 1982, Nada reflected that Syria is a country where the Brothers 'have endured a long and bloody story'. At that time, President Hafez al-Assad, father of the present President Bashar al-Assad, ordered a crackdown on the city of Hama which was a conservative Sunni Islamic stronghold and home to many members of the Brotherhood. Tanks and artillery were engaged in a three-week siege of the Old City, the rebel stronghold.

The killing that followed, in which most of the victims were civilians, was estimated at 35,000 people. It's regarded as one of 'the single deadliest acts by an Arab government against its own people in the modern Middle East'. Hafez Assad continued to rule uncontested until his death 20 years after the massacre. The Hama horror is often given as an example of Syria's appalling human rights history and it showed all the ruthlessness of the al-Assad dynasty as the Islamists of Syria were murdered 'as a nuisance'.

It was re-enacted on 1 February 2012, when protesters splashed red paint symbolising blood in the streets to mark the 30th anniversary of the massacre. As well as the 'blood paint', red dye was poured into the waters of Hama's ancient water wheels. Graffiti read: 'Hafez died, and Hama didn't. Bashar will die, and Hama won't.'

As the paint was being spilled, so was blood – in a chilling echo of the past, the killing was being repeated by and on a new generation. Bashar al-Assad's secular regime is controlled by Alawites who comprise a faction within Shia Islam. Most of the Syrian army are Alawites and they were convinced they were the ultimate target of the rebel uprising. They were fighting for their lives.

Throughout the first weeks of 2012, the city of Homs was reduced to rubble – virtually a funeral home with crushed buildings as coffins. While the world reacted with outrage, the regime kept on killing. The victims included the much admired American-born, UK-based war correspondent, Marie Colvin, who many believe was deliberately targeted because of her graphic reports from within the Baba Amr area of Homs where she died alongside French journalist Remi Ochlik on 22 February. The high profile casualties prompted more condemnation of the Syrian regime but bigger headlines didn't lead to a reduction in the killing.

For Youssef Nada, events past and present are another reason to pledge himself to resolution rather than revolution: 'President Bashar al-Assad's uncle, Rifaat al-Assad, was in charge of the army in 1982 and ordered them to bombard Hama. After the bombardment, which killed 35,000, they took thousands still alive to the prisons and tortured them to death.

'Today in Syria anyone belonging to the Muslim Brotherhood is condemned to death,' said Nada. 'Not to prison – to death. That is the law – official. Not instructions – the law. Meanwhile, in Libya, with Gaddafi it was the law of the jungle.

The Brotherhood's inner circle in Libya were well known to Youssef Nada from his time in Tripoli. He also knew the leaders of another faction which broke away from the Brothers and worked with the British and American authorities against the regime.

He said with deep feeling: 'It resulted in a sordid deal. It was a time of great turmoil with the IRA in Northern Ireland, and the British Government leaked some information to Gaddafi so he was able to catch the Libyans who were opposing him. It was part of a barter agreement. In return, Gaddafi gave the British information about the IRA – because he was arming them. I still feel disgusted about this. I don't know how the British could work with Gadaffi.'

Nada – who was closely involved in Libya's transitional talks in the immediate aftermath of the end of Gaddafi's regime in August 2011– says he is equally bemused by extent of UK-Libya relations which endured in the years after 25-year-old policewoman Yvonne Fletcher was shot dead by machine gun fire during a protest outside the Libyan Embassy in St James's Square in London on 17 April 1984. An 11-day siege followed and when it ended, all the Embassy officials were allowed to freely return to Libya. It has always been believed that WPC Fletcher was killed by a Libyan official who went on to become a high ranking member of Gadaffi's government.

The death of WPC Fletcher has never been forgotten, and following the collapse of Gaddafi's 42-year rule in 2011, one of the first legal moves by the British Government was to send Scotland Yard detectives to Libya in an attempt finally to bring to justice the alleged suspect in the shooting, Abdulmagid Salah Ameri, and those who helped and protected him.

Youssef Nada personally abhorred the way the policewoman's murder was dealt with: 'It was well known who killed Miss Fletcher from the window of the embassy,' he said. 'She was killed while doing her duty, and her Government negotiated in the interests of business, of money. They ignored her life, forgot that she was protecting her country. Ministers of the British Government sat with a killer of one of their citizens.

'But because of the oil they hugged and kissed Gadaffi and called him their friend. They displayed no morals or ethics or principles. Gadaffi blinded them with money, played them along, and they forgave him. A killer gives you some money and you forgive him. After killing your father and your mother, and your sister and son; giving money to prevent justice being done is a dirty job.

'Gadaffi was a chameleon, a changing personality for every moment. Governments cultivated him because he had power and money but he was a killer just like any mafia group. He worked with Mossad, the Israeli Intelligence. He gave them the travel arrangements of one of the leaders of the Palestinians, the jihad faction, and he was killed when he left Libya to go to Malta.

'He worked with the Palestinians and then he worked with the Lebanon. Then he jumped to the IRA, and on to the mafia in Italy, and then moved into the Arab countries, and when all this went wrong he went to Africa. The African leaders wanted money so they encouraged him. He returned back to the Arabs, to Italy, to the Americans. Any time he wanted, he could do a 180-degree turn. Anytime – because he had the oil. He had the money. He could make any deal, pay any ransom. 'From the legal point of view anyone who knowingly facilitates or assists the criminal to commit a crime is considered a criminal too. If such facilitating and assistance were intended to generate benefit then it is another proof of the intentionally performed criminal act. When the Western governments accommodate and assist and protect a corrupt dictator and cover his crimes in exchange of preferences and facilities of contracts or politics against the interest of his country. then those governments are all criminals. Look at recent history: British Prime Minister Tony Blair embracing that gangster Gadaffi and kissing his neck; Italy's Silvio Berlusconi kissing his hand and France's Nicolas Sarkozy bowing 90 degrees. America's Secretary of State Condoleezza Rice bowing her head and looking at Gadaffi's shoes!

'All this for what? Does Gadaffi have science? No. Does he have power? No. Was he capable of doing something good for the humanity? No. He was a thief who robbed the Libyan people's wealth and these people wanted to assist him to get a share of it. H was not the only criminal.

'He worked with everyone. There was no moral code. Abdelbaset Mohamed Ali al-Megrahi – who was convicted for his involvement in the Pan Am flight 103 bombing on 21 December 1988 over Lockerbie, with a death toll including those on the ground of 270 – took direct orders from Gadaffi.

'Al-Megrahi was his man and he was loyal to his man. When al-Megrahi was freed by Scotland in August 2009 on compassionate grounds that he had terminal prostate cancer [he died on May 20, 2012) he was treated as a national hero on returning to Tripoli. Naturally he defended the leader, the one who gave him orders.'

Libya is rich in natural resources – it has all the gas and the best quality of oil, and offshore the depths are not great, making it easy to access. In World War Two, Rommel lost the war in the desert for want of petrol for his tanks – but ironically, the best oil in the world was underneath the sand beneath his feet.

Youssef Nada went to see the demonstrations when Rommel arrived at El Alamein. He was 12 years old: 'The Egyptians were all shouting, "Welcome, welcome Rommel". Oh yes. All the Egyptians were on his side because they were under the occupation of the British. In the Arab world, and in Egypt, they looked on Hitler as a hero, not as criminal dictator, which is how I and most of the rest of the world regard him.

'Egypt has experienced its own dictators since the time of Pharaoh, 3,000 years ago when they built the pyramids. The Pharaoh was their God and they had to obey him until death. The people are used to being governed by dictators. But when Islam came to Egypt and the people experienced justice and equality they started to find themselves, until Muslim dictators were imposed on them – and the Pharaohs suddenly were turned into Sultans.

'In all but name, every Arab country is run by a dictator. It works differently in every country but it is still dictatorship. In Saudi Arabia, the royal family must have privilege more than the citizens, as if they came from Heaven and not from Earth.

'In Qatar, the Emir of Qatar [Sheikh Hamad bin Khalifa Al-Thani] is the boss – he runs the country. It is *one hand* management but I have to admit that the rights and needs of the citizens are his priority. Every person in Qatar is entitled to their own home and their rights. Sadly, this doesn't happen everywhere; on the streets of Jeddah there are people begging – and it is the same in Tunisia, Egypt, Yemen, Sudan, Jordan, Iraq, Morocco, Algeria and Syria. These dictators have the wealth to buy weapons and power but the people go begging. God said you have to help the poor, the sick, orphans and widows. Why should a Muslim and Christian interpretation of that be any different?

'The problem is the same problem with terrorism. How do you justify killing by taking a part of a phrase and saying: "God means that." You cannot say that. You are not God. The justification for war is a huge area for deception. It is usually an unholy mix of many things: dictators, religion, politics and belief.

'And then you have the tribes and the tribal habits mixed with religion. This is something so passionate and going so far back in history that few outside the area understand. The tribal strength is more than their religion. They have a stronger loyalty to their tribes, their clans, than to any national government.

'When they do battle they follow tribal rules not religion. The biggest tribe in this area is the Pashtun [the largest ethnic group in Afghanistan] which has different sects but the majority of them are related to the Pashtun – the power is the Pashtun. Afghanistan's other major tribe, the Taliban, is something new, but linked into the Pashtun more than any other tribe. They were guided by the Americans and Pakistani intelligence in the schools from which the Taliban elements emerged and grew at the time of the Soviet occupation of Afghanistan.

'The way of thinking is tribal; anyone who is not from the tribe is a foreigner. The Pashtun is a closed society and it is very difficult to exist with them. They might deal with you but you will always be an outsider, a foreigner.

'One of the Brotherhood, a Saudi university professor, who was troubled by events in Afghanistan went to help those who'd been hurt and mutilated. He went to help, not get involved in the fight. He had some money and received donations and he established some water wells and set up a repair shop for cars and equipment and assisted in a small hospital.

'He had an Afghani to help him with local knowledge and working with people and in his house. He had wide connections and brought in engineers and doctors. He was doing nothing but good. Then he found his Afghani servant was trying to poison him. This man saw the professor as a foreigner who dealt with people who were not of the tribe. He saw him as a danger.

'For him, and all the others, the tribe is everything. Religion, political power, Americans, Soviets – none of that matters. You cannot preach to them. Religion is something important but not everything. The religious factor is there but mixed with the tribes: you cannot talk to them, or try to convince them from the religion point-of-view alone. The Taliban isn't going to march into America or invade any other country. They want *their* way of life in *their* homeland, and not be instructed to live or think another way.

Youssef Nada said that the main aim of the Brotherhood is for peace and working together in society, not only for Islam or for themselves, or for the country where they live, but for the whole world. 'Not only that, but also to have "added value", as we call it in economics. I have a lot of "added values" which I gained not only from the Brotherhood but also from my involvement with other societies, nations, and cultures.

'There are those who are there fighting against change in society. Changes there must be but they must be introduced at a pace which will be acceptable, which will work. You cannot force change in society, in the ways of living which have existed for hundreds or thousands of years. You must take your time.

'The Brothers are also trying to give rights to women and have access to Western dress and music. In the schools they are trying to introduce a lot of things which are used in the West. Yet, by going too fast with change in the tribal regions you inflame in them more reasons to fight you. The faster you try to modernise the tribal regions, the harder the opposition will be. There are generations of habits, of rituals and religion involved and the more you to try to rush change the more they will want to keep their tribal world. It could be done in one hundred years but not in five.

'The West feel they are civilised and want to transfer this civilisation to others. Compare this with the occupation of the Muslim countries during the last hundreds of years following the Crusades: the West went to South-east Asia, the Middle East and India: hundreds of years of trying to change Islam or the way of Islam.

'How is it going? In those early days there were about 300,000,000 Muslims in the world. Today there are 1.5 billion. What happened is that in an effort to change the ways of the people they gave them more roots in their own ways. They failed to eradicate Islam. Instead, they found a way to live peacefully together; you exchange what is good in each other. That is how you have co-existence. The superiority of the others will not change, and could not change any society or religion.

'We cannot deny that in many ways, the West is better. But in some, not all. I see it most with the families. If I am a 16-year-old Muslim and I see a fellow teenager taking drugs or getting drunk and smashing up a car, I don't want to be him. My religion forbids me to do it. I cannot accept the culture that allows the drunken teenager to do that. When you see a father abandon the mother of his child and leave his responsibility, it is wrong. In my culture, the man is responsible for everything: it is not only the law, it is from the religion.

'The British were in Afghanistan 300 years ago and they tried to conquer them for about 50 years. They failed, and the Soviets did the same. The Americans in 2012 are doing the same and pulling all the West into this muddy area. There's only way to win — to respect the tribal inheritance which is mixed with religion. Slowly, slowly, you get them out into a better civilisation.

'Fighting and sudden change won't do it, neither will dealing only by logic and not the tribal roots. If the troops pull out there will be trouble for another 100 years. But if you want to pull out and settle the case – then buy time with an amicable state among the United Nation states operating together for the humanity. It is an alternative way which needs a great deal of assistance to work. But it can work.

'The West sees its way of life as uncivilised, backwards, and one which doesn't fit the century in which we are living. You can't bring about change by weapons or excluding factions who are more "uncivilised" than another. You have to put all the tribes in harmony with the world of today. You have to respect the religion and you have to respect the tribal habits until they themselves change it.

'They will have to. We travel on jets as well as camels. One night Saudi television broadcast a 15-minute videotape in which Afghanis were shown throwing rocks at the police and then charging into them. What we heard was that the fight was with the Taliban, not with the Afghan. That is yes and no. Yes, because the one at the front of the picture is in the Taliban; but no, because every Afghani thinks the same, whether he is Taliban or not – even those given salaries by the Americans and the British and brought in to be the new police, the new army.

'At any time you can expect the same to happen as happened to my professor friend and his Afghani helper. They are Afghani, they are tribal, they are Muslim. You take them out, you give them new habits which are contrary to their religions or contrary to their tribal ways of thinking, and one day you will discover that you were mistaken! There will be cyanide not mint in the tea.

'The way to go is with good manners to attract their sincerity, not force to create their enmity. If you are sincere in assisting them, then they will follow you. When you fight, they will come together against you. It must be their own idea to follow you.

'It will not be Obama but probably the next President of America who will decide if the United States leaves Afghanistan as a burned land. Before they left Cambodia, before they left Vietnam, they ruined them. That will be repeated. Vietnam, until now, hasn't recovered from the war. It will, but very slowly. There are many black spots in history.

'Two European friends were discussing about why Europe was involved in such areas; what was the benefit to Europe to fight in Afghanistan? The other said: "Our soldiers must be trained in real fights. That is their chance to be trained."

'Can you imagine that? That is politics. That is politicians. I couldn't imagine it when I heard it. They have to learn to kill? It is promoting fighting. We put labels on it. My advice to the peacemakers is to stop blaming everything that happens on Al Qaeda. If you want to implement a special agenda anywhere, don't walk in on the name of Al Qaeda and do it. That will backfire on you.

'We should leave the residuals of Al Qaeda to die alone and fight terrorism ourselves. Fight the violence as violence. Don't use the name terrorism – it's a crime, the same as any organised crime. Fight it as an organised crime without the slogans which make people who have nothing to do with it support it. You give the people the impression that Al Qaeda is fighting injustice: talk about organised crime, not terrorism, not Al Qaeda.

'Al Qaeda means "the base". The American propaganda machinery inflated this. They created an enemy to fight. They joined both of them, and the Taliban for one reason. They asked the head of the Taliban to surrender Osama Bin Laden. When he refused they invaded Afghanistan.

'From the beginning it was wrong to ask him to surrender Bin Laden because one phrase in the Koran says that the Muslim must not surrender anyone who asks for protection, although this is arguable if he killed somebody. They could have approached it with another way of thinking and achieved the result they wanted.

'You cannot have somebody who doesn't know anything about Islam talking to the Taliban. You need an expert, so when the Taliban insist they are following Islam, you can correct them. There will always be an interpretation to deal with a situation. Governments, leaders, must look to the future and not short-term gains for political reasons. History is history. They must look to the damage that will happen in fifty years or one hundred years. Not after ten years of this war.

'The occupation of the Muslim world has continued for five hundred years. They used every means to eradicate Islam from this area. Every means: the missionaries, the soldiers. Remember, when I was young in Egypt, if any European committed a crime they went to a special court, not the one for Egyptians. The result was always in the favour of the European. I witnessed this myself. It caused bad feelings. It's not a way to win harmony or hearts or have someone to follow your example if you treat them differently.'

What I believe Youssef Nada is pointing to is the gradual introduction of a liberal democracy, something far less headline making or flag waving than abrupt revolution which, arguably, is more revolutionary. And perplexing, for a vacuum must always be filled. In nations which are poor, with people who don't have equal rights, the attraction of a 'strong man' leader is a temptation to the thought that despots can be good for you.

But as Youssef Nada suggested to me many, many times: there is always risk in business and so, also, in life.

CHAPTER EIGHT

FINANCE AND FAITH

'*Capital as such is not evil; it is its wrong use that is evil. Capital in some form or other will always be needed.*'

Mahatma Gandhi

A long with such revolutionary thoughts, Youssef Nada is also a financial rebel, and, happily for him, a purist. The international research centre Pio Manzù, in Rimini, Italy, a consultative branch of the United Nations and Unido, paid the following tribute to Nada in its biographies of recipients of Italian Government Medals in 1992:

'*Youssef Mustafa Nada is one of the leading Arab entrepreneurs and financiers. He has built up throughout the world a trading network for commerce between the West and the Islamic countries, in Africa and in the Middle East. He has acquired an exceptional experience in banking and in foreign trade, a well-known figure in the economic, financial and political circles, not only in Europe but also in the Islamic countries.*

'*Even if he has spent more than half of his life in Europe, he is a respected and esteemed figure, occasionally consulted by the Islamic leaders.*

111

With business activities in over 25 countries, his company is well placed to stipulate contracts of both commercial and social benefit, which demonstrate Youssef Nada's broad knowledge of market mechanisms and commercial law.'

As a prominent and clearly successful figure in global business and finance, Nada believed in taking his religion into that world. Again it was his strict following of his faith and banking regulations which helped protect him when what he created crumbled under the weight of immense and untoward persecution and pressure at the start of the 21st century. Yet his trust in the value of Islamic banking, which reconciles financial management with the principles of the Koran, was never shaken. Under Sharia law ('*sharia*' translates, importantly for desert peoples, as 'the quickest way to water') the payment or acceptance of specific interest or fees (usury) for loans is not allowed. Investments in areas which contravene Islamic principles, such as alcohol production or operating casinos, are also forbidden.

It is one area of today's banking world where faith and banking can be safely used in the same sentence. There are several ways of investing money which doesn't involved interest, but the banker must be in control. After Youssef Nada became involved in the creation of the first Islamic Bank in Cairo with Saudi Arabia's Prince Mohammad Al-Faisal, he felt obliged to resign from the board, not only for political reasons but for technical principles. The Egyptian Government had insisted that funds were kept in a central bank as reserves and the bank would take interest for it. And there were other directives which clashed with Islamic banking.

So in 1988, when Youssef Nada began to build his own Al Taqwa Bank (the literal Arabic translation is the intended 'True Obedience'), he worked to circumvent any systems which would put him outside the Islamic banking rulebook. He wanted to create what he calls his 'pure' bank. At the time, Nada was a nine-digit businessman, in financial terms, with an annual turnover of US$3billion, and all the facilities to create what he believed would be a correct and honourable banking system.

He engaged advisor Paul Leonard of London-based Freshfields Bruckhaus Deringer LLP (known as Freshfields) – the world's second-largest law firm, in earnings – who was briefed to find a geographical base for Nada to run a bank within the guidance of Islam. Understandably, most of the locations he first suggested were in the Middle East, but his client wanted to be outside that region. Gibraltar, where a former senior government minister would be the bank's agent, was proposed but that too was rejected, and an offshore arrangement in the Bahamas was suggested.

Setting up offshore in the Bahamas at that time allowed a licence to operate in any country – the only requisite being you paid tax at your chosen location but not on all the banking activity. Fees were also paid in the Bahamas. Before the Bahamas Central Bank gives the licence to an offshore bank, auditors who are accredited by the Central Bank, must be chosen. Nada's representatives were accountancy firm Deloitte and Touche.

He was careful and diligent about his dual criteria: legality worldwide and working within Islamic banking principles. An Islamic bank has to split its operations between finance and economic activity (such as industry, agriculture or housing). The banking activity could take the form of *mudaraba, murabaha, istisnae, istizrae, musharaka*, or any other tool accepted Islamicly. An Islamic Bank can create channels to work in commerce and can buy and sell shares and currency.

Nada established a separate service company in Switzerland to create elaborate internal auditing procedures. It was authorised at the tax office in Bellinzona, the capital of the Swiss state of Ticino. He was offering services for the Al-Taqwa Group that included internal auditing and feasibility studies for the projects of the Group, including offshore banking called Bank of Taqwa in the Bahamas. He said proudly: 'I set it up in such a way that no one could ever say it is illegal. Everything was clarified in the paperwork.'

This style of Islamic banking was new. Investors put in their money on which they would have an agreed amount of 75 per cent to 90 per cent of profits − if there were any. If an investment by Al Taqwa went wrong, then the bank would lose its time and effort, and the investors their money. Profits were set against a final audit and reviewed by an Islamic legal committee.

Nada made all his conditions abundantly clear: 'I insisted in the written agreements that anyone who wanted to withdraw money must give a year's advance notice, for I had to have time to make profits. Also, that the majority of the funds were used to generate income and not kept in reserve. I had a contract which all investors had to sign. If they didn't, I returned their money.

In its first eight years, Nada's bank made minimum profits of ten and 13 per cent. 'I was running an ethical Islamic bank which was making profits for its investors under our law,' he said. 'You must not operate "usury" from the people. You must not clash with what is written in the Koran. The world economy is based on the usury as well as the activity and brains and work of people around the world. Part of usury is taking a big part of the work and energy and devotion and energy of the people to give to the elite and others.

'The shareholders of the companies are taking maybe 50 per cent on the backs of the workers who use their money to live, to pay for their homes and food. The investor gets money not for work but for money. Islam forbids this. It was also forbidden in Christianity but that's been forgotten. A Jew cannot take from his Jewish brother but he can take from others.

'It makes clear sense that you don't profit from the sweat of others just because you have money and the others do not.

This has nothing to do with communism or socialism; it is a matter of justice. In Islam everyone can have any wealth without sucking the blood or the sweat of others provided he pays *zakat* to the poor. Zakat is a fixed percentage of tax on wealth and income and in summary on the net worth of the person. Another form of zakat is paid at end of the fasting month of Ramadan. That's nothing to do with the state taxes but is paid directly for a specified category of the poor, starting within the family then neighbours and others.

'The Islamic banking system is only forty years old. It operates beside the usury system which was before Islam – and is why Islam prohibited it. It needs time to develop, to convince the people, not only the Muslims, that it is for their interests, to continue giving it a chance. When you study the economic crash which is now punishing the world, and the 1930 Depression, the heart of the reason was the usury system. Money was gaining money.

'In every pure economy, money and work must generate money. There is money and there is work and there is land. Land is the production facility. It used to be just for agriculture, but now it is also factories and other means of production. So we have the money, the work and the facility. This can generate the income but not only money to generate money on the account of the others. The product is the final thing.

'If only money is producing for you, it will be on account of the sweat of the others and the cost of the production facility. The manpower has to pay the professional facility. You don't give him anything to eat, just to live. You are sucking all the rest, not giving them the chance to grow up the same as you are growing up. No, you are feeding him, keeping him just to live. Even if he wants to own the house where he lives, he has to borrow and pay interest which costs him more than the value of the house, depending on how many years he can work and sweat to repay. The same goes for his children's education and health insurance and all aspects of life.

'It is a matter of participation. Money must not give money. Money and *work* will give money. That means if you have money, and you cannot operate it and I am ready to operate it, I am ready to work. I am ready to cultivate, I am ready to build a factory, to produce goods. You provide the money, I provide the work and then we share the profit and we share the burden. It is a mutual thing. For the bank, we used to take 25 per cent and the owner of the money would take 75 per cent. If it was a big amount, we took less.

'Islam does not oppose any wealth owned by one person or a group or family – whatever the size of the fortune – but it must come from clean and legal sources and must pay its duties of zakat and taxes. From the Brotherhood's point-of-view the economical benefits for the poor and middle classes must be superior to the political benefits in the international system. That is what the people want. Hosni Mubarak and his like worked it the other way, making the political benefits greater for him than the economical system for the people.'

There has been speculation all over the world that the Muslim Brotherhood want to rule with the Sharia. However, Youssef Nada explained that, from his viewpoint, the Brotherhood want to rule with democracy without contradicting with Sharia: 'That is the difference, the big difference. When you say normal democratic rule but without contradicting Sharia, you are open to a different interpretation of democracy as well as different interpretation of the Sharia.

'When we reject the bogus democracy we must also reject the bogus clergy. Sharia is a science. The same as any science any one is able to study it not only the clergy. They should accept criticism for their interpretation. Sharia is borderless and if Mecca and Medina are situated in a specific country it does not mean that the clergy there is more knowledgeable than others or that others must follow their interpretation. Since the early time of Islam the most knowledgeable clergy had never been from one county. We have to walk the talk and open not only the frontiers but also the brains. The question is whether we have to be in harmony with our feelings and emotions or with our brains and thoughts.

'In the 21st century we must accept the law but judge it in terms of the world we live in. We cannot be dogmatic and say this or that is the only interpretation. We cannot be limited to what worked in another century or what the honest and devoted scholars interpreted when they were riding camels and horses. Science, technology and time changed the human brain, changed our thinking in our interpretation of the Sharia. Sharia is what came in the Koran and was said or done by the prophet, but *Fiqh* [Islamic jurisprudence] is man–made contract agreements. No one can deny that today's men are more knowledgeable than last year's men. What is the value of knowledge if it is not there when it is needed?

'Sharia gave some social guidelines and defined some ethics and rules but did not interfere in all changeable life aspects. Predefined fixed rules could not be expected to be applied in circumstances, knowledge, technology, innovation which did not exist. The human actions and reactions in his life were left to his evaluation without breaching those rules and guidelines. Accordingly anyone who studied theology cannot and is not expected to claim that he knows or understand other science or technology to define which rule in the religion could be applied. Nowadays hearing or reading any subject is not enough to enable the person to understand it or to give his opinion about it. Specialisation and practice are essential in this complicated world where every second several problems appear. Moreover we cannot use politics in the divinity but he should apply the divinity in politics. Political life can be full of deception, hypocrisy and corruption which no divinity can tolerate, but if divinity is used in politics it can purify it and guide it to be honest, clean, useful and serving the communities.

'Ibn Rushd [Averroes] said that it is true that a Muslim must not deny what is known in the religion as the theologies said, but he is obliged through the Koran to use his brain to go deep in its explanations, reasoning, targets, timing and circumstances. We don't want to repeat what four or five ancient scholars did thirteen centuries ago. Allah said you have to think and you have to be mindful.

'The second Caliph Omar was presented with a confessed thief and according to the text his hand must be cut off. Omar asked him why he stole: "I was hungry and could not have work or food." The Caliph gave him food and forgave him following the *spirit* of the Sharia, not the wording. This caliph learned Islam and Sharia directly from Mohamed the messenger of God and he was one of the nearest to him.

'Let me borrow what Cicero the Roman statesman and lawyer said:

> *"A nation can survive its fools and even the ambitious. But it cannot survive treason from within. An enemy at the gates is less formidable, for he is known and carries his banner openly. But the traitor moves amongst those within the gate freely his sly whispers rustling through all the alleys, heard in the very halls of government itself. For the traitor appears not a traitor, he speaks in accents familiar to his victims and he wears their face and their arguments, he appeals to the baseness that lies deep in the hearts of all men. He rots the soul of a nation, he works secretly and unknown in the night to undermine the pillars of the city, he infects the body politic so that it can no longer resist. A murderer is less fear. The traitor is the plague."*

'It is both part of the problem and the solution in the current political situation and we should avoid the temptation of castigating one group as the villains while eulogising another individual or group as the saviour. We cannot close an eye to the wrongdoing of those we endorse while condemning the same ills in our adversaries. Neither the abuse of power nor communalism is the monopoly of a particular group or community.

'Civil society activists and the media in particular should be honest and truthful in their analysis. It is their honesty and integrity that will serve as the compass as we navigate our journey into the future in these difficult times. The influential stratum of society – this includes business, professionals, religious, cultural, academic and NGO leaders, apart from politicians – should condemn deception and injustice in unambiguous, uncompromising language. Politicians in particular should be as vocal and as vehement in denouncing the orchestrated lies and injustices and deception committed against peaceful societies.'

Youssef Nada said he understands the fears in the West about Islam and the Brotherhood, and says he and the Brotherhood must keep talking to answer all the propaganda which is made against them. 'Of course there will be fears after all the scare stories that are written. Many people talk with frightening language and have special targets. Some are inflating the shadow of the Muslim Brotherhood, and "the giant". They only see the giant, the "ghost".

'There are different ways of democracy in the world and if we follow the path of democracy, it doesn't mean that we have to copy one of the existing democracies. We can have one which fits our principles and at the same time the main pillars of the democracy differ in some details, but not in the pillars. We don't want to have a bourgeois democracy.

'If a king will come and make democracy and he is a king, the ruler, the only decision maker, the one who has the final word, the one whose blood is blue and the others red. That is not democracy. In somewhere like Qatar – a very small country – the Emir is doing his best for them but until when no one knows. He has more privilege than them but the people like him and they accept it. That is a bourgeois democracy. It fits Qatar but it is not comfortable in other places. It can work somewhere with a limited population like a big family – but not in normal circumstances.

'In Saudi Arabia you find 15,000 people within the dynasty of the king and the ruling family – that's out of 25million people in the country. "Them and Us! Have and Have Not!" – master and slaves who could be elevated or upgraded to employees or servants and lower category of creature but by all means not as the princes.

'In other countries like Egypt, Tunisia, Algeria, the bourgeois false democracy is no good; it should be public democracy. And we must never allow apartheid. In Egypt there are more than 80million people and 40 per cent are illiterate. It can't all be blamed on the dictatorships which came with Nasser and ruled the rest until Mubarak was brought down.'

In Egypt it began in colonial times when King Farouk governed 'but the key of government was held and turned by the British'. He went on: 'They imposed what they wanted but handled the population with soft hands. Nasser, Sadat and Mubarak imposed their will with iron fists. Both systems are evil. The education of the people suffered, with the result there was a vacuum in the intelligence. Those of the intelligentsia who did oppose were thrown into jail. Some clever people kept quiet – those who were loud were made silent through different means, torture, jails, confiscation of assets, denying employment or downgrading of their status. Among them were the Brotherhood.

'Some closed their mouths, and some rode a wave and served the dictators. The country was divided from the beginning into the illiterate and the intelligentsia. After Mubarak was disposed those who were illiterate and those half educated can do the donkey work – sorry to say it. Those who have to guide Egypt's development have the gift of education and the intelligence.

'Yet, those are the people who went with the regime and were well trained. They didn't use their conscience during the years of dictatorship so how can we trust them? There is apartheid there too. The people who were not trained are passive. To arrange a new system and to implement it, to bring the result out of the removal of Mubarak there had to be public democracy – but everyone in the country has to work too. That is the great challenge.

'The Brotherhood in Egypt has thousands of professors in universities; there are about twenty thousand PHDs. They have gone on from university. Also they have more than hundred fifty thousand teachers in the schools. Education is very important factor for us.

Strangely, and in my opinion – me personally, not the Brotherhood – we have a very weak point in being over-educated.

'When we began, the majority of the Brotherhood were peasant workers and students. Now a large part of us are elite – whether elite through education or the money point-of-view that is bad. You have to be relatively in balance it with the population. To be a popular movement, you have to be not only guiding the population, you have to be a part of it. You have to be one of them, to feel what they feel.

'I don't see any reason to fear the Muslim Brotherhood. But we have problems with two areas of controversy. One is with the Palestinian case. It is not only the Muslim Brotherhood but every Muslim on Earth is at heart with the Palestinians. The Brotherhood are convinced 100 per cent that the Palestinians are victims. Whether I can support them or not is another thing, but my belief is that they are victims.

'Even those who assisted in the creation of Israel in a moment of truth had the same opinion. Look at what President Eisenhower said in his radio and television address dated 20 February 1955: "The United Nations must not fail. I believe that – in the interest of peace – the United Nations has no choice but to exert pressure upon Israel to comply with the withdrawal resolutions."

'Also note the address by Secretary of State Dulles to the Council on Foreign Relations on 26 August 1955: "We still hope that the Government of Israel will see that its best immediate and long-term interests lie in compliance with the United Nation." We heard only speeches, but the victims continue to bleed.'

Youssef Nada is adamant that the Muslim Brotherhood are not financing Hamas [the Islamist political party that governs the Gaza Strip]. 'Members of the Brotherhood donate to some parts of the life of Hamas,' he said, 'but this is for hospitals and education and to feed the people. It is humanitarian aid. I have repeated many times that if I am true to my religion then I cannot ever aggressively commit violence. I cannot kill or maim or hurt in any way.

'If an invader came to my house, I have to surrender or fight to protect my family and my house. I can fight inside the house but I can't go outside to fight them in their houses. This is how I went to fight officially the British occupation of our country Egypt through the university and not through the Brotherhood. Officially. We had to fight for our freedom. I was once asked on American television if I accepted

121

that the Iraqis are killing the American soldiers in Iraq. I said to them: "Anyone who fights against the occupier of his country is a hero."

'The interviewer also asked, and repeated the question time and time again seeking the answer they wanted: "Do you accept that the Palestinians, whether right or wrong, kill the civilians, the women and the old people and the children?"

'I explained that it is clear in what God said, and what Mohamed said, that when you are in war – whether in Israel or Palestine or Egypt – when you are in war, you are forbidden to kill children, women, old people. You have to fight who is fighting you but you must not fight the weak even if they fight you. You must not fight children, old people and women.

'Supplying weapons? The Brotherhood could never be involved in that and not only do we not do it, Hamas is not expecting it from the Brotherhood. They don't want to bring any trouble to the Brotherhood. They must find another way for it. If the Brothers should be involved with supplying weapons there would be an endless war against the Brotherhood.

'Because of the political influence of the Brotherhood there are many who want to put us down. They want to catch one of the Brotherhood making some sort of war. They wanted to catch me involved in that, to accuse me of the crime of supplying arms to Hamas, but they couldn't and they didn't find anything – for it was never done or could be done.

'The Americans regard the Muslim Brotherhood as their fiercest enemy because the Brotherhood does not accept this situation in Palestine. This does not mean that the Muslim Brotherhood is against Jews, because we are not allowed to be against Jews, or to be against the Christians, or anyone. We understand that very well but we believe, and I also believe, that the Palestinians were victims and they are still victims.

'It is a game between the Americans and the Israelis. The Israelis are taking the power of the Americans and the Americans are using the

Israelis to keep the Middle East under their control, and in the end, the Palestinians are the victims. The international support of the case of Israel and the neglect, the closing the eyes, of the case of the Palestinians is the central issue in the Brotherhood. As I said, every Muslim in the world in his heart, whether he says it or not, is with the victims who are called Palestinians.

'And I have a puzzle: why do the Israelis all want to be in one place? In this time in the human's existence a nation can be wiped out by the press of a button, in a second. The perpetrator can be thousands of miles away and watch on a screen as technology does the dreadful job. It is against the Muslim religion, against our law, to be anti-Semitic. I am Semitic – how can I be against myself. The Muslim Brotherhood are also against atrocity.

'Israel makes itself an open target in today's world. If Gadaffi hadn't given the West details about the work of Abdul Qadeer Khan [the Pakistani nuclear scientist] then he would still be creating nuclear devices in secret. And he is not the only scientist. We don't know what is going on in North Korea.'

In November 2011, UN investigators said they had discovered a complex in Hasakah in the far North-east of Syria, very similar to a uranium enrichment plant Abdul Qadeer Khan had planned to build in Libya. It was the most solid evidence linking the creator of Pakistan's atom bomb to Syria. Syrian President Bashar al-Assad had constantly denied links with Khan. The renegade scientist, dubbed 'The Merchant of Menace' for his nuclear black market in blueprints and technology, has sold his expertise to Iran, North Korea and Libya.

Khan's Libya plant was never built, yet in 2003 in his efforts to come in from the cold by formally abandoning Libya's nuclear programme, Gadaffi handed over details of the plans, along with equipment and documents provided by the Pakistani scientist, to international inspectors.

Syria was believed to have abandoned its nuclear programme in 2007. However, when Israeli warplanes bombed what the CIA said was a nuclear reactor in a desert canyon east of the Euphrates River it was revealed it was built with North Korean assistance; it was a photocopy of a plutonium facility at Yongbyon that provided the fissile material used in a bomb tested by North Korea in 2006. Khan is an expert in uranium, rather than plutonium, technology, suggesting that Syria, like Pakistan, was going two ways to have the bomb.

In 2012, investigations were going on to discover what the 'Merchant of Menace' provided to Syria; previously his clients received the centrifuges needed to enrich uranium to weapons-grade levels as well as blueprints. He is said to have had dealings with nations including Algeria and Saudi Arabia.

It is a most fragile time, with events overtaking events as Youssef Nada considers our world future: 'The other great problem is the continuing misunderstanding of Islam which is filled in the researches and books from the Holy Wars until today. I sat with a priest and talked to him, opened my heart to him as a man who is committed to religion, who tries to accept what I consider it is coming from God. He is a Christian. I sat with him and talked to him as not corrupted. The man has his heart, his purity. Then I found he considered me an infidel.

'I didn't find this attitude only with the priest, I found it also with the fanatic Muslims. We are the inheritors of history since the time of the Crusades. Today we also have the problem of the economic riches of the area – resources which are very crucial to the world. The Middle East and the oil and the gas add up to the conundrum of our days – and nightmares. If the wealth from this is not in the hands of the consumers, their standard of living will not be as they want it.

'But always from the outside they came and put their hands in to take and not to share. Remember again what British Prime Minister Campbell Bannerman said in his Report on the area in 1907: "In the Middle East the people have the same religion, the same language... we have to divide them and we must never allow them access to science and technology."

Contemporary archive documents reported the Campbell Bannerman conference generally in these terms:

'*Experts from Britain, France, the Netherlands, Belgium, Spain, Italy contemplated the threats facing Western civilisation and concluded that the most pressing came from the South-eastern Mediterranean, and in their final report they argued that the Mediterranean was colonialism's vital artery linking the West with its colonies in Asia and Africa. Yet on the South-eastern shores of the Mediterranean was a nation united in history, religion and tongue, which was no threat to Western colonialism; it must be kept weak, divided and ignorant. The Bannerman committee saw a world divided into three blocs: the first entitled to material superiority was made up of the Christian nations of Europe, North America and Australia. The second, dwelling on the peripheries of Western civilisation and including Latin America, Japan and Korea, must be contained and pacified. The third bloc, of Arabs and Muslims, were to be deprived the fruits of technology and modern science.*'

More recently, an editorial in May 2009, in the influential *Al Ahram* newspaper compared then and now:

'*The Campbell Bannerman Report suggested establishing a state in Palestine echoing the views of the 1897 Zionist Congress in Basle and endorses the idea first suggested by Theodore Herzl of creating a strong Western leading country in the Middle East. A century later, at the conclusion of the alliance of civilisations forum, UN representative Jorge Sampaio said that the forum offered "a glimmer of hope" for a changed world. So far, so good, but then the second Anti-Apartheid Conference in Geneva, Western countries fought tooth and nail against any criticism of Israel, some even argued that any such criticism constitutes anti-Semitism. Having failed to move any criticism of Israel from the conference, the US and several Western Nations threatened to put a boycott. Israel started rebuking the Swiss president for meeting his Iranian counterpart.*

The Ambassadors of twenty-three European countries walked out of the conference in protest against Iranian president Mahmoud Ahmadinejad's comments. So how far have we come from the 1907 conference?'

Reflecting now on the Campbell Bannerman Report, Youssef Nada commented: 'The attention here was to limit Islam, but Islam was not the enemy. The enemy was from within. The worst came with the First World War and the Second World War. At that time, those at war were trying to bring the Muslim world on their side. The British took their colonies on their side. The French took their colonies on their side. Hitler tried to get them on his side, but the war was from within. The intention was complete. Today the intention is the same, but you don't know when it is coming.

'War is war. Even the winner is a loser. For us, for the Brotherhood, our duty is to avoid war whatever the cost will be, to always try and co-operate to avoid war – and that means we are ready to give and take. Not to dictate; not only to take. But there is a weak area: if any person or party has contact with the West or the Americans to discuss any solution without the participation of the governments involved, they are seen as traitors. They are considered to be collaborators – to be working with the enemies of the Arab countries.

'It gets even more perplexing and frustrating: an Arab government working with the West will accuse a group like the Brotherhood of being the enemy if they seek solutions. Can you consider it human, what happened in Jerusalem when the Crusades went there? The streets were full of blood. To awake the religious war is very dangerous. When they say the Muslims want to invade the West it is not good, it is wrong.

'I choose these words carefully: Islamists are not as they are portrayed; the Islamist is not the one who believes in violence or in terrorism. They are committed to Islam and to purity. They are completely against violence to other people. We don't even talk of people who are not Muslims other than "the people of the books" –

those of the Bible and the Tora, the Christians and the Jews. We do not consider them to be infidels!

'The word Islamist now is taken out of context to mean terrorism and fanaticism. But Islamist for us describes tolerant people who work for Islam in a good way – influenced by the conviction that the Muslim version of Islam is openness to everyone. This is what *we* call Islamist.

'I told an important politician, "It is true that I am an Islamist". He was shocked: "Mr Nada, I didn't think you'd be an Islamist!" He instantly believed I was a crazy bomber. It is ignorance, but it's hard to accept people who label as terrorists all those who follow my religion. And the geography can make it more difficult as in America.

'The Brotherhood in America work as hard as possible to be model Muslims but they are monitored and investigated by the FBI. Muslims are treated very badly in the United States and there is no explanation for it. It is against the American Constitution and it must be stopped – today it's used against Muslims and tomorrow it could be against anyone.

'Either you agree that everyone obeys the law and anyone going outside the law must be punished, but when somebody makes a mistake you should not invoke his race or his religion. It's been proved in history that religious war never achieved its target but led to attrition among all the participants. The main difference is that the weak are used to being weak and it does not make much difference to them but the strong will be weaker.

'Not only the Nazis but also the Romans tried to eradicate the weak Jews but they are still there. Then they tried to do it with the Christianity but the Romans fell apart and it was Christianity which survived everywhere. Christianity tried to eradicate Islam through colonising its countries for 500 years but now one-third of humanity adopts Islam.'

Nada cites the Koran, Sura 9:5: '*O ye who believe! Stand out firmly for God, as witnesses to fair dealing, and let not the hatred of others to make you swerve to wrong and depart from Justice. Be just: that is next to Piety: and fear God for God is well-acquainted with all that ye do.*'

'It is said that in Islam there is the Islamic law which governs Muslims but in my opinion there is no Islamic law. There are rules in the Sharia for some parts of life and the rest is open. The rest is left to your conscience and to your needs. Sharia gave some social guidelines and defined some ethics and rules but did not interfere in any of the parts of life which can change. And the world has changed! Predefined, fixed rules cannot be expected to be applied in circumstances, knowledge, technology, innovation which did not exist when such rules were made.

'A person's actions and reactions in his life were left to his evaluation, without breaching those rules and guidelines as his conscience dictated. Accordingly, theologians cannot claim to know or understand other sciences or technology to define which religious rule could be applied. In the 12th century of Averroes [Ibn Rushd] the philosopher was able to deal with medicine, astronomy, mathematics in relation to religion. It was limited – but today there is no limit.

'Today hearing or reading any subject is not enough to enable you to understand it or to give an opinion about it. Knowledge must be with specialisation and practice – they are essential in our complicated world. We cannot use politics in the divinity but we should apply the divinity in politics.

'Political life could be full of deception, hypocrisy and corruption which no divinity could tolerate, but if divinity is used in politics it can purify it and guide it to be honest, clean, useful and serving the communities.

'The Sharia rule is "everything in life is allowed except what is forbidden", not that everything is forbidden except what is allowed. The Sharia is very simple whereas today's life with all its ever-changing dynamics is complicated. For that reason Sharia comprises rules and guidelines which everyone should know and use as parameters to define what should or should not be allowed. It is for a person's and the community's advantage, but the priority is for the community.

'A human needs to be in harmony with his emotions, not only with his brain and thoughts. In Islam, non-Muslims have the right to adapt

128

their family relations and family law according to their religion, not according to Islam. That is exactly what the Muslims are asking in the other countries: that they will abide by the existing law, but things which are related to the family should be left to them.

'Those of the Brotherhood are open about all of this. In Egypt there are thousands of professors from the Brotherhood; outside Egypt there are more, those who were obliged to flee the country. In America, the majority are well educated and moneyed. In Europe many, many are the workers who came from North Africa, from Algeria and Tunisia. There are 100 hundred million Brothers from Indonesia and Australia to Finland, and from China to the United States. There is no place in the world that we don't have members. And they want to live and work and be together with others in a peaceful way.

'All my life, since I was a child, even before joining the Muslim Brotherhood, I was open to my friends. In a primary school where there were orthodox Copts and Jews, I was open to them and still am. I share with them our humanity. We differ: a Chinese or Japanese person differs from me, but still he is a human; I share with him so many things. I differ from him on some points, one of them is religion, but it doesn't mean that he is my enemy.

'Hate is planted on both sides. Hate will result in bad actions that will spread a wrong way of thinking, giving everyone the right to take the law in his own hands, the law of the jungle. There is no endless pressure without action and we will all pay for it, not just one side.'

Youssef Nada believes too much spin is put into the so-called information highway, and that Western governments are fed propaganda reports. Material is written to mislead the decision makers and constantly repeated to them. Certainly, the Internet is a contagion for debasement of ideas and so far there is no antidote. The powerful, the kingmakers, read summaries; they don't have time, sometimes the inclination, to go into the details. It is tragically Shakespearean and so resonant of Iago and Othello and the plot 'to destroy the Moor'.

'Those who are near their ears are manipulating them,' said Nada. 'They hear from one side, and they don't hear from the other side. Of all of what is written about the Brotherhood, about 90 per cent is not correct. It does nothing but cause resentment and trouble.

'When the communists wanted Arab support they defended us and we belong to the Left, and when the others wanted support us we were to the Right. When the Right started to attack Islam, the Left jumped on us – back and forward, for politics not religion and certainly not Islam. I have books here which say Muslims have two nations: either it is in the nation of Islam, or it is the nation of war. That is not true, but it is in books of religion.

'They say the Muslim want to invade and convert those who are not Muslims with Islam, or not to live in the country. Islam is contrary to that, but you find it stereotyped and repeated in many books. Some people take it as fact. That is one of the problems for the Brotherhood – that they are trying to take out all the rubbish which you can find in the name of Islam, and the little things are there in the books. The ignorant people with the religion, some of them take it as it is a religion, not that it is the opinion of those who are deviates.

'I have books here which were published in Egypt in 1905 about Islam, and about the woman in Islam. It is unbelievable – they take the sword and kill with it in the name of Islam. Our education from the beginning is about what God said and what was interpreted by his messenger, by Mohammed the prophet. This, we believe we cannot change. It dictates as coming from God. We, a cleric or a politician, cannot interfere and change the text, and say that God said this or that, or meant this not that. We cannot change the word of God or interpret the word of God to justify our actions. The problem of the Bin Ladens and the men of violence has come from that.

'I wrote an article in an Egyptian newspaper in which I was so clear about this. You can't imagine the reaction. Naturally, my people, they understand what I said, and they all agree with me. The others, how they started to attack me! They said I was not a proper Muslim! I had come out of the religion!

'Some factions believe in beating themselves, hitting themselves for their religion. No religion should want that in the name of God. Our job is to try and cool the environment of hate and fear, because that is where so many problems come from. I have good treatment from everyone, whether he is Christian or Jew, or Sikh, or Buddhist or have nothing to do with religion. I treat people well and it is returned wherever I go. The feedback which is coming to me from what is going on today is there are those trying to exaggerate extremes.

'They are attacking Islam as Islam to stop people from even practising their religion. The reaction is starting with small things here, which are exported there. There is fire flaring everywhere: it is a Hot War, not the Cold War. The flames of hate are spread, and on the television and in the newspapers, the stories are about the extremes: women being stoned, people being hanged for sins, the Muslims want to "invade" Europe. They warn that in fifty years Europe will be a Muslim continent.

'I have some visitors who ask me: "Why are you doing these things?" I can understand why they ask – on the Internet one example can be seen by one million people in a moment or two. But that one million only see that story, that version, they do not hear the others, which is why patience is important. Attitudes can only change with time. The Muslims are in the West and will continue to be in the West, whether the others want them or not. They are there and they will continue to be there.

'The world was created for the humans, not for special people with special places. And, yes, there will be those who will go on trying to create the fear, and to create the hate among the people. But now the whole world is collected together. You cannot stop any part of the humans to be connected with the other part. Races will move from place to place. The West moves to the Muslim countries. The black people move to the white areas of the other countries. The white people of an area are moving to another place; it is easy to move in our world today but people in Muslim countries cannot tell those from abroad: "You have to live in our country with our way of thinking and according to our religion." They cannot say it.

'It is the same in the West. The West cannot say to the Muslims: "You have live our way of life." It is wrong. It could never be implemented. Language is different and you must try to speak as they do around you. An American Congressman went to Egypt and met the US Consul who took him to a coffee shop. The Consul ordered in English; when he returned to Washington the Congressman wrote: "How can this man bring us the right information on which we base our policy if he doesn't know how to speak with the people? How can he understand them?"

'You must also know the law of the place where you are and abide by it. This is more important than the language. If he doesn't know the language which assists him to be able to live among the others, he will pay the price, not the others. If he doesn't know the law of the place where he is living, then the others will pay the price, not only he. Every person is different. Why are some looking for people to be a copy of the others?

'If we talk about the colour of us all and not about the religion and look to the history and the geography – black people were born in Africa would be very black. In Pan America, they are another colour; in the Middle East, another colour. Whatever the reason is, whether those people who have different colours or not, their colour has spread around the world. They were there during the time of slavery, or they arrived through trade, or were invaded or they invaded, by colonisation. But they spread every colour everywhere, so today you see a mixture.

'The movement of the different people happened, and it will continue to happen. No one can stop it. But when someone steps out of line you must not condemn all from that group. You cannot believe they are the same, clones, that every Muslim is Bin Laden, or Ayman al-Zawahri, or a killer. We are all the same: all humans. You cannot condemn all society because a madman, or a criminal or a terrorist was one of them.

'Now we come to the main point, which is the safety valve for the humanity: it is justice. When you commit a crime, it is you, not the people who lived with you, not the society from where you come. It is you. It's the nature of politics that you attack religion. For religious reasons you attack economy. For economic reason, you attack politics. That is the way which it goes. We must all be aware of it.

'I had an Austrian friend who was a banker and he lived in the period where the Jews were discriminated against in Austria and in Germany. He told me a lot of stories. How could it be justified that the government treated some of their nationals differently from the others because of religion? That because of his religion a man has to put a yellow star on his chest or a sign in his house or shop to show people he is a Jew? How were the government able to mobilise the people to follow such a treatment? What society does this and claims there is justice? It is this recent history which resulted in a war among the Christians. Fear and hate will create everything.

'It was not an easy war, the Second World War. About forty million were killed. Have we learnt any lessons from it? Listen to me! There is only lesson: we must always avoid war. But will we learn? Discrimination, fear, hate will come one day and it will be war. Yes? Finish with the Jews, start with the Muslims. It is the same principle. The next one will be America and Europe, and then East and West. Then it will be Muslims and Christians.

'There are no wise people to think about that, only those that are creating the hate and the fear. But people are following them. People followed Hitler in Germany. Education is a very important part for any leader anywhere. Not normal education, but peace and tolerance. In the Koran, God talks about all the humanity by talking about the sons of Adam – that means one family, one father, all brothers and sisters.

'I cannot go blindly to lead my life, and my family and my future to somebody who does not understand all these things. But politics brings anyone from anywhere. They are talking about invasion, and Islam coming with the sword, and how Islam wants to impose Islam in the West. But if you study the Koran, which is what the Muslims have to follow, it is forbidden to force anyone to be Muslim.

'People don't know that – that it is written in the Koran, not only once, several times: forbidden. But everywhere you hear the warning, even from the Pope. The Christians have to hear the Pope, or hear the Muslim. When the Pope says it, they will follow. But when Muslims say that it is forbidden by us, will he then believe that?

'The media is stronger than the power of any other thing on Earth. Where is the intelligence? Where are the academic people? Who are the Muslim Brotherhood? It must be explained so that there is no fear – for there is no need for fear. Where is the deception? From the Muslim Brotherhood or those who use religion in politics to bring fear? Who deceived? Again, the concentration must be on justice. Justice.

Youssef Nada said he was bewildered when he heard Barak Obama say, one week before his election as US President, that he was against the election in Palestine. Expressing disbelief, Nada added: 'He was taking part in an election to be President of the United States, and he's against an election in Palestine, while at the same time stating that elections are vital to democracy.

'The people must choose the person or group they want. Even if the Devil is elected, that is it. The fault is not of democracy but of the electors. If you are spreading democracy, defending democracy, you have to accept it the result you get. Do you want Nasser/Sadat/Mubarak or do you want Egypt? If Nasser/Sadat/Mubarak are out of the line, whom are you defending? You have to support them or leave the people to choose another one. And if they choose someone you don't like?

'By abolishing the Muslim Brotherhood or any group asking for a voice nothing will be achieved that will last. Many unbelievable things have been done in the name of religion and democracy since the time of slavery. What can you expect from a slave? To love you? To love his

his country? To love the government? To follow the law? If he were strong, he would have to fight for justice. If he is not strong, then that means he is a slave. You expect anything from the slave? You cannot have his heart.

'That is exactly what is going on now against Muslims. Exactly what is happening because someone's name is Mohammed or Mahmoud. They look at the name on the passport and they treat him accordingly. This won't diminish the number of Muslims or stop Muslims being Muslim. It didn't stop the Jews being Jewish.'

On 28 February 2012, America's Attorney General Eric Holder told the US Congress that the Justice Department was considering whether to review civil rights violations because of the New York Police Department (NYPD) surveillance of the entire American Muslim neighbourhoods. Although there had been many reports that the NYPD were operating secret programmes – created with the help of the CIA – to monitor Muslims, the Attorney General did not indicate any urgency in the review.

American authorities have built databases showing where Muslims live, where they buy groceries, what Internet cafes they use and where they watch sports. Dozens of mosques and student groups have been infiltrated, and police have built detailed profiles of Moroccans, Egyptians, Albanians and other local ethnic groups. The NYPD operations extended outside New York City to New Jersey, Long Island and to colleges across the North-east. Muslim students throughout the country have reported being 'stalked' on university campuses.

Youssef Nada said this enforces his argument that such behaviour leads to trouble: 'The Muslim military doctor in the barracks [in Fort Hood, Texas, in July 2009] who killed his fellow soldiers was not a terrorist; he did not belong to Al Qaeda, or to Hamas. He was an individual. He had seen something – treatment of his race or his religion or his origin. He didn't accept it. He became mad. He started to be a criminal, a killer. I repeat, but for a reason: whether it comes out in action individually, or with groups, or with factions, you have to go to the origin of the problem: injustice.

'In my opinion, the reason why religions were formed was to adjust the behaviour of the human. There are a lot of things in common between all religions, but you come back to justice. When you touch the humanity in the human, it will wake up, even if it was dead; even if it was dormant. When the world talks about the "Arab Spring" and asks what is next, the answer is the hope of humanity.

'We need a crystal ball to see the future for Egypt and for Libya and for Tunisia and Syria and all the world. But the hope is in humanity. People and not the politicians are what must matter. As I've said so many times, democracy may not be perfect but it is the most perfect thing we have for the moment. But you can't plant peace when, from time to time, you bring hate. We have to understand each other.'

CHAPTER NINE

DANGEROUS DIALOGUE

'We make a living by what we get, but we make a life by what we give.'
Winston Churchill, 1937

Understanding is not just a priority but a necessity in Yemen, which has always been coveted and cultivated more by its neighbours than itself. From Saudi Arabia in the north you go south-west to the critical end of the Arabian Peninsula to find this small, beleaguered nation – with the Red Sea to the west, and Oman to the east – which has been cursed with poverty, terrorism and separatism.

The Romans dubbed Yemen as *Arabia Felix* (Happy Arabia) but that's been a misnomer for a long, long time. Even the national habit of chewing the amphetamine-style mind-messing shrub khat (*Catha edulis*) doesn't appear to bring much joy to the population. Yet, outsiders take an interest in Yemen for its geographical access to Asia and potential for oil.

In the early part of 2011 there were protests, similar to those in Egypt and Tunisia, against the government of President Ali Abdullah Saleh who had survived waves of dissent and discontent since his long rule began in 1978. He was President of the Yemen Arab Republic (North Yemen) until 1990 when the nation was unified as the Republic of Yemen.

Youssef Nada has his own history with Yemen and President Saleh who was finally was overthrown at the end of 2011. He helped in the country's disputes and also in Yemen's relationships with Saudi Arabia because of his own ties to King Fahd.

The friction between Yemen and Saudi Arabia has always been about boundaries, about the land and, of course, what lies (or floats about) beneath it. Back in 1934 the kings of both nations signed the Taif Treaty which promised 'perpetual peace', but the lure of oil, the atrocities of civil war, and the new kingdom of Saudi Arabia meddling in Yemeni affairs, resulted in eternal wrangling.

The Taif Treaty established a common border between the two nations but the constant warring within Yemen escalated into similar conflict with its northern neighbour. The Yemeni civil war was so harsh and devastating to the South that finally only unification was an uneasy answer. The Republic of Yemen supported Saddam during the Gulf War and so put itself on opposite sides to the Saudis.

In turn, the Saudis helped rebels in South Yemen, which brought more strife and civil war in 1994. A year later the Treaty of Taif was officially revived, re-marking the far western boundary and establishing a framework for settling the last part of the disputed border to the east. Peace – but not for long. While the Saudi Arabia conflict rumbled, Youssef Nada was dealing with another problem that emerged for Yemen.

Eritrea, on the Horn of Africa, surrounded by Sudan, Ethiopia and Djibouti, is smack across the Red Sea from Yemen and Saudi Arabia. In that stretch of water sits the Hanish Islands, of which the bordering nations disagree over ownership. Mixed in with accusations of activity by Saudi intelligence agents, a Syrian charged with terrorism and some Israeli involvement, were the ingredients of a firecracker of a situation.

Working with Yemen approval, in 1995 a German concern began creating a hotel complex and scuba diving centre on Greater Hanish. A work force of a couple of hundred men moved to the island from mainland Yemen. The Eritrea rulers were horrified. They told the Yemeni to get out within one month – or else.

When the Eritrean ultimatum ran out and the Yemeni military forces and civilians had not withdrawn, Eritrea used aircraft and all the seaworthy vessels that they could muster, including fishing boats and a commandeered ferry, to land ground forces on the islands.

The Eritrean forces attacked the Yemeni contingent and overran the entire island within three days of combat. It was alleged that Israeli commanders helped in the invasion. During the fighting, a Soviet merchant ship was damaged by Eritrean gunfire after being mistaken for a Yemeni naval vessel.

All this was occurring with the ongoing threat of civil war exploding once again. It was a mess.

Youssef Nada did historic work on the case and was helped by the distinguished United Nations representative, Giandomenico Picco, with whom he became friends and co-wrote a book, *The Political Situation of the Red Sea*, about the dispute. Picco, the political secretary of the Under Secretary General of the UN, was instrumental in the release of Western hostages in Lebanon and the negotiations which ended the Iran–Iraq war. He represented the UN Secretary General in the negotiations of the Geneva Accords (1998) on Afghanistan and in the Rainbow Warrior arbitration.

The Muslim Brotherhood were constantly involved – directly and behind-the-scenes – in the long and ongoing problems of Yemen, which persist in the second decade of the 21st century.

The Brothers in Yemen contacted Nada and he used all his abilities to help because: 'Any Muslim country is our country and this is one of the principles of the Muslim Brotherhood'. Nada and his team conducted an intensive feasibility study of the affair, utilising maps and historical documents, and correspondence from the past with the British High Commission and the Italian Ministry of War in Rome, and valuable relevant documents from the Museum of Istanbul.

'Through our contacts we had aerial photographs and documents from the Pentagon,' said Nada. 'Many people from the United Nations helped me reach material which the government of Yemen did not know how to obtain. It cost tens of thousands of dollars but I was happy to spend such money on their behalf to get the truth of it. I looked at every detail, followed all the information we were able to gather, and we gave a bulging file to President Saleh. It was the information they needed to get them their rights.

'That file containing the delicate, deciding documents – all verified at high government level – won Yemen full ownership of the larger Red Sea islands in a ruling by the Permanent Court of Arbitration at the Hague.'

With his past associations with the Saudi rulers, Nada was able to deal with King Fahd's representative and directly with Yemen's President Saleh. He also met the Yemen Brotherhood leader, Yasin Abdul Azis, for two hours at London's Heathrow Airport – he took the same aircraft there and back – and then talked to King Fahd's representatives.

'I explained the fears that another civil uprising would destroy Yemen,' said Nada. 'I talked to the Saudis as myself, making suggestions; they did not want to talk directly to the Yemeni President but agreed that I should. I arranged a meeting at his home with President Saleh whom I'd not met before.

'I expressed the view that the situation between the Saudis and Yemenis was extremely critical and could erupt at any time with terrible consequences. I said that he'd done well in his war with South Yemen, so it was good time to have discussions while he was in a strong position.

'Pivotally, I showed that I had an opportunity to get him and the Saudis together to find a solution. He told me that all his life he was always ready to listen to others. He did not want to have enemies in spite the expulsion of Yemeni after the Gulf War. He would meet anybody to resolve future conflict. We set up the negotiations.

'The main problem was the borders set out by the Taif Treaty. The lines were blurred. The Saudis had asked for a corridor to be established from their land to the sea in the south, between Saudi Arabia, between Yemen and Oman. The latter had made a quick agreement which stopped the Saudis – who were very angry – from having no access to the Arabian Sea.

'You don't find in the Arab world a lot of people in politics or in business who understand all these complex problems. Maybe those who are in foreign ministries, they know a part of it which is related to their country, but they don't know the details which involve other countries.

'The Saudis were pressing, and a message came to me from King Fahd: "We must have a passage to the Arabian Sea, even if they lease it to us." It isn't far between their land and the Arab Sea. In the middle it is all Yemen, but at the right side is the desert they call Rub' al Khali ['the great sandy waste', the Empty Quarter] which is swimming on oil. It was a long negotiation but succeeded in avoiding armed conflict and protecting the interests of Yemen.'

After Youssef Nada had been thanked for his efforts at a meeting with President Saleh, one of the Yemen Muslim Brotherhood was asked to have a private talk with the president. He asked him: 'What are the demands of Mr Youssef?' When the question was passed on, Nada said: 'I answered: "This is a gift from the Muslim Brotherhood."

'The Brotherhood's main concern is always the interests of the people and the country. But that is separate to my business life. The Brothers in Yemen wanted to establish an Islamic bank and to give Bank Al Taqwa 5 per cent in return for our advice based on our experience. I refused to do that. I did not want to make a financial link between the mediation work I did as the Muslim Brotherhood: that was done for God.'

141

For those outside the Brotherhood, Youssef Nada believes, arguably quite correctly, that such a concept is difficult to grasp. We live in a world where all seem to pursue profit at any price and cashing in your conscience is a bargain. Governments do work with devils and the legacy of that is nowhere greater than throughout the Middle East.

Muammar Gaddafi, like some of his fellow dictators, did not just stay in power for so many years with his guile and his oil, but by fear-mongering politics. It was a simple equation: any person or group who opposed him were terrorists; any group that wanted to take away his power were intent on creating jihadist bastions on the shores of the south and east Mediterranean.

That kind of rhetoric gets noticed by Washington and London and Berlin and Paris – the message is that it's better to deal with the dictator/devil you know. It's a cruel game, as the departure of Gaddafi's regime from Libya has shown: a people tortured and massacred, a nation desolate. Untold wealth from the concrete palaces spread digitally to bank accounts that have their own private accounts. The dictator's family fleeing into next door Algeria, the catalyst for more international unrest and debate rather than humanitarian action.

The noise of those predicting Islamic Revolution – defined as Islamic takeover – always point to Iran of 1979. The other point of view can cite the modern Turkey in the second decade of the 21st century, but there are constant pressures on the rule of Prime Minister Recep Tayyip Erdo an.

Youssef Nada always pleads for tolerance and balance and mediation to resolve disputes, that the killing of one innocent person is the killing of all, as stated in the Koran. So, the saving of one is the saving of all. Yet having a good heart and mind doesn't stop you from becoming a target. After 9/11, when President George W Bush began his 'crusade' he wanted someone in his sights, and Nada was the bullseye.

BOOK TWO

BEYOND REASON

'The Devil can cite Scripture for his purpose.'
Shakespeare, *The Merchant of Venice*

CHAPTER TEN

THE CIRCLE SQUARED

'*But indeed if any do help and defend themselves after a wrong done to them, against such there is no cause of blame. The blame is only against those who oppress men with wrong doing and insolently transgress beyond bounds through the land defying right and justice. For such there will be a penalty grievous.*'

Sura Shoura aya 41–42

The dry framework of Arab revolution was ready to be ignited – which in a literal sense it was in the early afternoon of 17 December 2010. It was, as it so often is in history, one man's personal mayhem which set the dominoes dropping across the Middle East and North Africa.

Persecution simply became too much for 26-year-old Mohamed Bouazizi, who made his living selling fruit and vegetables from a pushcart in Sidi Bouzid, an impoverished spot of a place in Tunisia, about 200 miles to the south of Tunis. He had been harassed by police for most of his working life, routinely about pay-offs and permits, bribes and kickbacks, the tell-tale methodology of endemic moral depravity.

That Friday in December, a policewoman confiscated his weighing scales and inventory, thus effectively destroying his business. When he objected, she casually slapped him around. He marched off to the municipal buildings to complain but was given no help, given no consideration as a person. At the iron gates in front of the salmon-coloured provincial-capital offices he splashed paint-thinner about himself and lit a match. And a revolution: the tragic death of one brought more momentum than the demise of many.

On the first anniversary of his desperate suicide, Bouazizi's mother and sister said his dignity was more important than bread. Yet it was the inability to even buy bread, and the outlaw culture of the business world, by which millions and millions of Arabs identified with Mohamed Bouazizi. It came back to economics: he couldn't make a living because of petty bureaucratic corruption. On that the poor could unite, and also against the venal coterie of despotic rulers guilty of upmarket corruption and thieving billions of dollars.

Which is why, of course, Mohamed Bouazizi was not the first, nor will he be the last, anti-corruption martyr in the struggle against dictators. Many, many, many thousands of others have given their lives. At the beginning of 2012, the United Nations released a death toll from the previous 12 months of unrest. By unofficial accounts it was conservative, but it still comprised distressing arithmetic, with estimates ranging from 15,000 in Libya to tens of thousands in the evolving sadness of Syria, and thousands in Yemen, Bahrain and Egypt.

The casualties in Cairo alone were staggering, the broken bones and crushed heads, the disfigurement of minds and bodies, and more. A year to the day of Mohamed Bouazizi's self-immolation, military policemen, armed with electric prods and clubs, baton-charged protesters in Tahrir Square, beating them and setting fire to their tents. (*Tahrir* is Arabic for liberation and this square got its name in 1952 when Nasser abruptly shrugged off King Farouk and realigned power across the Arab world).

The images of a woman being stripped of her veil, being clubbed and kicked and stamped on by soldiers before being dragged along, half-naked, in the dust, surprised and shocked. What distressed and shamed so many was the invasive assault on her dignity. As she was pulled about, her upper body was exposed showing her Marks and Spencer blue bra: that violation seemed to epitomise the military's attitude of the Egyptian people as commodities in the grand scheme.

Again, one person's misery illuminated the evil going on. It led to unprecedented protests by thousands of women – many came forward testifying they had been abused and subjected to 'virginity tests' after arrest. One Egyptian general told American television viewers 'these women were not like your daughter or mine; these were girls camped out in tents with male protesters'. The army had to 'prove that they weren't virgins' otherwise they might claim they had been sexually assaulted.

The violence and anger followed the second round of voting in the first free elections in generations – the right for democracy – on 16 December 2011, when military policemen moved into the square at dawn. At least 14 people were killed and more than 300 wounded in street fighting – again a high cost for rebellion rather than submission. Twenty-four hours later protesters fled into side streets to escape the troops in that wicked-looking, Darth Vader-intimidating riot gear, who grabbed people and battered them repeatedly even after they had been beaten to the ground.

We were told that the ousted Hosni Mubarak's adherents within the army had, through their stooges, directly orchestrated the vicious backlash against the protesters: the motivation for daily events was never ever 20-20 clear. Your eyes and the television news cameras could record the adversaries, but not allegiances. What you see is not always as it is. The only thing certain was uncertainty.

The young, the liberal, these revolutionaries applauded worldwide by armchair pundits had harshly learned that you can light the flame but you don't own the fire. You only had to look across Tahrir Square at the lawlessness on display and wonder what the previous months of the Arab Spring had brought to Egypt. The euphoria which once

147

engaged the square had gusted away. It was military rule by men who wore their entitlement with their uniforms that held the momentum.

That entitlement, encouraged by the grace and favour of America, was so embedded that even several months after Hosni Mubarak finally succumbed to people power and stepped aside as President, the army was in control. But of what? Not of the economy; it was a diminishing return. Egypt's money, utilities and food were disappearing fast and with it credibility. What hadn't vanished were arbitrary arrests of those believed to be making dissident noises; the army courts remained one of the nation's more productive enterprises: more than 10,000 people went before military tribunals.

That awakening, the popular revolution by millions who had crowded Tahrir Square in protest in January 2011, was replaced by a belief that Mubarak was gone but not his regime, his dictatorial legacy. Indeed, almost all who had served him for three decades and worked with him closely as colleagues before that, were still in government, still grasping grimly on to their golden privileges, their economic empire and its network of extraordinary clubs, homes and hospitals. It was all part of a hugely protected and privileged subculture – a gilded cage, impervious to scrutiny, which Mubarak had spent years building to keep happy and content his loyal and obedient officer corps.

It becomes a habit. If they gave up power completely they would lose their lavish lifestyles and, perhaps, their lives. That is always a strong incentive to stay put and fight. As such, they found some sanctuary in the chaotic awakening. During the acoustic pandemonium across the warren of alleys and streets of Cairo, much chicanery charged into the confusion.

Most twenty-first-century Egyptians have grown up in a security state dominated by one person acting with military support. No one was able to express themselves without fear of retribution – even though with that repression came ruthlessness and incompetence, propped up by foreign dollars, which created long, long years of neglect and corruption.

ove left: Youssef Nada's father, Mustafa Ali Nada, who owned a farm and dairy ɔducts factory in Alexandria.

ove right: Youssef Nada as a teenaged student in Alexandria.

low: Youssef Nada at the 'Mosque in Munich' which was to prove controversial in the ᵥestigations and reportage following 9/11.

Above: As the Ayatollah Khomeini looks on, Nada points out to Mohsen Rafighdoost, Minister for Iran's Revolutionary Guard, plans for a satellite city near Tehran.

Below: With Anwar Ibrahim and the Malaysian opposition leader's family in 1995. In 201 Anwar Ibrahim was consulting Youssef Nada about an upcoming 'Malaysian Spring'.

bove: Youssef Nada meeting Indonesian President B.J. Habibie at his offices in Jakarta.

elow: Nada stands behind (*right to left, seated*) Muslim Brotherhood pioneer Ahmed elmi Abdul Magid, Mustafa Mashour, the fifth Supreme Guide of the Muslim rotherhood, and Dr Youssef Al-Qaradawi.

Above: Nada with Giandomenico Picco, the former chief United Nations hostage negotiator, who won the release of Terry Waite and Terry Anderson among many others.

Below: Nada with Swiss legal champion and member of the Council of Europe, Dick Marty, and Prime Minister Recep Tayyab Erdogan of Turkey.

Above: Douglas Thompson in Tahrir Square, Cairo, as protests were beginning following Friday prayers in July 2011.

Below: Youssef Nada in 1992 with Javier Pérez de Cuéllar, the then Security General of the United Nations, at a conference in Italy.

Above: Nada with Prime Minister of Tunisia Hamadi Jebali on his right, and his 'kingmaker' Rashid al-Ghannusi on his left. The Tunisian team went by government pl at the conclusion of the World Economic Forum's annual meeting in Davos, Switzerlan and called on Villa Nada on 28 January 2012.

Below: Youssef Nada and his wife with Ghaleb Himmat before the hearing of his case against Switzerland at the European Court of Human Rights in March 2011.

ove: Saddam Hussein's guards capture on camera his introduction to Youssef Nada in ptember 1990, before their long 'interview' in which Nada tried to persuade the tator to withdraw from war.

low: Youssef Nada with his friend Ahmed Idris Nasreddin, with whom he shared the ablishment of the Al Taqwa Bank – and a place on America's terrorist list.

Youssef Nada in a reflective moment on the terrace of his home in Campione d'Italia, overlooking Lake Lugarno.

When, on 11 February 2011, Mubarak was forced to step down after 30 years as Egypt's leader – to popular applause and some international dismay – a fervent liberation party began in Tahrir Square and all along the banks of the Nile. It looked a triumph for Facebook followers and Islamists and vice versa. Dictatorship appeared to be the only loser. Families hugged in the streets; children were grabbed from their sleep to witness unprecedented scenes and events. Egypt, the biggest (half of the 85million population are under the age of 25) and most politically important Arab country, had booted out a tyrant by the will of the people. The voice of the adored singer Umm Kalthum provided the soundtrack for this moment in history with *ana al shaab, ana al shaab* ('I am the people'). The army's troops, from the generals to the foot soldiers, were heroes; they had been loyal to Egypt and not to Mubarak – they had not shot at the protesters.

Such a result, such people empowerment, was hard to comprehend, even for those who watched the sun rise over Tahrir Square the following day and began clearing up, wielding brooms not weapons. The new day brought reality into the patriotic but erratic equation. It was too early for most to realise how harsh that could be, or how complex that equation truly was, and if solvable at all. The most vital unknown of all was how deep and dark were the roots of the ruling military elite.

Change needs care, for it can trap you like a maze – like the officialdom and long, slow paper trails of the Mugamma, the Egyptian government office complex on the south side Tahrir Square which comprises claustrophobic corridors, anonymous doorways, paperwork 20 floors high, and incomprehension. Many in Cairo maintain there are more dead souls in the Mugamma than in the City of the Dead.

The initial contest between Mubarak and those wanting change placed the military in the middle. With the people's goodwill, the Supreme Council of the Armed Forces (SCAF) took over and President Mubarak's long-serving defence minister, Field Marshal Mohammed Hussein Tantawi, became in all but name the ruler of

Egypt: the latest Pharaoh. But it was promised that this uniformed junta, which in reality had simply regrouped, was only to be in power until a new government was in place.

The bureaucracy of democracy is unwieldy, an ongoing incubi, but this time it was also up against the army's desperation to protect its autonomy and preserve its exclusive privilege. Talks went on in secret as political parties were formed or reformed and ducked and weaved their way around a brand new set of rules.

The ballot box and parliamentary life existed in Egypt from 1919 until Nasser's 1952 coup, but few recalled the bewildering democratic process of voting for the candidate of your choice and getting them elected. So, with the novelty of having a free vote, for the first time in living memory people voted without knowing the outcome, which was a shock to the constituency – and the system.

A new constitution, with presidential elections to follow, was needed. The 20-member SCAF insisted a new parliament would have no authority over the Cabinet and a civilian government would only be formed after presidential elections, possibly in 2013. The anthem of Tahrir Square – 'Freedom! Freedom!' – was ignored. Reform didn't happen. Emergency laws targeting any form of protest, from the streets to the Internet, became harsher and were augmented with new provisions. Activists and bloggers – to use Twitter was to defy – were jailed and civil-society organisations subject to official investigations.

The response was frustration and unrest which was first aimed at the failure to introduce political transition, but as the clock ticked on at what was perceived as the obstruction of the military to change, that they steadfastly remained Mubarak's men. Demonstrations were called against the army's intransigence. The Internet had tips on how to calm the effect of tear gas – use Coca Cola, not water to wipe your eyes; splash vinegar on scarves and paper surgical masks – and opportunistic street vendors were selling gasmasks at a couple of Egyptian pounds a protester. The cognoscenti knew something bad was on the way.

Coptic Christians gathered outside the Maspero TV headquarters in

Cairo were attacked on 9 October 2011, and around 30 people killed, some crushed to death by army vehicles. State-controlled television appealed for 'honourable citizens' to support the troops, and the usual goons appeared armed with Molotov cocktails and clubs.

After prayers on Friday, 18 November 2011, Tahrir Square was the focus once again. For nearly a week protesters fought state security officers amid the snap, clack and pop of canisters landing and then the belching sting of the tear gas, the acrid tang of riots. Much of the action took place in a fog, like the struggle for freedom itself. Twitter and texts brought more protesters, more trouble. What was eerie – more evidence of the insanity of turmoil – was that in the streets around Tahrir Square daily life went on, in the shops and the hookah/shisha cafés, amid the chaotic fanfare of the traffic. The majority wanted peace and stability and a fair and just government. Yet, in just four days, 33 people were killed and 1,732 wounded. The clouds of white teargas smoke, almost festive and bewilderingly deceptive given their nasty, often debilitating effects, could be smelled throughout central Cairo – along with the ever-present unsettling and disquieting aroma of both wealth and despair.

One demonstrator adamantly articulated the growing distrust of the ruling classes everywhere in the second decade of the 21st century: 'The military council says we have the right to peaceful protest but they're still dealing with us with violence. They are trying to kill people. When they catch someone they keep beating him; the police hire thugs to do this ugly work.' That would be an ongoing complaint, as it was becoming abundantly clear even to Arab Spring enthusiasts worldwide that Mubarak's leaving was a *symbolic* departure.

The management of the transition of Egypt from military to civilian rule was beginning to feel like an eternal quest. For many weeks the frustration had been palpable. Tahrir Square had been the gathering point for protest by all the disenchanted, the young, the Islamist factions, including the Muslim Brotherhood and the minority Coptic

Christians. Security forces had often reacted with violence and what followed was death, casualties and compromise. Yet by Election Day on 28 November 2011, the voters appeared in substantial numbers, creating patient, snaking lines throughout the provinces for the staggered, complicated electoral process.

It was a moment for which Youssef Nada had waited almost all of his lifetime. Yet he was uneasy, concerned that the Muslim Brotherhood's twilight life in politics had not prepared its Freedom and Justice Party (FJP) for government – especially of a nation ruined by mismanagement and an economy shaken dry by internal and external events. That is why, he explained, the Brotherhood never wanted total control but a coalition. He dismissed suggestions that the Brotherhood wanted power and not responsibility. Monopoly of power was not a present solution, rather it was all 'hands on deck' to find a way forward to improve the lives of the people, so many of them jobless and living in poverty, on a day-by-day basis.

The care of its constituents has always been a supportive part of the Muslim Brotherhood's structure. Its message is based on Islam and spread through charity work and the mosques. The Muslim Brotherhood, with affiliates in all Muslim countries, Europe and the United States, is led by professionals, doctors, lawyers, professors.

After decades of Government corruption, the Brothers are perceived at home as honest and credible leaders. Yet, constantly persecuted, they have been forced to work in the shadows – and that is not a solid, true training ground for solo government.

What confused matters was the emergence of the truly conservative Salafis and their strict Al Nour party. The Salafis hard-line purist views on female and Christian rights catch headlines, as do their intents about banning bikinis and alcohol, even in nations and areas economically dependent on their tourist industries. Many Salafi adherents were released from jail after the fall of Mubarak and the Al Nour party emerged stronger, with encouragement from Saudi Arabia.

Although the Brotherhood separates itself from Al Nour, any power-sharing would pressure the Brotherhood to enforce more extreme views. Youssef Nada believes it is something they had to something they will have to deal with. It's part of politics, part of life. By January 2012, and the third and final voting in Egypt's parliamentary elections, it was clear that the Brotherhood's Freedom and Justice Party would be the dominant Parliamentary party.

Youssef Nada insisted that the interests of all parties and people would be addressed in the formation of a new parliament, in a coalition or unity government. The Brothers would govern from the middle, listening out for the interests of Egyptian liberals – and the Salafis and other ultraconservative Islamists – and in doing so offer middle-of-the-road policies and calm the outer limits as Egypt readjusts its world axis. And calm Western fears of extremist Islamist pandemonium, which for so long had been an essential part of tyrannical blackmail.

The West's many years of questions about human rights and autocracy were brushed off by Mubarak and other Arab nation despots by claiming that if they were not allowed to stay in charge, the Islamists would seize control. America and others indulged in the game, with Israel always the elephant in the room. Now the Islamists are the emerging power and the West has to begin altogether new conversations.

By January 2012, the White House was publicly seeking closer and stronger associations with the Muslim Brotherhood. (It continued to quietly keep talking and negotiating with the military leaders as well). But by then, high-level talks had been taking place privately for many weeks as President Obama put to one side the lifetime of hostility toward the Brotherhood who were perceived to be irreconcilably opposed to United States interests.

It would prove difficult diplomacy in an American presidential election year. It was, for America, to be 'a historic shift in foreign policy': Egypt's autocratic governments had long had the full support of successive administrations including, in 2011, more than $1.3billion in US military aid. That would prove one of the most delicate issues in the change of power.

On 10 December 2011, the former presidential candidate and chairman of the US Foreign Relations Committee, Senator John Kerry, met members of the Muslim Brotherhood in Cairo. In that city on 18 January 2012, Anne Patterson, the US Ambassador to Egypt, also met with Muslim Brotherhood Supreme Guide Mohamed Badie and other senior leaders. At the same time, former American President Jimmy Carter was in Egypt for the elections.

As will be appreciated, for Youssef Nada, Jimmy Carter's presence, as much as America's political engagement with the Muslim Brotherhood, had enormous ironic stature. President George W Bush had called Nada 'a terrorist financier', and now President Obama was tipping his hat to the organisation which Nada has championed almost all his life. With his habitual caution, he counselled that the world should 'wait and see what happens'.

The policy change reflected the reality of the Islamist showing at the ballot box and an acknowledgement that the Muslim Brotherhood, so long vilified by powerful American politicians and shoot-from-the-lip television commentators, want a modern democracy and freedom of people and markets. The unknown phenomenon of the Al Nour party presents another challenge to the Muslim Brotherhood, and to Youssef Nada who has worked tirelessly and often risked his life for a peaceful conclusion to the decades of death he has lived through.

He is acutely aware of the international stumbling blocks involving Israel and Hamas and the Palestinian quest for nationhood.

In wild polemics, American politicians have painted the Muslim Brotherhood as a begetter of terrorist monsters like Al Qaeda, but they are in fact two very opposing movements. Al Qaeda scorns the Brotherhood for renouncing violence and in turn the Brotherhood expels any member who engages or encourages terrorism or the taking of a life. If you are motivated to do, so it's easy to make a circumstantial case to link the two, for some terrorists – like Al Qaeda commander and the late Osama Bin Laden's close associate, Ayman al-Zawahri – were once in the Brotherhood.

The Muslim Brotherhood's angry attitude to Israel, reflecting the majority public opinion in Egypt, is a negotiation hurdle, especially for Israel's United States sponsors. Some say Israel has no right to exist, others offer the two-state solution, but Youssef Nada believes there is another way, on the understanding that 'we are all humans'.

As such, there must be toleration. Certainly, the wave of free elections in 2011 revealed voters wanting Islamist-led governments five years after Hamas won in the Palestinian elections. The Justice and Development Party won a majority in Morocco's general elections. The Ennahda Party, under the guidance of Youssef Nada's close friend Rashid al-Ghannusi, triumphed in Tunisia. Nada advised the new leadership who visited him at his home in January 2012, at the conclusion of the World Economic Forum annual meeting in Davos, Switzerland.

Then came the long drawn-out – and arguably the most important election – the vote in Egypt. From the off, the Brotherhood's FJP took almost 47 per cent of the total Parliament which was dominated by the Islamist parties. The Al Nour Party, which only formed a political organisation a few months earlier, won nearly 25 per cent. A coalition of liberal parties was a poor third. Some observers argued that the Islamists were backed by the riches of Saudi Arabia (Al Nour) and Qatar (the Muslim Brotherhood) and 'bought' their vote. Others said they had blackmailed the illiterate population (40 per cent of Egyptians are without learning) in a 'vote-for-us-or-you-are-a-bad-Muslim' campaign. The reality denied much of that.

Abdel Moneim el-Shahat, one of the most outspoken candidates of the Salafist Al-Nour party, outraged moderate Egyptians with his clear calls for Salafi Islam – a strict interpretation inspired by Saudi Arabia's Wahhabi sect – to be made the law in Egypt. El-Shahat echoed Afghanistan's Taliban when he insisted historic statues of Egypt's pharaohs should be covered or destroyed because they amounted to idolatry, which is strictly forbidden in Islam. He angered many intellectuals by attacking the novels of Naguib Mahfouz as books 'inciting promiscuity, prostitution and atheism'. His views cost him a run-off vote in Alexandria when liberal, Christian and young voters supported the independent and Brotherhood-endorsed Hosni Dewidar.

The Muslim Brotherhood, so long outlawed, was very much party of Egypt's political mainstream, and with that nation as the standard bearer for the Arab world, it follows that the Brotherhood would act out the same role for the moderate Islamists. And that dismayed many who believed the angry and loud voice of the secular liberal protesters of Tahrir Square would be reflected at the voting booths. The past, especially such an ancient society, will always have strong grip on the future.

The Muslim Brotherhood never offered a presidential candidate or sought to be in total control of government. It was a prudent political choice, for the uphill task is to reverse the dismal economy and seek to solve the nationwide poverty and unemployment which got the protest movement started. Christians and minority liberals, and many in the West, were vocally dismayed at the thought of the imposition of Islamic law and social restrictions. The Muslim Brotherhood argues that despite its culture it is an inclusive party. With the Salafis included along with the liberals, few could doubt there could be pull either way from the Brotherhood's centre when finally, after all the decades, the iron regimes started by Nasser were bursting apart their uniformed seams, unravelling on prime time television.

The power of television, computers, and social media, in all that has happened over the past many months, is self-evident. TV screened the 'Arab Awakening' and for 24 hours every day the acts of protest and those of reprisal were played into homes worldwide or onto computer screens. Youssef Nada has used television to forward his point of view, as has his close friend Sheikh Youssef al-Qaradawi, with whom he spent time in prison. Al-Qaradawi was jailed for his allegiance to the Muslim

Brotherhood and the father-in-law of his younger daughter Hasna who is married to Dr Mohamed Youssef Al-Qaradawi.

Sheikh Al-Qaradawi is a hugely influential figure in Sunni Islam. He is often cited as a spiritual guide for the changes in attitude and regimes in the Arab world. An Egyptian, he took the citizenship of Qatar and from there he operates his own foundation in the capital, Doha. He also hosts a television show on Al Jazeera which gives him direct contact with a vast constituency running into many millions every week. His message is: 'People have to change from inside and fate will respond.'

Like Youssef Nada, he argues that the Islamist movement should take a middle road and avoid extreme impositions. He dismisses ideas that countries which rely on tourism force an Islamic dress code on visitors. He has suggested to the Salafi Nour Party to adopt new thinking: 'I told our Salafi brothers they are in their first political experience and have to deal with people with moderation, and I hope they will.'

Yet, as the story of Youssef Nada so clearly shows, nothing is ever 100 per cent straightforward. In an interview at the end of 2011, Sheikh Al-Qaradawi said the West had to, 'Think about how to deal with Islam, while Israel cannot continue to base its policies on force. Countries that are going through this awakening, and where Islamists rule, will be very wise in their dealings with the West and Israel but they will not accept oppression.

'Our brothers the Turks have been able to serve their country and produce an economic and social renaissance. They have won over secularism calmly. Turkey is the model of moderation and it's a model that Arab countries can benefit from.' And that sounds like reason itself. When asked about the reasons for his friend's problems – al-Qaradawi is banned in America – Youssef Nada has a one word answer: 'Hamas.'

Sheikh al-Qaradawi is persona non grata in the US for his support of Palestinian suicide attacks against Israel where he is despised. He condemned 9/11 and backed a religious edict allowing American Muslims to fight for their country, even against a Muslim state, but insists the Palestinian attacks are justified. He splits opinion by offering his.

It is stand-offs like that which Youssef Nada has spent his life facing and negotiating conversations about. It's a bringing together of opposites, of solving the puzzles of fate and philosophy. It's being a politician but also a statesman, for nothing in the Middle East is ever simple. It's a culture where loyalties, deceptions and deals over borders and territories, kings and presidents, are in centuries of archives, and interpretation is held in the hands of power.

Sheikh al-Qaradawi left Egypt three years after Youssef Nada, but unlike him he has returned to Cairo. In February 2011 – 50 years exactly after his departure – he went to Tahrir Square to pray, to the enthusiastic cheers of the crowds. Sheikh al-Qaradawi said: 'What's forbidden is desired and we Islamists were always forbidden. Islamist movements and Islamic preaching [da'wa] were fought and repressed, they had no luck, no place. Now that the tyrants have been removed, nothing prevents Islamists from taking their rightful place in the heart of society.'

You only have to view the evening news to know that something should and must be done to stop the carnage. It's through the work of individuals like Youssef Nada that there is talking as well as killing, and with that, hope. And always remembering that nothing is ever crystal clear, it's smoke and mirrors in the often startling sunshine which can blind good sense like some ancient curse.

Rational Islamists were quick to understand they could best achieve influence at the ballot box. The Salafis, who for so long regarded voting as supping with the Devil now, however reluctantly, believe it is their only hope to promote their views. There are some devoted followers, including religious scholars, who would re-establish medieval polity: this impotent thinking in the 21st century is disconcerting and a path to nowhere.

Of course, there are still those on both sides of the divide who believe conflict alone will bring an answer – the outsiders of terrorism.

People of reason in the East and West are disturbed – and continued to be so with the horrific attacks in Nigeria at the end of 2011and in 2012 – with violent acts which even saw Muslim against Muslim.

Much has changed since 9/11 and possibly the most sweeping carousel has been the Islamist view of democratic politics: it doesn't make you a bad Muslim to vote for your rights and live in a country where you are allowed to do that.

If there was one thing the young demonstrators fully understood and proved during the Arab 'awakening' was that the world has shrunk. Still, the men who held power, like Assad in Syria and the military hard men of Cairo proved as determined to keep it invoking martial laws and Pharonic ways to trump modern protest. It is an unenviable contest the one between mobiles 'phones and tanks.

Yes, dictators can no longer hide or cover-up their horrors with more horrors. Their misdeeds are only a text or Twitter away from being known around the globe and all the way back again but for some the death and horror and shame are of no matter. What happens anywhere is of concern to us all, as does what doesn't happen. For without change and understanding, there might not be a tomorrow to be concerned about.

What shocked and startled international opinion was the Islamist success at the ballot box. On 4 January 2012, a surprised *New York Times* reported: 'The Muslim Brotherhood is the most powerful political force in Egypt.' They might have added: and very much elsewhere. The Brotherhood members have been punished through the decades for their allegiance, their belief. If there is any sharpness in Youssef Nada's tone it is because of that suffering: 'The Muslim Brotherhood is not an insignificant little group. It is international. It represents the biggest Islamist group in the world. It cannot be restricted to what a regime wants it to be like.'

The Muslim Brotherhood is the Arab–Islamist organisation which motivates all others and their actions and thinking will show the way and indicate how our world will go – such a strong understanding of the Muslim Brotherhood is of the utmost importance. The conflicts will be between religious ambitions and the worldwide practicalities of building and rebuilding nations and economies. It's a high wire act. Like the life of Youssef Nada.

However you feel about the Arab Spring, the Middle East is changing swiftly, with summer, autumn and winter spinning into the years ahead. The Muslim Brotherhood had burst out of the margins, out from the ancient alleyways of politics necessitated by repression. Our world order is changing with it. It cannot do any less.

Chapter Eleven

Indian Summer

'*Each member of the Muslim Brotherhood anywhere in the world believes that he has a duty that he must fulfil within the general context that is drawn, which is: Call for God to bring you wisdom and good exhortation.*'

Youssef Nada, 2011

Cairo, July, 2011

One of Amal Zine al Abadeen's sons was killed by a policeman's bullet and another son sat in the military prison which those decades earlier had held thousands of members of the Muslim Brotherhood, including Youssef Nada.

The prison is no longer in the desert: it is part of Cairo which has spread out into the sand, a country more than a city now, with more than 18million people trying to find space to live. The traffic moves like cattle, pausing and agitated, suddenly fierce and frisky, bumper touching bumper everywhere you slowly go.

There's a road block at a corner of Tahrir Square and teams of security men who look like members of a pre-makeover boy band check identification papers and the car for explosives. Hosam, 23, the

161

same age as Youssef Nada when he was brought to Cairo, and also from Alexandria, is my 'guard'. He's nervous, watchful and chews his bottom lip when he concentrates before replying to questions. There is not one sign of any other security: no soldiers, no police.

'If the police come, they will not ask us any questions,' Hosam tells me. 'They will not speak. They will (he makes a pistol of his right hand and points it at his chest) go bang! bang! And to make sure (he points his hand at his forehead) they will go bang! bang! again.

'Many of my friends have been killed or injured beyond recognition and we are still waiting for SCAF [the Supreme Council of the Armed Forces] to implement our demands. It might be bang-bang! before that happens.'

Amal Zine al Abadeen's surviving son was beaten and arrested in a protest at that slow progress of change, a kettle of simmering frustration, protesting because the so-called 'Arab Spring' had not flowered into an overnight dream of democracy and happiness.

You can understand the anger and the upset. 'I've grown tired,' Amal Zine al Abadeen told all of us in Tahrir Square. 'This revolution has done nothing for us. I don't want money. I don't want anything like that; all I'm asking for is justice.'

There it is again: justice.

As we know so well from Youssef Nada, it was something of a lost commodity in Egypt throughout the military rule, years of so much change, with ancient glories gone to neglect and the population multiplying in a scramble to more than 81 million people (in July 2012), a huge percentage of them illiterate, most of them poor.

The crowds in Tahrir Square on the weekend of 7 July 2011, who had walked and driven and burst from the former Misr train terminal (renamed by Nasser in 1955 as the Ramses Railway Station) swelled like the Nile in winter rains. They had suffered the side issues of revolution, economic malaise, sectarian discord and rising crime with little return. You could feel the disappointment heavy on them like the broiling heat of the afternoon.

Members of all the major political parties, including the Muslim Brotherhood, were present. There was no obvious display of feuding about the constitution, elections and other highly and hotly debated issues. One of the crowd, 33-year-old paediatrician Dr Sherine Ibrahim, told me: 'Up to this day the justice system has not allowed any public access to the trials of Mubarak's people. Trial dates are being delayed, ex-ministers who are notorious for being corrupt are being acquitted, and we, the people, aren't allowed to be part of the process. Nothing has changed.'

There had already been many high-profile arrests, including Mubarak's sons and many of his officials. The country's hated interior minister, Habib el-Adly, was sentenced to 12 years in prison on corruption charges. Lawyers for some of the accused have blamed prosecutors for conducting a witch hunt. The counter to that was that at least 840 protesters had died and only one lowly police officer had been convicted, in absentia, of murder.

Adly's trial on charges of killing protesters has been delayed, a sign to some that the military council was unwilling to alienate Egypt's security services. 'They are trying to avoid doing this,' said activist Hani Shukrallah, with some prescience adding: 'They are afraid that once they start punishing these people, the whole security apparatus is going to unravel. Parts of it will go rogue, which is something they have demonstrated that they are quite capable of doing. The army does not see Egypt as a country in need of transitional justice.'

Indeed, many army officers believed there was a need to revive what they call the heritage of the Pharaohs. In Cairo and Alexandria in the summer of 2011 there was increasing talk of the need for a 'strong' leader, meaning another Nasser. Or Sadat. Or Mubarak. The more thoughtful, maybe cynical, believed the twenty-first-century solution would not involve a 'strong' president, but a person acceptable to as many groups as possible, albeit in reality a puppet of the military.

It was complaints about government behaviour like those which began the Arab Spring that reignited violence on the streets of Cairo.

Mohamed Sayed was killed on 29 January 2011, but the trial in his case was delayed three times and his family said they were offered more than US$16,500 to drop the case. Sayed's father, Sayed Abdul Latif, said they refused: 'We sleep in the street, and our children sleep in the dust, and the officer who killed my son is asleep in his house.'

It was into this environment that the Muslim Brotherhood joined in January 2011, in a display of unity with the young, Internet-led revolutionaries and an assortment of liberal, leftist and secular political forces. Only four months later in the city, the first general Muslim Sisterhood conference in 60 years was held. One of the speakers was Khairat Al-Shater, the deputy leader of the Muslim Brotherhood, who promised more female representations and movement to investigate leadership positions for women within the Muslim Brotherhood. Times were changing.

'Take to the streets on July 8: the revolution is still on', read graffiti plastered across Cairo. 'The demands of the revolution have not changed since day one,' said the 25th January Revolution Youth Coalition in a statement which added: 'It was not just about toppling the old regime but about building a state where people can have freedom, dignity, rule of law and social justice.'

'Dignity' was the one word everyone you talked to in Cairo repeated. It is top of the list and it would seem that from it, humanity would properly establish itself. Still, humanity is a difficult sales pitch, a complex feasibility study. However moderate and academically sensible you believe the views of Youssef Nada to be, they are often carried away by a storm of fearful and opposing arguments – and not just from Western commentators and politicians but from within his own Islamic world. The essential question always appears to be: 'Is he too good to be true?' Or, is it too true to be good?

In a world of shady motivations are there those who prefer conflict to ensure their own power base? Are all violent groups fighting for a misshapen cause, or are they just mere gangsters practising evil for profit?

When the co-ordinated attacks were perpetrated on the United

States on 11 September 2001, with two of four hijacked airliners being crashed into the Twin Towers of New York's World Trade Centre, the final death toll was more than 3,000. That number – or the numbers, the millions and millions, who have died in wars over the centuries – can never be truly evaluated. How do you mark up a human life? Any attempt will leave anyone with heart breathless, lost for words, for imagination. But what the events of 9/11 provoked was a war of blame, of cultures – a war, you wonder, if anyone will, or can, ever win.

Youssef Nada was picked out personally by US President George W Bush as a so-called 'financier of terror' through his Al Taqwa Bank, the Islamic financial institution he had so carefully established to be within the parameters of international banking law and practice. A Swiss author, Victor Kocher, with whom he became friendly, telephoned him from America where he was investigating the post 9/11 situation for his book *Terror Listen*. He spoke quietly: 'Mr Nada, I am in New York and I met a lot of politicians and people of the United Nations and also in the administration, and they said it very clearly that they targeted you to make the other wealthy Muslims fearful from financing any violent groups.'

Most certainly it seriously disrupted Youssef Nada's life and his business and that of his associates and employees. One moment he owned his world and the next the keys to it were snatched away and it was locked before him. He is convinced that as it became known that he was Muslim Brotherhood's International Political Contacts Commissioner, many of the world's intelligence agencies moved against him.

He'd always had an extensive list of powerful people wanting him dead. He believes the assault on him, his bank and his business empire, was to link terror with the Muslim Brotherhood. He told me: 'I have been one of the Muslim Brotherhood for more than sixty years. It is not secret. I am honoured to be a member. I believe it is the greatest honour in my life. I still pray throughout the day and night for those who brought me into the Muslim Brotherhood.

'The Brotherhood is an ideology which spreads everywhere and no one can stop it unless they can confiscate or assassinate thoughts. They can try, but thoughts cannot be confiscated or assassinated. Thoughts are inside the heads. They can't be whipped or handcuffed. Years of struggle means that people were killed for it, imprisoned and lost their homes and livelihoods. Families were broken, children became orphans, and women became widows. But we go on.'

There had been moves against Youssef Nada and the operations of the Al Taqwa Bank before the 9/11 attacks. He is a thoughtful man and not prone to paranoia or leaping to certain conclusions because of circumstantial evidence. He believes the continued disquiet with the Muslim Brotherhood, other than the misunderstanding of its peaceful purpose, is that, as he insists, as you cannot ban ideology, and as the group has emerged as an ideology, its existence is guaranteed. This brings more unease, because if you can't control thought you cannot conquer it.

Still, and fervently, Youssef Nada is convinced he, Bank Al-Taqwa and the Muslim Brotherhood were not the ultimate target of those linking them with terrorism and with bankrolling and supporting terrorists. He is convinced it is part of the constant derailment of any possible rapprochement between East and West, West and East, Islam and all other religions. He points out that the allegations were made against all Islamic movements: 'The Muslim Brotherhood are the predominant moderate Islamic group and as an ideology can never be defeated. Children can be orphaned and women made widows but you can't murder thought.

'Muslim terrorists twist Islam for their own agenda. The Muslim Brotherhood condemn terrorists. The religion we believe in does not accept what they do in the name of Islam. We want to take hate off the top of the list and talk of peace. Since the 9/11 events in America there has been little rational thinking. Yet, taking an American life is not more abhorrent – or against everything I believe – than the taking of any life.

166

It is written in the Koran that if you kill one innocent, it is as if you kill all human beings.

'For America, whose people always believed they were immune to such traumatic events on their own soil, the hoodlums attacking in New York and Washington on 9/11 revealed this confidence in their security was an illusion. This American Dream was shattered and they hit back indiscriminately. There was no stopping them.

'Europe struggled against terrorism for decades – remember Baader-Meinhof, the Brigate Rosse, the ETA, Cosa Nostra, and the IRA – and it didn't ruin the life of the Europeans. The governments took special measures which contained and absorbed the terrorism and it passed. But when something happened in the United States, the entire world has had to pay the price – and every day since.

'The events of 9/11 engaged a new wave of the anti-Islam movement. The Jews confronted such injustice in the past and in time they overcame it. In the 21st century it is happening more than ever with the Muslims. It is a circle and none of us knows what will come around the corner. We must find a balance by which we can all live together. I must be loyal to the country where I live and obey the law and accept the majority decisions. It is my obligation. But I have the right as a Muslim to have my mosque and follow my religion. But it is not easy – even Switzerland, the most civilised of the world nations, banned minarets. [In a 2009 referendum a constitutional amendment forbidding the construction of new minarets was approved by 57.5 per cent of the participating voters].

'Moawya, the Fifth Khalifa in Islam, replicated an existing Christian tower in Damascus for the first minarets in history: side-by-side, Christian and Muslim places of worship, Muslim country. No one objected. It was Christian Switzerland in the 21st century which stopped the minarets. The world's tallest statue to Jesus is not in Jerusalem or Berlin or London or Paris or Rome but in Indonesia – a Muslim country. They didn't say: "Take it out, we're not Christian." That is not the attitude of so-called fanatics and fundamentalists. Yet the Swiss outlaw minarets, which is planting hate, while we work to make peace.'

For Youssef Nada, the millions who have lost their lives in warfare since the 9/11 attacks are an ongoing scar on our world: 'There is no value for human life. If you can make retaliatory crimes we are creating a false and inhuman philosophy. When Saddam spread a lie and invaded Kuwait on the back of it, he was judged a criminal, an invader who must be repelled. When President George W Bush lied that Saddam had weapons of mass destruction, nobody questioned what right he had to take death and destruction to Iraq. Or blow up mosques and inform the Sunni the Shia did it – and set them to massacre each other. To murder and to create war. Nobody talks about what the Americans did – they only talk about Saddam.

'The Muslim Brotherhood were the first victims of Saddam. Before going against the Shia he went against us. Saddam hit one of the American boats in the Gulf and in turn the Americans invaded Iraq. It is important to me that I am fair, for I am providing facts. I must not defend the wrong which I must admit to and propose how to correct it. If there is anything which was directed wrongly in our history I have to accept blame.' Nada smiled when he added: 'None of us are all-knowing angels.'

Nada points to the Muslim Brotherhood's planning which began in 2009 for electoral reform and the Brotherhood's status in a democratic Egyptian Parliament. 'They said we are not going to elect a woman or a Christian to be President and I didn't agree. Everyone is free to elect whomever they think is good and reject the others. Vote for whom you want. That is democracy. Our enemies used it to attack, saying we were against women and Christians. We are not against them; everyone must have a chance to be on a ballot – it is up to members to vote for or against them. They are all citizens. The minority must have somebody to defend their rights and must feel that the Parliament is a citizenship.

'From the religious point of view it was declared a woman or a Christian can fill any position except the highest one [welaya ozma]. In our history, the Khalifa appointed the heads of the states but it didn't mean the ultimate one could not be a woman or of another religion. He is not one who was sent by God or a Prophet. His position was as an arbitrator. Like the story of the ruler's son who slapped the Christian boy: "Since when have you made the people slaves when God created them free."

'There is no superiority by religion. The Khalifa was not the high authority, he was an arbitrator. If people quarrel together, he sees who is right and who is wrong. It does not mean that he is a messenger of God. Or that he is the same as the Pope, the highest authority and whatever he says must be followed; that he declare forgiveness, and for people to go to paradise. We Muslims don't have that. I argued that there was no law to prevent the highest position being taken by a woman or someone from a different religion. It made a lot of trouble.

'Anyway, this *welaya ozma* is irrelevant because in democracy no one person can be the sole and highest authority whose orders must be implemented. Instead, the power is divided into three: the legislative, judicial and the executive.

'The Prophet was supported by the Angel Gabriel and the four who came after him were educated by him and chosen by those who lived with him. The authority of the others who came after the four either hijacked or inherited, and a lot of blood was spilled for its sake. They were able to make big empires but they also were living in luxury, while their people were in poverty. There is no other way to stop this injustice except to break this power and divide it in several pieces. This collapses the theory of welaya ozma and even the expression of *welaya* itself is open to many interpretations. The Prophet said: "Every one of you has the responsibility of others."

'I am talking freely, and even the expression of secularism which all the Brotherhood — as well as any faction attached to the religion — oppose is a problem for me. I do not oppose it, although I am against part of it. Barry Kosmin of the Institute for the Study of Secularism in Society and Culture breaks modern secularism into two types: hard and soft. According to Kosmin, "The hard secularists consider religious propositions to be epistemologically illegitimate, warranted by neither reason nor experience." However, in the view of soft secularism, "The attainment of absolute truth was impossible and therefore skepticism and tolerance should be the principle and overriding values in the discussion of science and religion."

'I agree, and all people with faith will reject hard secularism because it denies the soul and talks only of the mind. Soft secularism is more tolerant, as man can't reject his spirit and morals. This doesn't contradict with Islam. Ibn Rusha [Avorres] insisted religion and philosophy must be separated. He said that those with faith happily and wholeheartedly accepted their religion as absolute fact. Because others did not believe in God it didn't mean God did not exist. The believers believe and the secularists insist they cannot accept any evidence of its existence – Catch-22 – and therefore cannot accept it.

'The essential principles of secularism were defined by the Englishman George Holyoake in 1896: The improvement of this life by material means. That the science is the available Providence of man. That it is good to do good. Whether there be other good or not, the good of the present life is good and it is good to seek that good.

'The Muslim Brotherhood does not contradict that but we add to it: The improvement of this life by material and moral means. The religious code necessitates exploring and using the power of science for the happiness of man. It is good to do good. Whether there be other good or not, we also believe that the good in the present life is good and will be rewarded later; it is good to seek double good.

'We accept their theory and more, and the secularists reject our contribution which to me is a bonus. There is no reason to fight when we could co operate on the common ground. It is rigid thinking which makes disputes. Like those who follow Salafism, which applies theology in an unbending way even though it is man-made and not from the Koran. It makes no allowance for living and understanding each other in the modern world.

'When his power was under threat, Mubarak encouraged strict Salafism to spread in Egypt. He wanted to make trouble between Salafism and the Muslim Brotherhood and make hate for Islam. It was a policy of divide and rule by encouraging the promotion of extreme thinking which would turn off the majority who'd be disgusted by it.

'When I criticised them in a Cairo newspaper, instead of answering the points and entering the debate which I created about their behaviour and thinking, one of the Salafism leaders attacked me personally. He pronounced on me: "Youssef Nada: God correct him. Or cut his neck." And this was a man of God talking!

'I argued against their insistence on a woman covering herself with a burqa – and looking like a ghost in the street. And against their opinion that Shia are not Muslims; I explained that they are the same as the Sunni even if they differ from us in some practices of Islam. They had attacked Jews and Christians and I said we have to respect them because in the Koran we have to respect these religions. If any Christian or Jew makes a mistake it doesn't mean we call all that religion an enemy. The religion is one thing and its followers are another. If some crazy Muslims twisted Islam and are wrong, it doesn't mean that Islam is wrong. The same goes for Christians and Jews.

'The Koran says: *Those who believe and those who follow the Jewish scriptures and the Christians and the Sabians, any who believe in God and the last day and who work righteousness – on them shall be no fear nor shall they grieve* [sura 2 aya 62].

'In another chapter of the Koran the same is repeated as follows: *Those who believe and those who follow the Jewish scriptures and the Christians and the Sabians, any who believe in God and the last day and who work righteousness – shall have their reward with their God. On them shall be no fear nor shall they grieve* [sura 5 aya 72].

'One of the deficiencies in our culture is that inner criticism and different thinking is not accepted and considered a deviation from the mainstream. I believe that criticism is very important for any group or society to be creative and avoid errors and develop new ideas and standards.

'The head of the Muslim Brotherhood is the Supreme Guide who is elected from the best qualified candidates. If he makes errors the whole organisation must not bear the consequences. He must be alerted to his mistakes and asked to correct them. It does not bring shame on him. The shame would be to allow him to get away with the mistakes.

'Abu Baker, the Prophet's companion, in his speech after being elected the first Caliph, said he was installed to lead, even if "I am not the best one. If you find my deeds are correct please assist me and if not you should adjust me."'

Those who defend the censorship of criticism say any dissent must not be public, as that weakens unity and reputation. I say it will widen the dialogue to create the best results from as many brains as possible. A leader is a public figure and must hear the public. All must listen to each other.

'The people of experience must be allowed to transmit their knowledge. At the same time, the young who have their vision must be able to put forward their ideas, understanding and learning. They have to present their arguments with unity and respect. If the new generation accepts democracy and their religious obligations they have to give the last word to whom they elected as the decision-maker. After a resolution is made, everyone must accept it and implement it, even if it is contrary to his opinion. He is a member of a society and he has to abide by its resolutions. From the Islamic point of view the Prophet said God's hand is with the majority.

'In Islamic teaching there's no barrier to the Muslim brain being creative in the interpretation of the religion as it applies to knowledge being gained as time moves on. When the second Calipha Omar was preaching in the mosque he was interrupted by a woman who told him he was mistaken and explained why. He looked out to the congregation and said: "The lady is correct. And Omar was mistaken." The Prophet in the battlefield asked his troops to redeploy. One of his officers asked him if that was his or God's opinion. He said the tactics were his idea. In that case, said his commander, we will stay where we are. The Prophet told him: "You know your business. Do what you want." Even the Prophet can't play God.'

Youssef Nada is acutely aware of the ever-brighter spotlight being shone on the Muslim Brotherhood with so many political changes in the Islamic world, on the varied interpretations of Islam itself. 'I know you wonder why the Muslims, after more than one thousand years, can't agree on everything – they do on some points. I suppose it is being human.

'Sunni Muslims had four important scholars during the first 300 years of Islam to interpret and explain the teachings and the Koran. They were split on some matters and it led to divisions and created factions. Those four did a very important and difficult job – they had to travel throughout the Middle East to verify the story given to them from the Prophet. It was hard, with many miles and many months of work. Today we can have all the information in one hour, even one second of time. We appreciate the hard job which they did, but it doesn't mean that we have to stop there.

'Some of the matters involved are crucial because they have formed strong barriers between East and West. One of the most controversial is punishment for crimes and the interpretation of criminal law. The other vital question is the Islamic attitude to women, the rights of women. It is written in the Koran that men are the supporters of women through their financial responsibility towards them and the preference God gave them – in their physique, their muscles. Women and men were given the same brain, the same soul.

'In the Arabic dictionary you will find different meanings for "stewardship", including supporting and strengthening. Men chose the definition which worked with their gender and made it as a sword of superiority – a weapon to deny women equality.

'The Koran was first presented in the Arabic language and is a reference in the language. The way it is phrased in the Koran, men cannot escape their obligation, the "more" they have to give is in the taking on of the heavy duties. It doesn't mean superiority because it does not say God made men in a higher position than women, but that the man has the responsibility to care and maintain the life of the woman – and for the family and for all the expenses.

'If the woman has an income or property, or if she is working, that is her money. She has no obligation to give any of it to the family. Only the man is responsible for that. If he gives the woman anything, he has no right to take it back. For example: I have this building. I gave it to my wife. I cannot, when I am angry with her, or I am desperate for money, demand she gives me back the house.

'Men don't have the right. A man must protect a wife from anyone who wants to harm her. It's not her responsibility to protect him. If these things don't exist that means that he has no superiority. Nowadays, the man doesn't have this superiority. It is in the Koran in a lot of verses, that they are equal in everything. Today women work: any idea of superiority in these circumstances is a manifestation. It is modernisation. It is not a matter of religion. Yet, in my opinion, all the rights of women today are spelled out in Islam.

'Those who are interpreting our religion just to stop modernisation are wrong. Old brains are fine – not old-fashioned thinking. We must have fresh ideas – if we don't bring something new to the life we are not living. It's everyone's duty. The Prophet said we are responsible for our seven neighbours, as they are the same as family. Today we must be responsible for many more neighbours – good sense tells us to adapt all aspects of the culture.

'A telling example of this is in the uprisings in Egypt in 2011. The Egyptians, whether Christians or Muslims, were on the streets and in Tahrir Square asking for their liberty. They were opposing Hosni Mubarak and his military rulers because of the corruption, and that is very clear in our interpretation for the religion: we must not allow corrupt people to govern us and to ruin the economy.

'The Saudi interpretation – based on the old brains – which they chose and tried to spread when the people were in the streets against Mubarak, was that the people had to obey the head of the state even if he crucified you or whipped you or confiscated your money. Today nobody can imagine that the religion can order you to accept that. Otherwise, you will get out of this religion and try to find another religion. Anyone with a new brain would!

'Some scholars went on to verify the Saudi interpretation but it is a convenience for dictators and despots. The Muslim Brotherhood maintain it is wrong to obey tyrants. Other groups stay with old-brain dictates because they are backed by the tyrants and it furthers their cause: "Do not disobey me – it is against God to do so!"

'It is nonsense. There is an expression among Muslims that dying in the way of God is a wish of every good Muslim. We say not only dying in the way of God, but living in the way of God. Those young people who were killed in Tahrir Square, when they confronted Mubarak's Government died in the way of God because they wouldn't accept the brutality of the dictator. They defended their rights and we accept that, for they both lived and died in way of God. It's equal.'

CHAPTER TWELVE

THE CONFUSION
OF WISDOM

*'Without freedom of thought there can be no such thing as wisdom and
no such thing as public liberty without freedom of speech.'*

Benjamin Franklin, 1722

Nowhere is the debate about the aims and goals of Islam fiercer
than when it centres on God's law – Sharia. It has been
interpreted by clerics and scholars and reasoning for centuries, but
what disturbs huge sections of society is the fear that Muslims want to
impose this style of judgment on everyone, everywhere. Yet, as Youssef
Nada points out, in the Muslim world, like any other, the laws of man
or religion can be made to accommodate any given situation. Corners
are not so much cut as eradicated.

'Take the case of Osama Bin Laden when he was based in the Sudan
and the Sudanese refused the demands of the Americans to extradite
him,' explained Nada. 'The Sudanese were not governing according to
Sharia or Islam, but at this point they relied on it to defend their
position. When Bin Laden was there and the Americans asked for him
they gave him the possibility to escape. They were relying on the point

in Islam that they must not deliver a man to this enemy, because he came asking for protection.

'Al Qaeda are killers, as was Bin Laden, and they came out of the religion. They are against all humanity. This I believe. But the Sudanese produced a good point about the principles of our belief. It is a delicate puzzle for those who do not have to wrestle with it, with their conscience and their religion, only seeing such a circumstance in black and white. I understand that but we must have the wit and patience to investigate all of the puzzle, find the balance between hardline thought and that which is more adaptable to the world today, the one we live in.

'There is a point everyone is talking about: that Islam is against democracy. In my opinion it is completely wrong. There is no one democracy. There are many types of democracy. Democracy in Switzerland is not the same as democracy in Italy or in England. The democracy in Switzerland says the last word is for the population by referendum; in England it's through Parliament. There are many different democracies and there are weak points but they try to correct it. Why are Muslims not permitted to adapt their way of democracy? Why do they have to imitate the democracy of others and not make their own?

'The attack on the Islamic Sharia is becoming greater all the time. It is not a matter of the Muslims wanting to change it; there are others who want them to say that it is unchangeable. There is a fear it is being manipulated rather than Sharia being seen as a system which can be adapted for the 21st century. The attack on Sharia is coming on four fronts: the treatment of women; the punishment; the reasons to accept going to war; the economic system.

'It produces questions and dilemmas. Under Sharia, in business, interest is forbidden: the present international banking system is based on the interest. Even in democracy you don't find one system of inheritance, so why not accept also the way of inheritance in Islam? We come back to the principle that man is responsible. Superiority is an obligation rather than a right. When you analyse this superiority, you find it empty. It is only an expression without any real power. If we look to the material point-of-view, the man is sacrificing for the woman, not the other way.

'The new interpretations of punishment in Islam are supported by the behaviour of the Prophet and the khlaifa and from different phrases of the Koran itself – that the replacement of punishment rules. Punishment in Islam is not for punishment, it is to stop the individual from hurting society. We as Muslims have to follow what God says and what the Prophet says. Anything else is man-made.

'We believe that God sent a messenger to the Prophet to teach him the rules which he wanted to be followed. He got the legitimacy from God, the Prophet, but those who came after him and entered into protecting this and that, all that was done after that is man-made. We have the right to discuss it. We have the right to change it. If it needs interpretation then we are free to interpret the same as those who came before us; they don't have the monopoly for it.

'There is a way in Islam that traditional punishment should be replaced by another way which could reach the aim but in a different way. It could be harsh but not involve brutality; it is up to the new brain of the people to bring something fresh and not follow the past. The target must be reached, but with different means.

'We accept that when we say punishment, that means the law, the legal structure. What I believe and the Muslim Brotherhood believe is the law must stop what we regard as crimes. You say that this is not a crime, it is up to you. That is your way of thinking. That is our way of thinking.

'Democracy is still developing. It doesn't stop. I don't say Islamic democracy. I say democracy and that's what we called for in Egypt – we accept democracy but it must not contradict with the principles of Islam because the majority of the people are Muslims. If you make a type of democracy which contradicts their belief, they will not accept it. We move away from that if we say that which does not contradict the principles of Islam, then you must have the correct way of interpretation of this Islam which you don't want to contradict.

'You have to avoid the monopoly of interpretation: this a very important point here. If we say what does not contradict with Islamic principle, if it is democracy, and the majority accept it, this item becomes the law. The new Parliament will say that this contradicts with this. They are free to say that. Someone else will say both of them are not correct, and it doesn't contradict. That is democracy. No one must have the monopoly for it.

'Here you must have a special system to judge about the interpretation and explain it to those who do not have the means to verify whether it is against or for. The man in the street cannot say whether it is contradicting or not. Muslims are not living alone in the world. They are living in the world with other societies and other religions. How they will behave with the others and how they will treat them and accept their treatment?

'The Greeks and the Romans did not keep all their commitment with the other peoples. The Pope gave his permission that an agreement with the Turks could be broken because they were of a different religion. In Islam it is not accepted to do that. In Islam, if your enemy has another enemy and he comes to you asking for protection, you must not give him to his enemy. You are to protect him, even if he is not of your religion. We live in a confused moral world and the questions and challenges are enormous. But we must not ignore them. We have to change as the world spins and changes.

'The Muslim Brotherhood started in 1928 as a nucleus of seven people in the Suez Canal zone. During this time the Brotherhood struggled to exist – sometimes allowed, sometimes not.

'It was in adolescence, just starting to develop. It grew in every way by each generation. The founder, Hassan al-Banna, was a teacher, and the first members were university students, followed by professors as it expanded. The new generation is different; remember the harsh treatment during all this time when the Brothers had to defend themselves. Always they had to think how to defend themselves.

'And no more so than in Egypt. I feel for all those young people who were hurt or killed in trying to win freedom. I also despair. When the people went to Tahrir Square in Cairo, so then came a helicopter and then a jet fighter plane from the army.

'I have a friend whose son was driven over by a tank and the side of his face crushed. I have visited him in hospital in Lucerne and Vienna several times and I cannot sleep through the night without seeing his face, his injuries. It is not only his terrible suffering and that of all the others that is disturbing, but that it might be for nothing.

'After Mubarak was kicked out, who came but the leaders of the army. Who made them leaders? Who chose them? Mubarak. What was the basis of the choice? Loyalty. Corruption. Can you imagine that those who were loyal to the dictator and living in luxury and promoted in a corrupt system could give what you are expecting?

'I now live outside Egypt and I can look and judge logically but not emotionally. It is eighteen months after such events and nothing is happening. What were the people expecting? That the generals are angels? That they will give them what they ask? When you judge with your experience and knowledge, with history and the facts which are there, you have to say "wait and see".'

When Mubarak first came to power after Sadat was killed, Nada met one of his advisers, Mohysed Al-Said Hammad. He was a marshal with the army and a medical doctor. His wife was a professor in agriculture and was teaching in Riyadh at the women's university. Nada met him in Mecca and he told him: 'You can change the history of Egypt and you can do the best thing you can do for your country and your people.'

Hammad asked how, and Nada replied: 'Because you have the ear of the president. He has his political advisers but they play one against the other. Politics is not your life, so when you say something political maybe he will listen to you more than the others. The problem was that Sadat had blood in his hands. He killed some people and others took revenge and killed him. Mubarak came with no blood on his hands. This man can start a new era between him and the population. We understand that the ruler cannot meet all the aspiration of the people. There are international positions. There are limited resources.

'But if Mubarak is open with the population and doesn't use an iron fist we can arrange to have the leader of the Muslim Brotherhood Omar Al Telmesamy make a demonstration with one or two million people and come to the Presidential Palace and with a list of what the population wants. This list could be discussed beforehand. Some items that the people want can be immediately implemented. Some he can say he needs time, especially the economy. Not everything can be done in one order. He can promise to look at everything and order it if he can. But give him time.

'This way the co-operation between the population and the ruler could be there. The goodwill could be there and he has representatives to convince the people with what he cannot make – not only by orders and conflict and power. That is a chance not to be pushed, to use the intimidation methods with the population to keep them silent.'

In response, Hammad told Nada: 'It is better to write what you want and I give it to him.' Nada pointed out that it was well known that Mubarak didn't like to read, but Hammad insisted and Nada said: 'Okay. I will write to you three quarters of a page, and if it is needed, I am ready to come.' Hammad agreed and said: 'We'll meet again after one month here in the same place to see what happens.'

When they met again, Hammad told Nada: 'You put me in trouble!' Nada looked puzzled until Hammad explained that Mubarak had said to him: 'Are you mad? You want me to meet Omar Al Telmesamy of the Muslim Brotherhood! You know what the Americans and Israelis will say? Do you know what will be the result if the Americans and Israelis know that I met him? And you want me to meet him in public!'

To this, Nada replied: 'That is the way Mubarak was thinking and that was in the first two months of him being in power. Interpret it as you want, I gave you the story as it is. The situation, I had explained to him. It was short but concentrated: because he has no blood on his hands it is very easy for him to be popular. To have the means to discuss with them not to use the intimidation – all this was in the letter. It's the beginning of a new era. That he is a hero, not a ruler like the other side. I didn't say dictator – hero, not a ruler.

'But he did not want to upset the Americans and the Israelis. And he knew that meeting would do it. He had been part of the government for a long, long time and their support was his main interest. The Americans regard the Muslim Brothers as their fiercest enemy and there is only one reason: that the Muslim Brotherhood does not accept the situation in Palestine. But we are not against the Jews or anyone else – we do not support the situation.

'Palestine? They put some streets, highways around it everywhere, and they put settlements in their land. It is not a country, not a state. How can you define that it is two states? No way. In my opinion there must be confederation, not two separate states. Two states, not separatist states. One country, like the United States. The people must start to live together. In time they will be used to it together.

'As it is, Palestine is a shame on humanity. They are doing it in the wrong way, a way that can never end. You say make two states and then you take the land and you cut it in pieces. You don't give them water and say which state it is for. If it is done with a sort of equality, it could be accepted.

'Once you accept the injustice, you have to accept it for all. Not just for one race, one country, one people or one geographical area. You either accept it or you reject it. There is no one type of Federation. You cannot make one state. Give them the essential things for life, to consider them as citizens. One of the main reasons to be loyal to a country is that this country is giving you rights. That is what I see here in Switzerland. These people are very, very loyal to it, even if not everything is given, at least there is a level to start. There is an opportunity for everyone to prove himself not to discriminate him because he is Palestinian or he is Jewish.

'Both of them are injured. Both of them need justice. Both of them are victims. One is more than the other. One is victimised by someone else and the other victimised by the other victim. Okay, but still the other is a victim. Either it is justice or injustice – there is no half justice. There are a lot of factions in politics which are taking no such regard.

'In South Africa the injustice is still there because one bows to the other. One was accepted to bow and the other accepted to relinquish some things. Look to where Mandela was and where he is and what he was doing before. Anyone who wants to live in peace must understand the expression of "compromise". Mandela accepted compromise. Yet the American administrations put a condition in this area that Islam must be oppressed. They could gain more if they didn't touch the values and beliefs of the Muslims. Even if some of the Muslims are twisting Islam's interpretations it is the business of the Muslims to correct that.

'If this corrupted version is used for crimes they should fight it as they fight any crime but not to put all the faith and its followers in one basket and discriminate and fight them. The twisted interpretations of Islam are all around us. It's not just that non-Muslims do not like it – we don't like it. We are against it. Even in the minds of some of the Brotherhood the residuals of the old interpretations still exist and they are coming from the same society.

'I am not talking about secularising Islam. It is modernising the Islamic way of interpretation but not secularising Islam, at the same time, living in the 21st century. That is exactly what I mean. I have lived all my life trying to help people as much as I can. I was very cautious. I was law obedient and I worked very hard participating in the economy of nations. I never did anything against America, against any power anywhere except Nasser, Mubarak and Gadaffi. Although I say it is permissible to use violence against someone if you are defending your life or your country, I never used violence in my struggle with them.

'You look at the Muslim Brotherhood history, with the rulers in the Middle East. In Syria in 1982 they attacked them in Hama and killed 30,000 people in two hours. After that it was a police state and continued to be a police state, even after the uprising following the Arab Spring. We are all victims of the propaganda machine, we are caught in the middle. Normal people, law abiding people, are trapped between the madmen of terrorism and the dictator governments intimidated by them.

'They see the threat of Islam and Al Qaeda, this "ghost" everywhere. Whenever they see any people praying, they believe they belong to Al Qaeda or they are terrorists. You know my opinion on Al Qaeda, that they are killers and they came out of the religion. They are against all humanity. This I believe. But, they are not much. They are not giants, they are criminal clowns.

'For these people of nothing the authorities insult all the world and treat everyone as criminals in the airports. George Bush said: "Either you are with me or against me". And everyone followed him. Why does the world accept it? Those ministers and governments and security in every country, how can they cooperate in that?

'They've made it almost impossible for decent people to go about the world and their business without jumping through endless security hoops. And no matter what they do, the people who intend evil will find a way. It is good people who have been harmed. Also, the restrictions and regulations imposed on the business world all contribute to the difficult situation in the financial markets, which, in turn, causes problems and legal questions.

'The regulators of the European Union produce lots of laws that are difficult to implement in complex banking structures. Unfortunately banks do not have a lobby of support these days and banks are blamed for financing terrorism and the world's economic misery.

'The politicians are terrorised by the American administration and

185

they are following their instructions blindly. Anyone who objects either will lose his position or they send him a hotel maid who will accuse him of inappropriate sexual behaviour. The speed of the money cycle is the most important factor the banks could use to assist the economy and to forward rewriting their losses and bad debts through hot money. When the movement slows down everyone will be uncovered and the crash is unavoidable.

'A whole way of life has vanished, a good and honest way of doing business. I was walking in Vienna, the home of some important clients, and by chance one of them saw me and shouted: "Stop! Mr Nada we want to discuss some business. Come." We were near the biggest bank I dealt with. I entered the bank and at the first desk they organised the meeting in a private room with tea and coffee. No one was asked for identification. The banker saw me and that was enough.

'Now, the cameras are everywhere. Steel bars are on the windows. They are insulting not protecting the people. The prevention is silence. Why not study it and use it: wait until the robbers attack the bank and then you catch them. If you spend it for prevention, nobody will escape. It is like the explanation for illegal incarceration and torture – you cannot stop these bad men without getting the information from them any way you can. Yes, we want to protect the society from the other side, the dark side, but these people are human and we must not torture any human. Legally it is prohibited but it will continue. A lot of things came from the values of our age, our century.

'Film on television from Syria two days ago showed demonstrators handcuffed behind their backs and sleeping on their faces in the street. The others were being beaten on their backs. One man moved and was shot in the head. Bang! Just like that. Bang! Who is talking about torture? Where is he? Is it true that the world is prohibiting torture? Why is everyone in the world closing their mouths? Why is there no action? Everyone knows. Everyone sees it, but nobody is doing anything about it – because those who can stop it are doing it also.

'What of the "peremptory norm" (*jus cogens*)? The nations and communities of the world say that torture and slavery are never permitted. This compelling law was set to say that such things can never be allowed by any means but it is ignored, and that breaches the Vienna Convention. Those who do it, argue that torture is used for a reason: to get information from a criminal or a politician which is needed to prevent crimes. These reasons for torture are well known in history.

'If they are accepted as a reason, then why would they prohibit the torture? Don't prohibit it. Don't make hypocrisy. If you believe that it is essential don't be hypocritical and squeal: "That is not good. That is not human. We have to stop it and make agreements and make treaties and…"

'I see in the races how the horses are whipped when they run. What is the difference? That one is animal and the other is human. Is there any difference? You bring the human down to the degree of an animal. If that is needed why be hypocritical and prohibit it? Or at least you say, it is allowed in cases of so and so, and forbidden in other cases. I can understand that you have to isolate a criminal from society and not give him a chance to harm society. Then you imprison him.

'I can understand that you find any way of − I don't want to say "punishment" − I want to say isolate him from the place from which he might harm. This I can understand. But to torture him! The problem should be for the Americans more than for us; more than for the whole world because it is their history − the crimes which were done all over the world by the US administration.

'It is strange to see the change that has happened. When I used to go to the United States, or I travelled elsewhere, and my neighbour on the plane was American, we'd talk. I felt these people had a special quality and they were knowledgeable and I felt respect for them. Now, everyone talking with Americans feels that he is talking with the CIA or the FBI.

'The reputation of a very important country − a country which could change the world for the better − has been damaged, changed for the worst. Whoever becomes president, they will not be able to penetrate the system, Republican or Democrat, it doesn't matter which one. I can say that; I will die soon. Others cannot say it. It is important for me to put on record these testimonies.

'For information – or rather, disinformation – reaches the ears of the US Senate and the president daily. It presents the Muslim Brotherhood as coming to invade Europe and America and the Western world. It presents Muslims as an ongoing enemy because of their faith. Give me another brain to understand it, because my brain can't. Not only me: everyone. Why accept the faiths in other religions but discriminate against one-third of the humans on Earth, humiliate them and treat them with this method by labelling them that they are Muslims? What do you expect from them? What is happening now?

'It started by them saying there are some bad Muslims. Okay, true, just as there are bad apples on every tree. But then it was all Muslims. Now, it is Islam.

Up and up and up. It is a time bomb. We have to save the Muslims and we have to save the world from this time forward. You might ask: the chicken or the egg? You forget the most terrible wars which happened were not caused by Muslims. Why are people coming to condemn a religion of one-third of the humanity because some clan of 1,000 people of Al Qaeda?

'If you start to find a way for peaceful co-existence in the world irrespective of colour and religion – as it is said in the charter of the United Nations – that is the best way to live. This has not been implemented but it is the way to live in peace. There is no other way. We must convert the discrimination to co-operation.

'It began badly. First we had Judaism and then the Christians came but the Jews didn't accept Christianity. Next was Islam which neither the Jews nor Christians welcomed or acknowledged, but Islam accepted them both; not only accepted but respected that the religions are coming from God. We have obligations towards those who believe in these two religions; we have an obligation to protect the way they worship; to respect the way they implement their life according to their belief.

'The Christians accepted to live and accepted the other religion, with differences yes; denying some of it and accepting some of it, yes; but they accept that it is a respected religion. Islam accepted both; not only accepted but respected that the religions are coming from God. We have obligations towards those who believe in these two religions; we have an obligation to protect the way they worship; to respect the way they implement their life according to their belief.

'Some people attack the expression "Allah". Can we as Muslims attack Jesus. No way. That is our Prophet; not only yours. You say that he is the son of God, but we respect him the same as Mohammed. Moses for us is our Prophet, not only the Jewish Prophet.

'All those we admit were sent by God, we have to respect them. Not only to respect them, but protect them, although the religions have some modifications which we don't accept: a respect for someone else's belief. It is not only of respect – I have obligations towards you but you have no obligation to me. You consider me an infidel and I that you are faithful, but you change it sometimes.

'Christians believe in God and the Son and the Soul. We believe that God is one. This belief doesn't mean that we don't respect Jesus. We have great respect; not only do we have great respect, if we don't have this belief and respect we are not Muslims. The first page in the Koran says: "Those who believe in the message which came to Mohamed and the messages which came before him."

'Who is guiding the world? – Those who don't know anything about Islam. They just have a picture about Islam from the Crusades fixed in the history of the brain. Over many years children have been taught this and these are the facts to them. They inherit their belief. They hate Islam without looking into it.

'This situation through generations has built a wall between us one but when you go to fair-minded people who are looking how to make peace, they know we have to co-exist with respect, as it is

189

written in their religion. This wall is still there. There must be a change of attitude.'

Youssef Nada maintains there is now a 'huge' problem within the Muslim community in Britain, with the inter-mixing between religion and the traditions: 'The majority in Britain from India and Pakistan, even the Muslims from the Middle East or the Far East or in Europe, feel there is a difference between them and those Pakistani and Indians. A Muslim in Tunisia would be agog to listen to the belief and instructions of the steel-spined, backward clergy of Saudi Arabia. But the special position of Britain is the variety of different cultures, not different religions.

'Rashid al-Ghannusi, the progressive Islamic Movement leader, was in London for 22 years and returned home to Tunisia after the revolution. He told me how he went to a mosque near him in London. The Imam, the one who should be most knowledgeable, couldn't read the Koran. His language and pronunciation was all mixed up. He didn't understand the religion he was teaching. And this was done by a Muslim.

'What about the British? You see homeless people in the Underground, many bad things. Is this England? It's not. It is something from within England, but it doesn't mean that it is England. There are also universities, churches, good politicians. But the newspapers and books focus on the bad things.

'Surely, it is better to find a solution to the problem. We have diagnosed a problem which is there. We have to concentrate to reach the solution for co-existence and avoid not only war, but society discrimination and then jumping forward to co-operation. Jumping to love and then jumping to the last thing, peace.

'We agree on that, so where to start? To adjust what is there. A big problem has been created, not just in Europe and not only in the Middle East, but in the whole world.

'Now, we, not the Christians, not the Europeans, I say we, Muslims in Europe, have a problem. That is very important point. Life in Europe is not the same as the life in the Middle East where the people work and go to see their family and enjoy themselves spiritually. In Europe, the production machine is consuming the human. Everyone from the early morning is at his work and spends maybe only one or two hours in his home apart from sleeping. His wife is working. Maybe they see each other two times or three times per week; sometimes per month. The children go to the school alone.

'Once I was in the restaurant here and it was night. A boy about eight years old with his bag on his back was sitting at a nearby table and the waiter without asking brought him food and he started to eat and when he finished, he started to read a book. After about half-an-hour, his mother came, kissed him and took him home to bed. That is the family life. It is completely different from family life in the Middle East.

'I don't say this is better or this is better, but I say that the Muslim who comes here, has to live this life. They have to work day and night. Then his soul rumbles and he wants to go to pray just to be connected with God, or connected with his religion, or at least to purify or satisfy something internally. He goes to the mosque. He goes to Friday prayers.

'And the man who preaches makes a speech. But who is this man? Is he educated? There is a problem here, not only for the Muslims but for the whole country where they are living. In the mosque, if this Imam preaches hate then it is hate. If he preaches revolt, then it is revolt. If he preaches explanation or interpretation of the religion from a book, which could contradict proper Islam?

'This has resulted that in mosques some people are preaching hate and some people are – I don't want to use it the word, but it is the one that is understood best – terrorists. This puts a wall between the Muslims and the country they are in and the other religions. These activities cannot go without reaction. The host country cannot have people from their population or their citizens or their guests attacking them in their places of worship.

'To adjust this, the idea came to some politicians that it is better to produce Imams locally: he can represent Islam and at the same time not conflict with the community. The idea is good, but how to implement it? If it is seen that the new production line of Imams is to serve politicians who want to contain Muslims, that will not be accepted and will bring hate to the country and government.

'This plan has a double edge for me. It is important, but the Muslims themselves have to select those familiar in the European way of life and system to be educated in Islam. Then, they can be the bridge between both and at the same time keep the faith for those who want to keep their faith. Not Imams made by their culture, but adjusted to live with others. That is one of my targets – to stop the rubbish being spoken and issued from the mosques.

'Listen to this story of how an Imam can find power to tell people what is good and bad, what is true and false, and how to live their lives in a pure way. A poor man wanted to have work and went to a mosque. He eats and sleeps there and there is a library so he reads too. He cannot go deep in what he reads but he gets some information. Then they consider him Imam. They consider him knowledgeable and then he can say what is correct and what is not correct; what is acceptable in Islam and what is not acceptable in Islam. They follow him. Suddenly, he is the law.

'The majority are religious but don't know much about the proper methods of practising it in their daily lives. A lady goes to the mosque to see whether the Imam can mediate between her and her husband. Another couple love each other, they want to marry, but the documents are not there and they don't want to commit adultery. But they want to marry according to the system of marriage with two witnesses, and the Imam does that. But he must be capable, specialised, well educated. If his behaviour is accepted by the others, then everyone will follow him. Then I'm not afraid of this Imam. On the contrary, he will reflect the message of co-existence and of peace between the different cultures, religions, neighbours and in the schools. That is the one that I need.

'If you have one tailored for those who are against Islam and one tailored for those who have the ignorance of Islam, both of them will ruin both sides. If the decision makers want to tailor Imams with their belief, it can never be accepted. It would be a waste of time and it will encourage more hate. The other Muslims will think that they want to infiltrate our religion by those Imams.

'Whether you want to change the religion of those people or you want to teach them the peaceful co-existence, you want them to be a photocopy of you, or you want the people to respect all the common principles of the humanity. Obedient to the country, protect the country, law obedient. Respect the others. Assist the neighbours. Do something for the society. What more do you want? Teach your children that your way of living is not the only way of living. And that old and new can mix.

'My eldest son has only two Muslims among his friends. He is very social. One of my daughters doesn't believe in organised marriages but she assisted her friend in one with the nephew of my shipping agent. The guy looks handsome and his body is not weak or fat. My daughter said to me: "Daddy, why not try to convince him and my friend to marry." I said: "She and you don't believe in arranged marriage."

'My daughter replied: "No, but she tried with two others and she failed. What do we have to do?" So, I went to see the man, Roberto, and talked to him. I am not good at going around a subject. I was quite plain speaking: "Roberto, when are you going to marry?"

'"Uncle Youssef. I had a girlfriend and I spent with her three years but we haven't married."

'"You want to see another one?"

'"I know a lot of girls Uncle Youssef."

'"I know. At least somebody you know her family. You know she is well educated. I am trying to see if it fits you or not. I will arrange a dinner."

'"I don't believe in that."

'"It could happen, why don't you try?"

'They married and she has a baby now. You see how my daughter worked for it. That is life for us today. We are busy people. But we should take time to look out for each other and not to do harm. And listen to good and wise people.

'The priest is no messenger of God. There is only God who can forgive you, not the priest. We believe we are in direct line with God and God will accept return from your side to him. We have a phrase in the Koran that says: "What good will God will have if he punishes you? What will God gain from punishing you?" It is the same for us. What good or gain do we get from punishing rather than helping each other?'

CHAPTER THIRTEEN

SPOOKS AND WHISPERS

'*I have never found, in a long experience of politics, that criticism is ever inhibited by ignorance.*'

British Prime Minister, Harold Macmillan, 1957

It is still with some bemusement that Youssef Nada glances through the *Corriere della Sera* each day and finds it hard to agree with its promotional boast that it is 'among the oldest and most reputable of daily newspapers in Italy'.

A story which appeared in *Corriere della Sera* on 11 November 1997, continues to haunt his life. If you had the time today, you could read fragments of it scattered like leaves without trees throughout more than 250,000 Internet websites.

It began in public with a tale which one of Europe's most eminent politicians, Dick Marty – the former Swiss state prosecutor and the head of the legal committee of the Parliamentary Assembly of the Council of Europe – describes as 'coming from a book by Kafka'. Marty, a world-renowned figure in the battle for human rights, says he was dismayed by what had happened: 'Unfortunately, these are true facts set in the 21st century in member countries of the Council of Europe, under the auspices of the United Nations.'

The newspaper article, by Guido Olimpio, was the flowering of whispers, rumours and innuendo which had been orchestrated around Youssef Nada and his deputy and friend Ghaleb Himmat and their Al Taqwa Bank.

Nada as a prominent – and visible – member of the Muslim Brotherhood, was used to personal attacks. It had been reported, and repeated in several books, that he'd been recruited by Nazi intelligence during World War Two, had been an active spy against the British and helped Haj Amin al-Husseini, the Mufti of Jerusalem, in his support of Hitler.

Youssef Nada was nine years old at the time in question. When I asked him what had been the response when this was pointed out to authors and publishers, he said with a shrug and a smile: 'They changed my birth date. They made me a little older. I became a 15-year-old Nazi spy.'

The Albanian-born journalist Guido Olimpio, who was 54 in 2012, said in court in Milan (in 2002) that he had given sworn testimony to the US Treasury Commission and Congress Security in 1996 on terrorism financing. The names of Youssef Nada and Al Taqwa Bank were mentioned by him. He also said he had connections with the FBI.

In his *Corriere della Sera* article Olimpio alleged that the Al Taqwa Bank and Youssef Nada and his associates were 'bankrolling' the Palestinian militant Islamist organisation Hamas, and other groups – they were responsible for 'The Treasure of Hamas'. The assertion, and the lighting of a simmering fuse, was that the bank was a fund for terrorists. The report was, in turn, the catalyst for a media bonanza. The ringmasters were in business. And almost everyone worldwide joined the circus.

Olimpio, a onetime *Corriere della Sera* correspondent in Tel Aviv, wrote that the Al Taqwa Bank had 'donated 70 million (US) dollars to Hamas'. He suggested Al Taqwa was the principle source of funding for

Hamas. He said the bank was supplying money for the activities of Islamic groups including Alnahda in Tunisia, the Al-Gama'a al-Islamiyya in Egypt and the Algerian FIS. He claimed some of an Al Taqwa 'donation' to Hamas of fifty billion Italian lira had been siphoned off in a mysterious way; the bank he said was 'the financial engine of the Islamic parties with planetarium capacity'.

He said Youssef Nada had appointed Ghaleb Himmat as the person to look after Hamas and other groups, including Al-Gama'a al-Islamiyya. In late 1997, Youssef Nada and Ghaleb Himmat sued Guido Olimpio in the Italian courts for libel. Fourteen years later, in December 2011, the court ruled against Guido Olimpio – under Italian law a libel case could not be brought against the newspaper *Corriere della Sera*. The writer was ordered to pay tens of thousands of Euros in actual and punitive damages to both litigants. Youssef Nada donated his portion of the payments.

Youssef Nada had been aware of moves against him and the Muslim Brotherhood in a propaganda campaign, some of it subtle and some more obvious, during his years living in Europe. Nevertheless, he had gone about his business openly and held meetings at his home in Campione, Switzerland. If there was any secrecy or security around him, it was to do with visiting dignitaries for whose safety he feared. Some diplomats or national leaders would arrive by private plane or helicopter, and precautions were always taken to prevent any attack on them. Permits were arranged for one airliner to land privately to protect the security of a national leader.

If any of these important men had been kidnapped or shot going to or from his home, it would have been world headlines and a credibility and personal disaster for Youssef Nada. So he sent cars to escort their cars and he would usually drive his visitor himself 'to be with him if anything was to happen'. Throughout all of this he never carried a weapon, and neither did any of his colleagues. He did, however, own a licensed gun.

197

In 1981, Nada's long-running adversary, Colonel Gadaffi, set-up an assassination squad to 'take out' his opponents living outside Libya. Two of them were murdered – Ramadan in London and Al Khodeiry in Milan – and police caught the killers. On a hit list they found the name of Youssef Nada. The Italian police visited his home and advised him to get a gun licence. He did. Two pistols were bought for him in Como and the police collected them and delivered them to his home. He put them in a safe where they stayed for nearly 20 years, never oiled or used. So, it was a shock when he received a phone call from a banker friend in Lugano on 11 November 1997, to be told of a newspaper report that he was a man involved in the trade of terror.

Nada recounted what happened: 'He asked me whether I read the article about myself in *Corriere della Sera*. I said no. He said it is very bad, I should read it and give it to my lawyer to take action. And so it began.

The lies were spread everywhere, whether for envy or hate, knowingly or intentionally or not, whether hired to corner the Islamist activists, or motivated politically or financially, or for their own professional agenda or their countries or those who presented Olimpio to America to give false testimony.

'The accusations were false – nobody could prove otherwise, because it was simply not true. But their lie became bigger and bigger, like a snowball rolling down a mountain, the avalanche had begun. It was orchestrated and broadcast in many, many outlets. Most seriously it was misinformation which was repeated, fabricated stories made even more hysterical, and spoken of as fact to people in power, especially in America, in the White House and the Congress.

'The US Treasury copied the lie that we gave $70million dollars to Hamas. The capital of the bank was just $50million dollars, and we were regulated by one of the biggest auditors in the world: Deloitte and Touche. They are not blind. When they investigated and audited our accounts they can see everything. And our auditors' reports went to the Central Bank of the Bahamas. They are also not blind. But these accountants and auditors were not interviewed by the press or asked about our accounts. Instead, the world's press highlighted the Guido Olimpio article in *Corriere della Sera*.

'Agence France Presse (AFP) mis-stated that *Corriera della Sera* wrote that about $60 million in international contributions were moved into Al Taqwa and went from the Malta and Lugano branches of Al Taqwa Management Organisation (ATMO) to Osama Bin Laden and Al Qaeda. In fact, Al Taqwa and the entire group never had an office or contacts in Malta. I've never been to Malta. In Lugano the Al Taqwa Management Organisation (ATMO) never received money except from its principle Bank Al Taqwa and never transferred money except for payments of local salaries and expenses. The international news agencies interviewed all the leaders of Hamas and they declared that all the articles' allegations were groundless, and Hamas didn't even know that Al Taqwa bank or group existed.

'In our denial to *Corriera della Sera* we clarified that all what concerned us and Al Taqwa group, Bank Al Taqwa, its president Youssef Nada, and his deputy Ghaleb Himmat as indicated in the article was totally false, fabricated and baseless. They published the denial, but it was summarised.'

On 25 November 1997, Nada and the bank received this message from the chief editor of AFP: 'In reference to your denial of the *Corriere della Sera* article, you will find here a fax quoting your communiqué that we put out on our wires on Tuesday 25th, including one from Jerusalem recording a denial from (the) Hamas movement. It was sent to the same clients who got the first information on October 20th. I personally drew the attention of some of our most important clients onto this information. A story in Arabic was also put on AFP wires, on the bases of your text in Arabic. I hope this will settle the case to our mutual benefit. Sincerely yours, Yves de Saint-Jacob, Editor in Chief.'

Also in November that year, Youssef Nada was contacted by Richard Labeviere of the Télévision Suisse Romande, the chief French language station in Switzerland. They wished to talk to him to follow-up the article in *Corriere della Sera*. As he was involved in legal action against the paper and the writer, he turned down the request.

Later that month, there was a horrific event at the Deir el-Bahir archaeological landmark across the Nile from Luxor in which 62 people were killed by terrorists from Jihad Talat al-Fath. Six gunmen disguised as security forces were involved in a 45- minute killing spree in which many Swiss tourists and a five-year-old British child and four Japanese honeymoon couples died.

Some months following what Youssef Nada called 'the sad inhuman barbaric terrorist attack in Luxor', Télévision Suisse Romande aired a documentary film by Richard Labeviere which included unrelated footage of the Luxor and other attacks. It was a replay of allegations in *Corriere della Sera* with added interviews. Labeviere turned the film into a book – which Guido Olimpio later used in court as 'evidence' to justify his original article on which the film and the book were based.

Youssef Nada regards Labeviere's work as 'fantasies' including the obligatory Nazi slur, this variation that he'd been a member of the Abwehr, German military intelligence in 1940 and worked for them in Egypt in the 1930s. This was later picked up in 2002 by author Kevin Coogan who had Youssef Nada (born 1931) as a Nazi agent in the 1930s. The eminent Signora Carla Del Ponte, the Swiss Federal prosecutor who was the chief prosecutor at Slobodan Milosevic's war crimes tribunal, and Dr Urs Von Daeniken, the security chief of the Swiss police, appeared in Labeviere's film. Both were asked why they hadn't opened a case file on Youssef Nada and Al Taqwa following the events they presented in the film. On film, the two say there was no concrete evidence to do so.

On 26 May 1998, Nada telephoned the offices of the Government officials who'd appeared on television and asked for a meeting. In a fax on 2 June it was arranged. Simply, they said there was no evidence in the film which would make them investigate Youssef Nada or Al Taqwa. However, Dr Von Daeniken sought information on two suspect transactions to Turkey and Sudan he was investigating. Al

Taqwa co-operated with his team and were given the all-clear by Swiss officials.

In view of the number of Swiss citizens killed in the Luxor attack, Carla Del Ponte, as Federal Prosecutor, went to Egypt to head up an investigation. Not surprisingly, Youssef Nada was singled out by Mubarak's government, as he appeared on their 'outlaw' list.

Later, Carla Del Ponte was adamant when she was quizzed about the case by the Swiss newspaper *Corriere Del Ticino* on 1 June 2006: 'Information came that might be connected with Nada. We investigated the case for thirty days and we couldn't find a connection with Nada. Then we decided to make it thirty one [days] to leave no stone unturned and to invite Nada to meet us and to discuss it with him. We came out that Nada and his Al Taqwa have nothing to do with terrorists. I personally took charge and we found not the slightest indication; we were scrupulous and we found nothing. Nothing. Nothing whatsoever.'

Some of that information has appeared on Youssef Nada's website for some long time, but the contents of the *Corriera della Sera* article have constantly overwhelmed the statements. It is to an extent understandable, as Olimpio's story included all the ingredients of some spectacular and bestselling thriller: international banking and terrorism intertwined and set to a backdrop of paradise islands in the Bahamas, the Swiss mountains, and the ongoing wonderment about what really goes on in the Principality of Liechtenstein. And to prove the point that if you repeat something enough times it can become accepted, Youssef Nada found himself cast in the unlikely and unfortunate surreal role of a character in a John le Carré intrigue.

'On 9 December 1999, I arrived at Atlanta airport flying from Zurich and transiting to Nassau in the Bahamas. I didn't get there. US Immigration officers stopped me and didn't allow me to board the connecting flight to Nassau. They put me back on the same Swissair plane to Zurich. When I asked them for the reason I was told to contact the nearest American Consulate. I looked in my Italian passport and discovered that they had written the code number *217.4'6'A7811 5412 ATC 212 '0'* in it.

'Back in Italy, on 15 December I called the US Consul in Milan and went to meet him. When he saw the passport he said I had to apply for a visa and give him everything written about me in the media, translated into English, and my bank and other financial documents, plus my company's registration documents.

'I laughed: "Do you want me to bring you half a dozen trucks? I don't want to go to America. All I wish is to clear my name." I don't know the reason for what had happened, there could be a mistake or false information, but still, I applied for the visa. After four months, on 27 April 2000, I received a letter saying they found me ineligible under section 212'a"3"b', which states in part that "any alien who has engaged in terrorist activity or is a representative or member of a foreign terrorist organisation is inadmissible. The allegations of the Italian newspaper that you were funding terrorist organisations could be the basis for a refusal under section 212'a"3"b', you may hire a lawyer in the US and deal with the INS directly."

'I went to meet the US consul again. He was very cool and said I should apply for a new visa – that is the official procedure and if I didn't accept it he couldn't help me. I left him and I sent him a letter stating my story for legal records and sent another letter to the Immigration and Naturalization Service in Atlanta, Georgia, explaining: "My biggest worry is not travelling to USA or any country but just clearing my name. I am prepared to go through any investigation whether formal or informal to answer any question could lead to clearing my name."

'After two months more, on 23 June 2000, I was notified from Atlanta that what had happened was "per instructions from the head office in Washington DC", and my letter was being forwarded to that office.'

On 3 September 2000, Nada sent another letter requesting the answer and seven months later, on 8 February 2001, received this answer: 'You have asked us to advise you whom to contact to discuss your case. The appropriate person would be the American Consul in your country of residence. Thank you for bringing this matter to our attention and affording us the opportunity to address your concerns.'

Nada again contacted the US consul in Milan, on 30 March 2001, and gave him copies from the correspondence with the Justice Department. He answered on a small yellow paper Post-it: 'No further action can be taken on your case until you initiate a new visa application.'

Nada did just that: 'On 22 May 2001 I applied for a new visa according to the consul's advice. On 13 June 2001, I faxed him trying to get appointment as he did not answer my letter and application and I could not get him on the phone and I did not get any answer. I decided to wait. What more could I do? I was not impressed by American efficiency. Did these people know what they were doing? Nothing seemed to get done either quickly or accurately. An example of how things go wrong, and how bureaucracy can damage so much mistaking fantasy for facts.'

The scandal enveloping Youssef Nada and his Al Taqwa group was to be harsh on him and his business. His was an Islamic bank and for some, that alone was an alarm going off – another element of the always gripping fear of the unknown. And then there was the Mudarabah Account in which the traditional investment account is replaced with one in which the customers' funds are invested in Sharia Compliance Islamic assets.

When he'd established the bank with great caution and care for the legalities in 1988 he was required to have a Swiss citizen on his board of directors. The Swiss journalist and Islamic convert Ahmed Huber filled that role – and Youssef Nada said he had only ever known him as good man – but it emerged amid the rumours that Huber had a history of vocal support of Hitler.

It also didn't help the public relations when it was publicised that a bank member was Francoises Genoud who'd once managed post-war Nazi assets and was the publisher of Joseph Goebbels' diaries. Nada had never met Genoud. A bank founder and director was Ahmed Idris Nasreddin, an Ethiopian who was honorary consul of Kuwait in Milan, a board member of the Islamic Center of Milan and president of the Islamic Community of Ticino.

That one of the most admired legal scholars and Islamic activists, Yousuf al-Qaradawi, was also a founding member of the bank didn't dilute the acidity of the stories storming around and over Al Taqwa. Against that – and think of public perception – six shareholders in the bank were related to Osama Bin Laden, including his sisters Huda and Iman Bin Laden, respectable business people but nevertheless family members. And that didn't help the mountainous uphill public relations task either, especially as Nada believed the true purpose of the stories about him was to connect the Muslim Brotherhood to Al Qaeda. He never ever wanted to break any law for fear of being jailed on criminal and not political charges.

The Italian secret service, then the SISM (Servizio per le Informazioni e la Sicurezza Militare which became the Agenzia Informazioni e Sicurezza Esterna in 2007) had also been investigating the bank since a controversial 1997 Italian newspaper article.

It all broke out in *Corriere della Sera* on 7 November 1997. For Youssef Nada, who had worked so hard to establish what he regarded as supremely ethical banking, the following weeks and months were heartbreaking. And dumped on top of his troubles was the financial crisis penalising South-east Asia.

But the horrendous publicity alone was devastating, as Nada recalled: 'The echo was heard everywhere. The bank clients, shareholders, banking and financial institutes continued to call and write asking and worrying about the effect. There was a run on Bank Al Taqwa for withdrawing funds and closing *mudaraba* (an ancient form of financing practised by the Arabs before the advent of Islam) accounts and postponing and cancelling deals. New remittances dried up.

'It is well known in the banking business that rumours or

negative media reports against any bank, whatever its size is, means the beginning of the end of its life. A parallel disaster started in our investments with the crisis in South-east Asia where the economy and the financial markets in the countries of the area also crashed. Our investments there during that time were about US$500million.

'The bank never inflicted losses before and as I said was distributing dividends and *mudarabah* profits between 7 and 10 per cent a year. Withdrawals by clients to the end of 1997 totalled US$36 million. At the end of 1998 the withdrawals were $100million.

'The losses were great. The bank's Islamic legal committee, the general assembly, and the management agreed to invoke the *mudarabah* contractual conditions, and to stop withdrawals until all the *mudarabah* remaining assets were liquidated in order to determine who lost what.

As I said from the day the bank started, our policy was to make sure that all the bank clients knew and signed that they accepted that they were dealing with Bank Al Taqwa Bahamas, which was responsible for their *mudarabah*, and that Al Taqwa management in Switzerland was only doing the internal auditing not the banking activity.

'When the losses became evident, less than five out of the bank's thousands of clients refused to wait the liquidation of their *mudarabah* remaining assets to evade deducting the losses. Two of them initiated claims against Al Taqwa Management Company in Switzerland to avoid the implementation of the *mudarabah* contractual condition with the bank.

'This was reported to the relevant authority, the Swiss Federal Banking Commission. They investigated the case and appointed Price Waterhouse Cooper to check all the activity, documents, contracts, and the accounts of Al Taqwa Management. At the end of the investigation the Swiss Federal Banking Commission gave us a clean bill of health and asked us only to change the company's name, and it became Nada Management.

'One of those clients whose claim in Switzerland failed, initiated another civil claim in the High Court in the Bahamas against Bank Al Taqwa. The court rejected his claim and ruled in favour of Bank Al Taqwa. There are no banks in the world who never had disputes with some clients, which is why all banks have a legal department.

'That was the only claim we faced in the court in our 13 years of successful business. Sadly, he had the headline-grabbing name of Bin Laden. He was Ghaleb Bin Laden. It is well known that all Osama Bin Laden's family had nothing directly to do with him, disowned him and none of them was considered a terrorist. Their businesses still prosper. All of them are respectable, educated, civilised people. But the name? People think what they think, and say and write. I don't really know what their agenda is or who they really are. Spies? Agents for governments? I don't know. I am open with everybody. I speak the truth always. That is who I am.

'I have had to defend myself – that's all. What they are doing, and for whom, is not interesting for me. Definitely, they have a special agenda, but which agenda? I don't know. I never met them. I don't consider them very important, but it is true that their accusations put some oil on the fire.'

On the website which Youssef Nada maintains to answer his critics, and often vehement detractors, he has posted the following:

If it was said that I am an engineer... it is true.
If it was said that I am a businessman... it is true.
If it was said that I am a banker... it is true.
If it was said that I am an industrialist ... it is true.
If it was said that I am a real estate developer... it is true.
If it was said that I am a politician... it is true.
If it was said that I am an activist... it is true.
If it was said that I am an Islamist... it is true.
If it was said that I am a democrat... it is true.
If it was said that I am a socialist... it is true.

If it was said that I am a terrorist or financed terrorism or had any
link to terrorism… it is false, a deception and misleading, as such
things are contrary to my belief, faith and all my way of thinking.

That last statement is something Nada has had to make clear many,
many times, since 11 September 2001, when he became embroiled in
the legacy of that awful day of the attacks on New York and
Washington DC when the world stopped for so many and changed for
millions more. It was when the world was turned upside down and we
all paused in a twilight zone while the rules of the global power game
were rewritten. It was also when President George W Bush began what
he called his 'war on terror' and his 'crusade'.

One of the first civilian casualties of the American President's
onslaught was Youssef Nada. And he was to learn his fate the modern
way – from television. Nada was in his smart office building in the
central business area of Lugano, Switzerland, when he first heard the
news of what was happening in America on September 11.

When he had the facts as they were known on the day, he gave
comments to newspapers full of condolences and expressing his
disquiet at the criminal perpetrators for the 'the barbarian inhuman
act'. In return, he was attacked as covering up his own 'bankrolling of
terrorism' by making such remarks.

As the 9/11 investigations began, suspects' names were circulated to
all the banks worldwide, with instructions to report anything related or
connected to any of them. Al Taqwa checked and found no matching
names, but similar parts of names and families. They complied with
instructions and handed over a report and relevant documents to the
Central Bank of Bahamas. The Central Bank gave them to the
Bahamian Attorney General who sent them to the FBI.

The shivers of nightmare were beginning.

On 21 September, just ten days after 9/11, Youssef Nada was
informed that the Swiss Ministry of Justice and Police had received a

request from America for legal assistance in investigating Youssef Nada and the Al Taqwa group. Youssef Nada was concerned but calm. What had a man with no guilt to fear? As it turned out, fear was the fuel for his nightmare.

He was telephoned on 29 October 2001 by the American Consulate in Rome who reminded him he had written to Washington to clear his name and get his 'Section 212'a"3"b' linking him with terrorism explained and rectified. It resulted in an arrangement to meet FBI agent John Cosenza at the US Consulate in Milan a few days later. When he arrived, Nada was brusquely told by a guard to wait in a queue in the street. He pointed out that he had an arranged appointment but was again told to wait. He said to the guard: 'Nada doesn't stay in the beggars' queue,' and left.

The FBI called Nada several times to apologise for the misunderstanding and a meeting was re-arranged with Cosenza and Linda Viti, another FBI agent based in Rome. 'I took with me a copy of the file which I'd given to the central bank,' said Nada, 'and I explained to them my discussion with the consul who wanted me to bring documents which could fill trucks. I said to them that if the gentleman does not know about finance more than his salary, his mortgage, the food, his and the cost of his wife's dresses, how can he understand a banker's financial documents? And how can I bring them to him?

'They asked about what was in *Corierre della Sera* and other questions about me and Al Taqwa and the Milan Islamic centre and Mr Nasreddin. They wanted to know about my family and my activities – if I was as a politician or banker. They obviously had information from somewhere or someone. It was as if they spoke from a script. It was the beginning of the "fishing" season…

'On 5 November 2001, Mark Hosenball of the American magazine *Newsweek* called me and asked many questions about Mr Nasreddin and the Milan mosque, and asked our lawyer's name and phone number. He called the lawyer and informed him about his conversation with me but he was not accurate. When the lawyer told me, I asked him to officially send the corrected transcription, holding him responsible if he made any changes. The next day I called John Cosenza and informed him about this conversation.

'On 6 November, Mr Nasreddin arrived from Morocco and I went with his son to pick him up from Milan's Malpensa airport. On our way back to Lugano the Swiss frontier police stopped our car at Chiasso. They knew our movements. They escorted us to a guarded garage and checked every part of the car. It took about two hours. When I arrived home I phoned my lawyer and fixed appointment to see him in the morning.'

That next day a lifetime of patience and dedication was warped beyond reason and imagination. President George W Bush's avowed crusade became irrevocably personal for Youssef Nada.

Yet it took a little time before Nada was asked for the key to his nuclear shelter.

CHAPTER FOURTEEN

THE CRUSADE

'Every nation, in every region, now has a decision to make. Either you are with us, or you are with the terrorists.'

President George W Bush, in an address to a Joint Session
of Congress and the American people,
20 September 2001

Still feeling greatly perturbed by the Italian–Swiss border incident, Youssef Nada left the Villa Nada in Campione d'Italia at 8.30am on 7 November 2001, and began the drive down the mountain to his lawyer's office in Lugano. From there he put in calls to his own offices but there was no reply.

He placed a call to the mobile phone of Ghaleb Himmat but again got no response. Puzzled, he called Himmat's home where his daughter Hadia answered. There were special agents chasing all over and around the house, she said; it was like a police convention.

He heard her being instructed to speak in Italian not Arabic. She said her father had left for the office but she hadn't been allowed to call him. Nada put a call through to his own home and the situation there was the same. A policeman came on the telephone and asked his whereabouts. Within minutes he and his lawyer had a 2pm appointment with Claude Nicati, the Swiss Deputy Federal Prosecutor at his offices in Lugano. Nicati was a jobsworth. A file was open on his desk. He went through routine questions: name, birth date, father and mother's names, address, profession. Then a financial quiz show began.

Q: What work is the company Al Taqwa Management doing?

A: Internal auditing of the mother company Bank Al Taqwa and feasibility studies for its projects.

Q: From where does the company get its income?

A: From the mother company Bank Al Taqwa.

Q: In which currency does the bank pay the company?

A: In US dollars.

Q: What do you do with dollars?

A: Convert the dollars into Swiss Francs and pay the company's expenses.

Q: No. You convert the dollars to Swiss currency – what did you do with that cash?

A: We never withdrew cash, we pay the salaries and expenses through the banks and against bills and every Swiss franc was paid through the bank and registered and audited.

Nicati then produced an Al Taqwa Management statement of the company's account with Bank Del Gottardo, underlined with red, blue, green ink, and continued his questioning:

'Is this statement related to you company?'

'Yes.'

'Here you can see $200,000 dollars arrived and was converted to francs, cashed and debited; and here is another $300,000 dollars and here $500,000 dollars and so on. What you did with the cash?'

Youssef Nada remained calm: 'Do you understand accounting?'

Agitated, Nicati swelled up, very much Switzerland's Chief Prosecutor, and spluttered: 'What do you mean?'

'If you understand accounting, I can explain to you, but if you don't understand accounting, how can I?'

Nada continued that if Nicati looked at the statement he would read at the top a US dollar account. When any amount is converted to Swiss francs it should be debited to the dollar account and the value in franc goes to the Swiss franc account. Converting the dollar into Swiss francs necessitates debiting the dollar account, but it does not mean that the francs were cashed and disappeared.

Nicati: 'Does that mean that the company has another Swiss franc account with the same bank?'

'Of course we have.'

'If I ask Bank Dell Gottardo, will I discover it?'

'Yes, of course.'

Nada said that he asked many times what he was being accused of; what would be the charges against him? 'All I ever got as an answer from Mr Nicati were the same words: "You will find out later..." (Nada waited until May 2005, when he sued him in the Swiss High Court).

'He recorded our discussion in the interrogation protocol, but in a style which was selective and summarised. I became aware that the man in charge of investigating the banking case lacked the knowledge of finance and even basic accounting. I remembered the American consul who had no financial abilities other than his domestic affairs.

'Despite that, I expected that among his team he would have banking and financial and accounting experts who would be able to understand, unearth, and discover that we were victims of characterless persons who are unqualified for any noble job. Here I was again: the same sorry story. They shuffled pieces of paper they didn't comprehend.

'Suddenly, Mr Nicati was distracted. An aide whispered in his ear and he looked at me and said he was stopping the interview – the interrogation would go on another day. He needed me to go home to open my safe and the nuclear shelter [all newly-built houses in Switzerland had to have such shelters under planning law] and I had the master keys.

'I went home with my lawyer to find in the house about 20 men and women, police people in uniform and plainclothes. My wife was dealing with it extremely well, despite being alone with only a few people who worked for us, and the way the police had stormed the house. They had a map of the places they were going to invade: my home, Mr Himmat's and the offices. We were all in the headlights.

'My library was a mess, the books were all over the floor. There were officers from five different countries – I could hear American accents, English, Italian, Swiss German and Arabic. I spoke loudly in Italian above all the chatter and talk and noise: "This is not legal!"'

'The raid was to me full of mistakes, not correct. The aide who had interrupted the prosecutor took me aside and introduced me to an Italian judge who was brought to validate what they were doing. He told me in front of the judge: "Our actions which you considered legally full of holes are legal." I replied: "I can see that it will take time to prove whether it is or not."' It was, as time was to prove, the most accurate and prescient comment of the day.

That afternoon, as the security services turned Nada's home into something resembling a jumble sale, it was morning in Washington DC. President Bush appeared on television and named Youssef Nada and Al Taqwa as funding terrorism. America, the president pledged, was going to 'starve' all those associated with Al Taqwa. He gave the impression that it was 'some bank somewhere and a banker' – and both had names difficult to spell and pronounce for the folks in Iowa. Whatever the thinking, the message was abundantly clear.

(Swiss prosecutors had described Youssef Nada's home in Campione d'Italia, where he had lived for more than 30 years – a lavish sanctuary from a turbulent life – as the 'foreign ministry' of the Muslim Brotherhood, and claimed that he had been instrumental through management and financial help in setting up Brotherhood branches throughout Europe and America.)

President Bush had assumed a combative, macho stance on behalf of America: at this point the sensibilities of – and consequences for

– anyone else was not a concern. After 9/11, President Bush gave the FBI powers all but identical to those they were granted by President Franklin Roosevelt after the Pearl Harbour attacks 60 years earlier.

The question was, whether President Bush's remarks and America's subsequent actions were a personal attack on Youssef Nada and his Al Taqwa group, or pointed at the Muslim Brotherhood. Nada defended himself and his belief against the most extraordinary odds. He is still doing so, in the second decade of the 21st century: his name had been attached to monstrosities he says he could never condone never mind participate in.

'When the President of the United States spoke that way it was not only a problem for Nada – it could happen to anyone. How can you prove that you are innocent? With that attitude you are guilty until you prove you are innocent. It was very clear from the expressions George Bush used when he began this aggression on the Muslim world that he was setting religion against religion and politics against religion: a crusade. Naturally, when he says "some terrorists", we all accept that for we are all ready to fight terrorism.

'No one should blame the Islamic religion. Bin Laden had nothing to do with Islam. George Bush is a Christian, but Christianity did not bring war and death to Iraq and Afghanistan. Both sides use religion to support their actions when it has no true place in what is being done.

'After September 11, no one dealt with anything involving Muslims in the West the way it had been before. President Bush spoke, Prime Minster Tony Blair spoke, and they said it was not a war against Islam. They said that, but we saw activities which went against those declarations and new laws appearing all the time. They targeted Muslims or those moving from Muslim countries.

'Some universities refused to take students, not on the basis of their academic qualifications but because of their names, their Muslim names. There were laws targeting foreigners, and the word "foreigners" is quite flexible. Instead of saying the war is not against Islam, they said the laws were against terrorism. Well, the Muslim Brotherhood believe that terrorist operations which hurt peaceful people and the country in which they live are considered a deviation from Islam. They are not acceptable. Even if you are at war it is not your right to kill a child, woman or an elderly person, or to set a tree on fire.

'On what basis do we agree to terrorism? It is fear of Islam, not fear of us. Should we change our religion? Islam is the strongest thing that people could have. Whoever accepts Islam must be strong.'

Nada said that when he was interrogated and his home raided on 7 November 2001 it was like being back in Egypt many years before when he was asked repeatedly for his name, father's name, mother's name and address. 'I had done nothing wrong but they put me in prison. I was used to being treated illegally by a dictatorship, but it was a shock for it to be repeated in Switzerland.

'This time they confiscated my documents, blocked my credit cards, all my assets, properties and bank accounts everywhere in the world as well as my movements, and held me under house arrest in 1.6 square kilometres in Campione. No charges at all. Where was the law? Where was democracy? Was it democratic Switzerland, the country that is famous for being committed to the law and human rights?

'All the accusations against me, I cannot do and I have never done. I was innocent and I could hold my head high. I always have. But the purge of me went on. The inquests were open everywhere and America had initiated those inquests. What had been said did not come from President Bush only. Juan Carlos Zarate, the Deputy Assistant Secretary in the US Treasury in charge of investigating terrorism later gave a testimony at the House of Senates, and said unbelievable things about me. Much of it was copied from *Corriere della Sera*. And he said I personally gave money to Osama Bin Laden in late September 2001.

'Mr Bush and America and the rest of the world are searching the planet for Bin Laden! I casually go off and hand him cash! They cannot find him but I can and send him money in the air that drops directly over his head. Do not ask me how, I do not know.

'For a long time, certain forces were trying to associate me with terrorism. The signs were there but I ignored them, for I believed I had nothing to be afraid of. I had done nothing wrong. Some people or agencies – and certainly Mubarak's secret agents – were trying to construct something against me and the Muslim Brotherhood.

'All corrupt regimes use the same methods, the same tactic to victimise their target if they cannot assassinate him: invent lies to smear your target, spread them until they become facts. It had a familiar ring for me as events unfolded.'

It was at Ghaleb Himmat's home, down the hill from Youssef Nada's villa in Campione, that Swiss investigators found a document which infamously became known as 'The Project'. In the volcanic environment in the weeks and months following 9/11, the untitled Arabic document dated 1 December 1982, was seized upon by what Youssef Nada regards as mischief makers. Like a flag, it led a cavalcade of conspiracy, of accusations across all media.

These included the French-Swiss newspaper reporter Sylvain Besson to whom the document was illegally leaked by Swiss investigators. It was he who dubbed the document 'The Project' and called it 'the Muslim Brother's strategy plan for invading the West'. It was – he claimed in articles and later, a book – the template for an Islamic takeover led by the Muslim Brotherhood.

In the original Arabic version of the document, there is no mention of the Muslim Brotherhood. In that form it was a detailed strategy for the furtherance of the international Islamic movement. There were 12 key points, one of which was broadcast in conflicting reports and stated:

To accept the principle of temporary cooperation between Islamic movements and nationalist movements in the broad sphere and on common ground such as the struggle against colonialism, preaching and the Jewish state, without however having to form alliances. This will require, on the other hand, limited contacts between certain leaders, on a case by case basis, as long as these contacts do not violate the [Sharia] law. Nevertheless, one must not give them allegiance or take them into confidence, bearing in mind that the Islamic movement must be the origin of the initiatives and orientations taken.

Youssef Nada found the hysteria around 'The Project' extremely disconcerting: 'The stories taken from it were not as the document said. I received many, many tracts about politics and religion over the years, as did Mr Himmat. Today they come from the Internet and you can click a button to erase them. In those days they came in the post and you put them to one side unless they were of some interest. Mr Besson conjured that this was the Muslim Brotherhood's secret project but no, it was not. It was Mr Besson's big project. And he made money from it.'

The Cambridge scholar and author Alison Pargeter, who has researched political Islam and radicalisation and been an expert witness in America and the UK in terrorism cases, was not as excited as Sylvain Besson. She gave this verdict: 'In spite of the allegations, this document is a fairly mundane wish list and would appear to be largely an expression of intent that reflects the optimism of the time.'

What Youssef Nada calls 'The Hurricane' went on howling. Ghaleb Himmat, who had been involved with the Islamic Centre in Munich for more than a quarter of a century with the support of his friend and partner, felt obliged to resign his leadership of the mosque at the centre when he and Nada were accused of bankrolling Al Qaeda. Too much had been made of the mosque as 'a fermenting centre for Islamic aggression' and Himmat left in 2002 – long after 9/11.

The story of the 'Mosque in Munich' came up in different books with 'political intelligence' from the German authorities. The writers also had access to Special Branch files. Yet, for Nada it had all been innocent: 'When I met Mr Himmat the mosque did not exist. Muslim refugees who had gone to Munich from the Soviet Union after World War Two had failed to establish a mosque, and when he arrived Mr Himmat was instrumental in getting one built, for it was needed. When you are a foreigner in a place it takes time to make friends and for Muslims a mosque is somewhere to go, like students on a university campus.

'Mr Himmat was a co-founder of the centre and he put a lot of energy and time and years in it. It was not easy then – and it's not any better in the 21st century. Planning permission – a license – for a mosque in a European city can take many years, although mosques established from Saudi Arabia, like one recently in Rome, have little difficulty.'

Part of it, Nada believes, is that the propaganda of people like Sylvain Besson persists: 'I read a report about the attitude of the European Union towards Islam in Europe. They took it as a Bible for them – that the Muslim Brotherhood want to invade Europe. I cannot understand which stupid brain can accept that.

'Not one thing said about me was true. Those who said it had the loud voice, power and agenda to spread it everywhere. The Swiss Federal Prosecutor and the Swiss police were instructed by the Americans to start an investigation, and when they opened a file they were desperate to find a reason for doing so. They admitted that. They said to find the reason they can only lie.

'I am talking about 21 September and 24 October 2001. Mr Claude Nicati, the Swiss Deputy Federal Prosecutor wrote: "Although these people were overloaded by intelligence and media reports and with information from intelligence agencies we contacted big and small countries they couldn't find anything against Nada and Himmat."

'When the Federal Prosecutor started the investigation he boasted that he had allocated 20 per cent of his office and 20 per cent of Federal and local police investigators only for our case. Imagine – 20 per cent of the power of the police and the prosecutor's offices! When he started to dig he started naturally in Switzerland. Then he asked for legal assistance from many countries. He couldn't find anything to prove what he'd been told and he said to me: "Where are the accounts of the bank?" But from day one, I gave all the information; from day one I answered all the questions.

'Finally, he saw that all the information, all the "evidence" had been supplied by the Americans and he was being asked to find "evidence" that didn't exist to create a case that should never have been brought. The Americans never gave him anything. They couldn't accuse me of making banking activity without licence. The documents are there.

'The Swiss prosecutor complained about the vagueness of the information provided by the Americans. In one interview with the Americans they accused me of not cooperating because I wouldn't provide information which would implicate me. They wanted me to give them evidence that I had done something wrong!

'A letter from the Swiss prosecutor to the Americans said he was "more than disappointed" not to get more information – detailed information on me and Bank Al Taqwa which he'd been promised on a visit to Washington. He said: "All the information we have is coming from you." And that was nothing. They said that the Bahamas didn't co-operate with them but the American investigators took all our files, not photocopies, all the original files from our representative, the Registrar Office and the Central Bank there. But they said "the Bahamas didn't co-operate".

'The Americans claimed we'd special associations with Al Qaeda – and delivered cash for them! Cash! They pushed out fantasies: I'd moved funds to Jordan. The only time I was in Jordan was in transit in Amman on my way to talk with Saddam Hussein in Bagdad. It was also claimed that I'd financed a plot to kill tourists at the Millennium Celebration in Jordan. That was more nonsense.

'They accused the Al Taqwa bank of providing financial aid to

Khader Abu Ghoshar and Abu Musab al-Zarqawi. A newspaper said that I financed al-Zarqawi to blow up the festival for the Millennium. Other supposedly reliable sources said the Bin Laden family invested a big amount of money in Al Taqwa and it disappeared in suspicious circumstances. That was put in the investigation report. Osama Bin Laden's brother Ghaleb Bin Laden invested in the bank and he tried to take it before the time in the contract and made a case against us in the High Court in the Bahamas; the court dismissed the case.

'It was not a secret but it was in the official report as if it was all about funding terrorism. This make-believe information was being said around the US Senate and into the ear of the president. I believe all that has happened to me is because they wanted to connect the Muslim Brotherhood to Al Qaeda through me. That was always the intention. This is what is in the files that get on the desk of the American president, the Senate and other world leaders. That is the information they act upon.

'Communications involving Swiss prosecutors and American officials said that Mr Himmat and I were "suspected of participating in a criminal organisation: in particular they are alleged to have made payments to a terrorist organisation from 1981 until 2001". Here they said "criminal organisation." In another communiqué they said we were funding Al Qaeda. In 1981 Al Qaeda didn't exist. So how can they say that?

'The investigators said in their exchanges that there was not a lot of information and they had to rely on expectations. As for us funding terrorists they said: "The position of the investigation up to now does not indicate anything of that and we have to differentiate between the hypothesis and reality." There was another communication which said that according to the information and documents they had, there was reason for doubts about the worth of the investigation.'

In January 2002, the US Treasury Department sent a letter to Swiss authorities claiming Youssef Nada and Saudi government adviser Ali bin Mussalim had provided 'indirect investment services for Al Qaeda, investing funds for Bin Laden, and making cash deliveries on request to the Al Qaeda organization'. It said the 'assistance' continued until 'late September 2001'.

Ali bin Mussalim, who died from cancer in 2004, held Saudi ministerial status and carried a Saudi diplomatic passport as an adviser to the royal court. He had a reputation for financial deal-making throughout the 1980s and 1990s, including an attempt to corner the world silver market and acting as a go-between in a multi-billion dollar deal between the Saudi and French governments.

'The letter which came from the US Treasury to the prosecutor in Switzerland said I was funding terrorism with Ali bin Mussalim. He was a diplomat in Saudi Arabia and was an adviser to King Fahd and I knew him and I was in contact with him. He was appointed by the king to be the link between me and the king.

'I believe a great part of what they said about Ali bin Mussalim is true. I don't know it for certain. From my follow up with him and his position, it could be. He was in very close contact with Prince Turki, the head of the intelligence during the time of King Fahd during the Afghan Mujahideen war with the Soviet Union. The CIA and Prince Turki were cooperating to assist the insurgents during the time of the Soviet Union. They said that Ali bin Mussalim was financing it. Could be – I don't know. They said he was promoting the military deals between Saudi Arabia and France, and he got $70million commission. It could be, but I had nothing to do with it.

'My connections with Ali bin Mussalim were exclusively to do with King Fahd and trying to resolve the problems with Iran and the Soviets. He was in his own business and I knew nothing of that activity. He was rich. He died in a Geneva hotel. I knew him, but I didn't have any connection with his money or his activity. He was well-known in Saudi Arabia. Very well connected to Fahd. Fahd appointed him to be my link with him. The investigators took a piece from here and a piece from there and put it together and mixed a bad tasting salad.

'The Treasury said I was involved with Mamdouh Mahmud Salim, who they said was a co-founder of Al Qaeda. He was arrested near Munich in 1998. I never had any contact with him or any of his group. He was not a member of the Brotherhood. They said they had information that he had a line of credit from Bank Al Taqwa and from a bank in Dubai. They said he made withdrawals on a secret Bank Al Taqwa account. We never had any secret names or numbers.

'But the US Treasury said there were secret Bank Al Taqwa accounts that nobody can have access to. It was nonsense. We couldn't withdraw from a Dubai bank – we had no connections with banks there. They never named a bank in Dubai. How could it be that the cashing bank was not mentioned and not prosecuted? What they said was false information but they asked me about it, digging to see if there was any iota of truth to what they had. I had never heard about Mamdouh Mahmud Salim's name except from the prosecutor. Then I read the documents which came from the United States. They also indicated that information came from prisoners who were put under duress.

'I can understand it, for I witnessed such things when I was in the military prison. They used to knife the body of the prisoner until he would say whatever they wanted him to say. Not the truth. They said what they wanted to hear to stop the pain.

'Another report said my Tunisian nationality was a fake. I had the papers to prove it was not. Accusations fluttered about all the time but with nothing to bring them to rest. I challenged then and I defy now anyone to prove those accusations.

'The Swiss officials were acting at all times for the Americans. The American chief investigator of the case, David Kane, came to my house here. There were four men with him, one from DIGOS (Divisione Investigazioni Generali e Operazioni Speciali), one from SISMI (Servizio per le Informazioni e la Sicurezza Militare), the third was from the financial police and the fourth from the regular police authority.

'I didn't blame America or Americans. I blame the Bush

223

administration. All their actions were based on fantasies – not facts. The Swiss interrogated me about all the "Islamists" everywhere: about my nationality and how I obtained it, about my family, about my fortune; about everything – but they never said to me a single word about Hamas. Because they knew that I had nothing to do with it.

'I pitied them. They were professional civil servants trying to do their job, a job that was dictated on them. They couldn't refuse it; they had to obey the orders and to comply with it. "Go and fish. Go and dig. You don't have anything, but you must find something." They could not put their hand on any evidence to support the allegations simply because it didn't exist. Still, the fabricated stories were circulated through newspapers, films, televisions, books, the Internet, security reports, and testimonies in the US House of Representatives.

'Al Qaeda is their ghost and from a ghost they created a monster of which to be frightened. It was all so far-fetched. There is a big problem now in the eyes not only of Europe and America. After all the propaganda, when some people see Muslims praying they believe some awful act is about to happen, terrorism is coming.'

CHAPTER FIFTEEN

THE BANKRUPTCY
OF FREEDOM

'I don't see how you can separate faith from moral values. I also don't maintain that you have to be Christian to exhibit those characteristics in private live or public office.'

President Jimmy Carter, 1976

On 11 September 2002, four days after the raid on his home, Youssef Nada went to London to record a series of interviews with Al Jazeera television and was questioned closely and professionally by Ahmed Mansour. The result was screened in a series of ten one-hour programmes which drew a worldwide audience of more than 40million viewers.

He believed that because of the onslaught on his life and liberties he should defend himself publicly. He remained reasonably cool and calm. It was a test of character, for throughout all the investigations Youssef Nada's reputation and that of his closest associates were ruined. The Bank Al Taqwa went into liquidation in January 2002, and the investors lost their money.

Nada personally lost $350million, yet he insists: 'Thank God, I was mostly treated well, except when I was in London and Scotland Yard arrested me. After the interview with Al Jazeera I went back to the Hilton Hotel in London but the door key card wouldn't work. I went down to the concierge who asked me to wait a moment. After about five minutes he gave me another card.

'Entering the lift I was confronted by several men who I asked if I was Mr Nada, I nodded 'yes' and one of them said: "We are from Scotland Yard. You are under arrest Mr Nada." When I asked why, they said I should go to my room. There were five of them and they started to search the room. One of the Special Branch men asked me to bring my bag. It was Ramadan, and I said I first had to go to the bathroom and then say my prayer. They told me to leave the door open. When I had I finished he said to me again: "Bring your bag." I replied: "No, if you want to bring it, bring it. I am the age of your father. If you don't want to carry it, throw it through the window or don't take it." That was very harsh. But he got the idea.

'Then he told me I was not allowed to be in England. I said to him: "I'm sorry but I am European and I believe London is in England and England is a part of Europe." They said: "No. England is England. You are not allowed to come here. Your name is on the list at the United Nations." They took me to a police station and counted and took my money and other belongings and put them in a plastic bag.

'They put me in a cell and when I entered it I had a strange feeling. Very strange. There was what we call a *bankeena*, a couch with plastic mattress. The cell was better than the one in the military prison in Egypt. I had my Koran. I started to read and then I tried to sleep but it was very, very cold and I had to knock and ask for a blanket. After fifteen minutes I was still freezing – the blanket was like paper. I asked for another but it didn't help. The third time he said to me: "Don't ask me for more because I don't have another one to give you."

'After about three hours he opened the door and said I had the right to make a phone call to anyone, anywhere. I didn't want to make trouble for my Brothers and my friends in London. I didn't want them to come to me in the prison, to show themselves, because I wasn't sure what was going on. I called home to Campione and told them what had happened.'

His family called the Muslim Brotherhood in London who engaged a lawyer. After talking to Scotland Yard the lawyer told Nada: 'They have nothing against you but they are going to deport you today. Nobody can ask them why, they don't want to say, but if you stay, they have to say. If they deport you, nobody can ask them.'

'I chose to leave London,' said Nada 'I was listed on the United Nations blacklist. All my assets and all my money were frozen – and my movements. My life was blocked.'

CHAPTER SIXTEEN

COLD COMFORT

'Al Qaeda is just a parenthesis, a most dispensable one in the history of Islam and the Arab world. Not a culmination, but an aberration.'

Jean-Pierre Filiu, *Ten Lessons From the Democratic Uprising*, 2011

Youssef Nada's view of Al Qaeda and its high profile leader Osama Bin Laden, expressed while all the storm of accusations swept around him, was not hugely popular. He maintained Al Qaeda was not a cohesive terrorist outfit, not some monolithic organisation, but a small bunch of demented people excusing their merciless actions by citing Islam, which in turn Osama Bin Laden franchised out.

He also believes that international jihadism was manufactured as the new entrant in a 'hot war', filling the vacuum left by the dismantling of the Soviet Union. The 'army' of Al Qaeda and the threat it posed had been hugely exaggerated. It was a controversial viewpoint as President Bush launched his war on terror, and the 'experts' – on Afghanistan, Iran, Iraq and all points east – who not so long before had known Arabic as only a blend of coffee, went into punditry overdrive.

From seeing Al Qaeda nowhere, the intelligence experts saw it everywhere, and this led to the American–Anglo invasion of Iraq – on the so-tumultuously discredited evidence of weapons of mass destruction, and the UK government's 'dodgy dossier' – which created a new combat zone for East to taunt West and vice versa, and a disastrously draining war there and in Afghanistan.

It is some very small comfort for Nada to have been proven correct, albeit a decade and more later. The endless errors made by Western governments in their efforts to understand the phenomenon of jihadi are now accepted as such by many in the West.

Government actions across the globe have brought stories, some verified, and accusations of atrocities, of infringements of human rights and constant discussions over the 'war on terror' and rendition.

George W Bush's extrajudicial detainment camp at the US Naval base at Cuba's Guantanamo Bay, established in 2002 was, despite Barak Obama's pre-presidential promises, still in business a decade later. The role of America as the world's policeman has been severely diminished. None of this helps eradicate hate and distrust. There are dirty tricks – in the East and the West – by those with calculated and mercenary interests in retaining the status quo.

Information and fair-minded study and learning – and the revolutionary events of 2011 and into 2012 with Malaysia and the re-emergence of vindicated Opposition leader Anwar Ibrahim – showed the public and the policymakers that there are Muslims who are not violent and who can achieve radical differences in their world without it. There had been inspired efforts to keep Anwar Ibrahim's politics out of play in his country, and until 9 January 2012, when he was acquitted in the Malaysian High Court, he had been on trial in Kuala Lumpur for 11 months on spurious charges of sodomising a male aide. Immediately after, he was on the election trail aiming at taking over Malaysia leadership from Prime Minister Najib Razak.

He is on the same wavelength as his friend Youssef Nada. To Nada, we are all human, to Anwar Ibrahim we 'are all sons of Adam'. He says his leadership model for Malaysia is like that of Turkey and says he has similar hopes for Islamic democracy as its Prime Minister Recep Tayyip Erdogan. The prospective Malaysia leader said: 'I talk about the "Malaysian Spring" but our route will be elections.'

That attitude is toward a world living peacefully together, co-existing, live-and-let-live. But there is an enormous task ahead to get people talking rather than making instant judgements. A glance around the blogosphere of the Internet instantly reflects the bile, the cauldron of hate and the true lack of understanding.

There is hope, but Youssef Nada – talking to me at his home in Switzerland – said he continues to count the cost: 'Those who were killed, who were obliterated. Who lost their brain or their bodies or both. What can you say, Mr Thompson? I am alive, I am here, sitting beside you. The two million who lost their lives in Iraq – the widows, the orphans – those people, what do you say to them…?'

Yes, it's difficult to find an answer. It's dispiriting, because of all the politics that fell about him and his life, Youssef Nada was distracted and sometimes fearful of helping people in need. He showed me the details of such a case in his computer files. A woman whose husband had spent ten years in a Moroccan jail accused of terrorism had been advised to contact him. The family had written to Micheline Anne-Marie Calmy-Rey (she became only the second female President of the Swiss Confederation in 2007) but wanted direct intervention, and now they were at the Villa Nada.

'They knew I had contacts with the royal family in Morocco,' said Nada, 'a link to the king, and previously I would have made inquiries and tried to help. But now I was very cautious. Anyone can come to see me, man or woman, Arab or European – I won't close my door to anyone.

'This man's wife came and asked me to intervene but I couldn't. Maybe he is connected to a terrorist group, maybe he is innocent. I don't know. It is not me who can judge. If it was in my normal days I would do what I could even though I didn't know them. It is not the same now. There is no way.'

231

His caution is understandable. Who knows in today's world what any action will bring. Even what is a crime? Or even more difficult – a 'hate' crime? During his time of being branded a terrorist banker, Youssef Nada formulated his point of view in this way. It reflects how furiously disappointed he was that the justice to which he wants the world to aspire to was so sadly absent in his case. I think his words show much he suffered from the treatment he received, how much it hurt to see values which he treasures dismantled around everything he had worked for, everything he loved.

'I understand and accept that legal cooperation among nations is important to protect the world from terrorists and bring them to justice,' he said. 'I reject the assisting in injustice for political reasons; that creates fear and hate and they are the seeds of violence and terrorism. Is it fair and just to accuse someone without evidence but with shady, misleading information? I expected the rule that everyone is innocent until it is proved that he is guilty.

'I believed that when you defend justice you are defending yourself; that when you protect the law you are protecting yourself; that those who are entrusted to protect justice could not be condoned if in any case they act with injustice; that injustice cannot sit on the chair of justice. Justice does not change for colour or race or nationality or religion. The main difference between civilised and primitive society is that civilised society is concerned with the protection of the other's rights. The law is formulated to regulate the boundaries between the rights and obligations. The pillar of justice is that it must not only be done, but also seen to be done.

'As I have said, I met with the investigators from the US Treasury, the FBI, the CIA and the Swiss Federal Prosecutor and police staff. I assured all of them they were misguided. I was guilty of nothing. None of them has ever admitted they were involved in a chain of misleading information and accusations – or been able to produce any evidence against me.

'Although I have reservations regarding their conduct, I don't feel that they are enemies; I believe they are professionals exercising their duties. All their interrogations of me were about our business, political, social, religious activities, and connections and even taxes. Nothing regarding the initial false accusation of financing Osama Bin Laden or his Al Qaeda or hijackers or Hamas or terrorists.

'I've lived and worked in Switzerland for many years during which I have enjoyed love, equality, tolerance, respect of humans, animals, nature, and values. I enjoyed the sincerity and the friendship of doctors, engineers, lawyers, lawmakers, bankers, politicians, activists – men and women of the country who represent the top and cream of human values.

'I was forced to liquidate my bank and companies and I was stripped of all my human rights, wealth, and health. I was smeared in the media all over the world, prevented from movement, denied permission to pay taxes, legal expenses, health insurance. And even the money in my pocket was confiscated by the London police acting like Fagin's pickpockets. This was done by the order of the UN Security Council.

'The UN dictates that those on whom the sanctions should be imposed are defined, according to Resolution 1267 of the UN Security Council, as well as the Federal Swiss ordinance of 30/11/2001: "Taliban, Al Qaeda, Osama Bin Laden, terrorists and those who are connected with, or assisted or financed them".

'That wasn't me! I had nothing to do with all those items. The Swiss, the Americans and others were misled by others for their own reasons. It went on until the American president was misled and designated us on 7 November 2001. After the events of September 11, the American defence system included highlighting and designating any suspects anywhere without any verification.

'Inserting my name on the list stripped me of all my human rights, freedom to work, health, reputation and directed the entire world to treat me as a criminal and terrorist. They had the power to damage but never the courage to correct the damage they caused.

'The Swiss Federal Court prosecutors pursued my case for more than three years and did not specify their accusations about being connected to terrorism. They unjustifiably kept the file open before they were forced to close it and declare they had no evidence for an extended time of three-and-a-half years without closing it, or referring it to a judge. Accordingly the Prosecutor was forced to close the file and declare lack of evidence.

'The only country in the world which prosecuted me was Switzerland, not Italy, not the USA. The Swiss admitted on 23 October 2001, the very same day of opening their case, that investigations through many countries had proved futile. On 2 November, the Swiss Federal Prosecutor applied to some countries to search our houses and offices and confiscate all documents and send them to him. Five days later the Swiss–USA task force coordinated actions against us with the USA, Italy, Lichtenstein, Bahamas, Great Britain, Germany, Austria and Saudi Arabia.

'All these countries raided our houses and offices, seized our documents and froze our money. The news was on every international television. After these actions, President Bush himself announced our name, accused us of financing terrorism, inserted us on his terrorist list and ordered our listing on the UN terrorist list.

'Since 7 November 2001 until 31 May 2005, they interrogated, contacted all the world, investigated all banks and entities connected to us, examined our political, financial and Islamic connections. In spite of all those efforts and time they did not find any evidence of any link or finance, or even intellectual connections to terrorism or the Taliban or Osama Bin Laden or Al Qaeda. In their internal periodical reports they repeatedly admitted lack of evidence and first proposed closing the file on 19 August 2003.

'Mr Juan Carlos Zarate, the senior US Treasury official, made several visits to Switzerland during those years to follow the investigations. He didn't want the file closed. After one visit in 2004 he said his agents were working with the Swiss. Shortly after that the Swiss prosecutor

Claude Nicati announced incorrectly that "sufficient evidence for our involvement in terror financing was found".

'On 31 May 2005, they complied with a Federal Court ruling and closed the case saying there was no evidence. The next day they made a media announcement that the case was not closed – only suspended. I still don't know how this contradiction can be explained. Two days after the file was closed, the US Treasury said that "procedural action" did not "in any way affect the designation of Youssef Nada as a supporter of terrorism or freezing of his assets". They didn't stop there: "The United States has a strong evidentiary basis for the designation. We remain committed to ensuring that he is not able to support terrorist networks and that his assets do not fall into the hands of terrorists".'

This evidence was never given to Swiss authorities who had constantly requested it. America supported their listing decision by arguing the UN had blacklisted Youssef Nada; they didn't say the UN listing was carried out at their instigation.

Juan Carlos Zarate, the Deputy Assistant Secretary in the US Treasury, repeated the allegations against Youssef Nada and Al Taqwa in sworn testimony to the US House of Representatives on 2 February 2002. A month later, Youssef Nada wrote to him via the Swiss prosecutor challenging his statements and requesting supporting evidence for them. In response, the Swiss Federal prosecutor replied in writing to Juan Carlos Zarate:

'I was more than disappointed when I received your letter. This does not give me more information than what I have and the only explanations I received are so general and without details that I cannot use them go on with my investigations.'

The statements which were made and not supported by evidence included – and to read them is to see why such testimony to the American House of Representatives so upset Youssef Nada – 'charges that US$60million was collected annually for Hamas from all parts of the world were moved to an account with Bank Al Taqwa'. And another: 'The Malta and Lugano branches of the Al Taqwa Management Organisation received money from Kuwait and the United Arab Emirates for Osama Bin Laden.' And another: 'Jordan has accused Bank Al Taqwa of having financed a network linked to Bin Laden and of plotting terror attacks against Western and tourist targets during the millennium celebrations.'

When confronted with the lack of support for their claims – at a pedantic level, Al Taqwa never had offices in Malta – the US Treasury responded in writing:

> *The information we released is not calculated to satisfy the traditionally standard of proof applicable in criminal investigations or prosecution either in USA or in Switzerland. We based the reference to the reported Hamas $60million in annual fundraising revenues transmitted through Bank Al Taqwa upon a report published by the BBC on October 17, 1997. That report stated that approximately one-half of Hamas' annual fundraising revenues had been lost and cited* Corriera della Sera.
>
> *To the extent that the information provided herein is not responsive to some of the specific questions you asked, we don't currently have releasable information that is responsive to your questions. The information available regarding the Malta branch of Bank Al Taqwa is derived from media reports published by Agence France Presse on September 23, 2001 and Indigo Publications on March 16, 2000. Those reports characterised the general flow of financing from contributors through the Malta and Lugano branches of Bank Al Taqwa to Osama Bin Laden*

The absurdity of the response – intelligence gathering from newspaper clippings – provoked a disenchanted response from Youssef Nada: 'Their evidence is no more than poison pen, baseless media articles. Juan Carlos Zarate was not the only one who made such testimony to the American lawmakers: David Aufhauser, the General Counsel of the Treasury on 26 June 2003, repeated the same unfounded accusations in the US Senate. Steven Emerson on 18 May 2004, made his testimony before the House Financial Services Committee and repeated the same symphony as if it is one orchestra with several players raising the tune with intervals of one year. The Congressmen and the Senators, as they are the guardians of the democracy, must investigate and clean up the records which are now part of reference. I am banned from travelling to testify and present my documents in the USA.

'It is well known that one of the intelligence duties of spies is to collect information from the media and analyse them. But the intelligence should be intelligent. In my case, the poison pen news was intentionally leaked – it was done through political pressure not professional skill. They were relying on phantoms and influenced by Islamphobia.

'They deviated from the line of rules and justice, picked up rumours and considered them reliable facts. They were repeatedly told the accusations were unfounded but they enjoyed the press coverage and the blessing of high-powered civil servants. They had the power to harm but lacked conscience and sense of direction in doing their job.

'The investigators knew nothing about accounting and banking, and they started to investigate accounts and banking. They knew nothing about geography and they went behind borders. They knew nothing about history and they started to investigate historical cases. They knew nothing about the sectarian factions and they started to investigate their connection. They knew nothing about the Islamists and they started to investigate one of their important people. They knew nothing about the Muslim Brotherhood and they started to investigate one of their elders.

'When they tried to overcome their lack of knowledge they were misguided. Their experts knew more than they did, but it was shallow material and those providing it had an agenda. And that agenda was spread around the world. My case was handled internationally although guided by Switzerland and dictated and supported by the US Treasury and the FBI. They called on help from the Bahamas, Britain, Italy, Germany, France, Austria, Liechtenstein, Saudi Arabia,

Egypt, Syria, Jordan, Kuwait, Tunis, Palestinian Authority, United Arab Emirates, Yemen, Spain, Pakistan, Afghanistan, Malaysia – and more for all I know.'

With wry weariness, Youssef Nada reflected: 'I did feel – you might think correctly – that the world was against me. It was tough physically and emotionally: to have lived a long life trying to do the good thing and then for this to crash around me for no wrongdoing on my part? No evidence. No truth. Sad, very sad for me.

'And what of all the others who were unable to fight back or who were destroyed before they could? There is a difference between the fabricator, the liar and the deceiver but all of them share the same characteristic – they are not noble. Such shameful misleading can mean the loss of health, or wealth, or even every human right, life and dignity and respect.

'This is exactly what led to the Iraq war, where hundreds of thousand lost their lives and others are facing the same destiny. The destruction of the infrastructure which took tens of years to build – water, sewage, electricity, schools, hospitals, streets, ports, airports – all the needs for twenty-first-century humans to live.

'And all because of a "dodgy dossier" – as the British media called it – that Saddam Hussein had weapons of mass destruction and was a danger for the Iraqis and the world. It sent a population, 27 million people, back to the Stone Age.'

The bank and businesses operated by Youssef Nada and his colleagues were ruined following all the accusations and press reports, but what he describes as 'the two competent authorities' – the Swiss Federal Banking Commission and the Bahamian High Court – stopped the actions brought against them on the grounds that there was no case.

On 24 October 2001, the Swiss Federal Police wrote to the Deputy Federal Prosecutor saying that they 'could not find any specific connections between us and any terrorist organisation to confirm the media reports'. Yet Nada's prosecution in Switzerland went on for four years, and in 2012 he was still seeking retribution to correct 'the worldwide damage caused within their sovereignty and territory'.

It comes back, as it always does, to justice. 'Our rights according to the local Swiss law are compatible with our rights according to the UN declaration of human rights, adopted and proclaimed by the UN General Assembly and committed to by Europe and Switzerland. I agree that the whole world must cooperate to fight terrorism, but if this fight is to be justified it must be lawful. It must not victimise innocent people.'

The situation was raised by the Swiss permanent representative at the UN, Peter Maurer, in his address to the Security Council. It was also brought up by the Swiss Justice Minister, Christopher Blocher, when he met John Ashcroft who was President George W Bush's first Attorney General and helped created anti-terrorism policies adopted after September 11.

Despite this, Youssef Nada notes: 'Nothing was done. The barbarian terrorists are cruelly stripping innocent people from their properties, rights and life. Civilised society must not be dragged to follow their ruthless behaviour when they fight them.

'The mechanism of blacklisting legally and correctly must be dealt with. It must be implemented without giving the totalitarian governments, wherever they are, the means to eliminate their political opponents by designating them without justification. Our names were listed without any evidence against us. The criteria used against us provided no fair hearing of our case, no route of appeal – and no way of getting compensation for the ongoing damage to our health and moral and economic well-being.

'Italy is my country of citizenship and it never prosecuted me, never accused me: it executed legal assistance requested from Switzerland to raid our houses, confiscate our papers and hand them over to Switzerland. Italy was not the country which coordinated what happened to us. The countries which did that were Switzerland and the USA.

'It's true that I am an Islamist. I am proud of that. As an Islamist I believe that any type of terrorism including what happened on September 11 in New York, or later in Madrid or in London, or anywhere, must never be condoned. Justice must not punish the law-abiding Islamists if killers hijack Islam and use its name for terror. The Islamist did not give any mandate to those criminals to execute ruthless and cruel actions in their name. There is a need to have efficient ways to regulate globalisation, for without any control it dramatically increases the lack of balance and of justice in the world. The world must not leave its existence to the discretion of authoritarian rulers or the whims and fancies of racist politicians.

'The Muslim Brotherhood are part of those calling for globalisation and world order. The main difference is that our call is not based on race, language, colour, or privilege to those who are powerful – similar to the ancient domination Greeks or the Romans – it is based on justice, tolerance, peace and equality.'

Although his extensive work and social life – more than half a century of worldwide activity in religion, charities, trading, banking and industry – was so rudely interrupted, Youssef Nada wants to continue being an ambassador for good.

'I want to continue in the line of which I devoted my life,' he told me. 'My faith, structure, skill, contacts, background and experience were and will be useful to open dialogues, extend bridges and lead to more understanding and cooperation between various countries, politicians, factions, and religious groups, healing rifts, and building bonds through respect and tolerance. I did it before, and I shall continue.'

Yet as of 2012, Nada remains on America's terror list. Which begs the question of when is a terrorism figure no longer one?

In August 2002, the George W Bush administration designated the Italy-domiciled Ahmed Idris Nasreddin – Youssef Nada's friend and founding member of the board of Bank Al Taqwa – as a prominent financier of terrorism. It said he was a pivotal moneyman in Al Qaeda's international network. The United Nations followed the US lead and ordered its 190 member nations to freeze the assets of Nasreddin and his business holdings and ban all contact with them.

On 14 November 2007, the same administration, without any fanfare, removed Ahmed Idris Nasreddin and more than a dozen of his businesses from the official blacklist; the UN did the same almost immediately after. There was no public announcement by anyone or organisation, or explanation other than notice of 'an updated list of enforcement actions'. What had changed?

'You cannot for five years refer to someone as an international terrorist financier, seize all their funds, tell the world that this is a major-league bad guy, and then suddenly change your mind without public explanation,' said lawyer Jonathan M Winer, a former Deputy Assistant Secretary of State for International Law Enforcement. He added: 'In order to have credibility, you have to explain to the world what has happened, and you have to justify both decisions. Was the initial decision a mistake? And if it wasn't, how do you justify the new decision? It screams out for a full explanation, and none has been provided.'

When asked, the US Treasury Department did not discuss the case but said in a statement that both the listing and delisting were 'appropriate'. The Treasury's Office of Foreign Assets Control 'reviewed all of the information in its possession, including the information upon which Mr Nasreddin's original designation was based, additional information, and Mr Nasreddin's submissions in support of his delisting petition'.

The Treasury said that 'a primary basis' for Nasreddin's designation as a terrorist financier was his 'support for Youssef Nada, co-founder and co-director with Nasreddin of the prominent Bank al Taqwa, and Nasreddin's support for the bank itself'. The change in 2007 was because 'Mr Nasreddin no longer fits the criteria for designation because he has submitted signed statements to the Office of Foreign Assets Control certifying that he has terminated any business relationships with Nada, Bank Al Taqwa and any other designated individuals and entities, and that he will have no such dealings in the future'.

A former State Department official who took part in the global designation of Ahmed Idris Nasreddin and Youssef Nada when he belonged to the United Nations Al Qaeda Monitoring Group, said the US Treasury provoked more questions than answers as to why one of the men was being taken off the blacklist after so many years: 'They seem to be saying that he was a bad guy but that he has renounced being a bad guy. If that's the criteria, wow, a lot of people will try to get off the list.'

Unofficially, Treasury officials said that many people do get off the list where 'circumstances warrant'. If they appealed, individuals went through a 'very fact-based inquiry'. They said that Ahmed Idris Nasreddin's case was not unusual. Yet, despite being taken off the UN list, in 2012 Youssef Nada remained on the American list. No one, it seems, will admit that putting him there and turning his life and world upside down was an error, a knee-jerk to events, albeit catastrophic ones. It has been said and written that he's guilty of much, but he has not been officially accused or charged with anything. It's been a long limbo – Kafkaesque, indeed.

CHAPTER SEVENTEEN

WAITING FOR JUSTICE

'Any state belonging to the Security Council has no problem adding a name. All it has to do is to tell the sanctions committee an individual supports al-Qaeda or some other terrorist network, but doesn't have to provide any proof.'

Dick Marty

Youssef Nada has a library of paperwork relating to his blacklisting – just a fraction of what has been generated since the aftershock following the events in New York rocked his life. He can relate it at will: the movie unspools constantly in his mind.

It is an unsettling narrative, for throughout no evidence is presented – other than that from newspaper reports – to support any of the conjecture in the case. The word was that material would be forthcoming, but the waiting had absurdist shades of a Samuel Beckett play. Overwhelmingly, it appears that everyone – all the nations involved – simply wanted to keep each other content that they were doing something about terrorism.

That intent sabotaged Youssef Nada's life, as he explained: 'One week

243

after 9/11, the media started to attack me. The attack intensified after the raid on my house and offices on 7 November 2001, and George Bush's declaration on television that he will starve us. Five years passed, then we applied to delist our names from the Swiss blacklist; our request was rejected. My efforts in the media battle were not enough. I went to the court and they ruled that although I was denied my human rights, and living as under house arrest, Switzerland must abide with the UN Security Council resolution – even though it contradicted Swiss law and the constitution. It was so totally political.

'When I contacted my Swiss friend, Professor Dr Sebastiano Martinol, for advice he said the only politician in Switzerland who would be prepared to go into this jungle was Dr Dick Marty, and within three days he'd arranged for me to meet him. Being a former prosecutor, he naturally wanted to verify whether what I said was true or not. I gave him all the material and he was satisfied. He was well-known in Switzerland from his days as a young prosecutor when he was dubbed 'the Mafia Hunter' when he broke up drug trafficking gangs.'

In 1987 Dick Marty received an Award of Honour from the US Department of Justice and the International Narcotic Enforcement Officers Association. From 1995 until 2011 he was consecutively elected to the Swiss Council of States for Ticino; from 1998 until 2011 he was a member of the Parliamentary Assembly of the Council of Europe. In 2005 he led an investigation by the Council of Europe into alleged illegal CIA secret prisons in Europe. It brought him under scrutiny by America's 'special services'.

The Swiss politician used satellite images and aviation logs to discover if the 'rendition' of terror suspects for possible torture, or illegal secret detentions, had taken place in any of the Council states. Working with Italian prosecutors, their investigations led to the indictment of 20 CIA agents and Italian military security officers for clandestine collaboration in the kidnapping and the rendition of terrorism suspects to secret prisons in Egypt, Jordan, Romania, Bulgaria, Iraq and Afghanistan.

At the end of September 2009, Youssef Nada's name was removed from the United Nations Security Council's (UNSC) terrorism watch list. He said: 'Our case was the only one in Europe that involved cooperation between twelve states, led by the Swiss Attorney General in response to a request by the US and under American supervision since September 2001. They could not provide any proof of our involvement with terrorism financing, as was alleged by Washington. So we brought a case against the Prosecutor General, whom the Swiss Supreme Court rebuked for being late in notifying us of the charges. Investigations were dropped on 31 May 2005, after he admitted to the lack of any evidence.

'Nevertheless, America refused to remove our names from Washington's terrorism list or the lists compiled by the UNSC, the EU and the UK. Switzerland, as a member of the UN, announced that it was bound by the UNSC resolution and would not be able to remove our names from its lists at the moment.

'Dick Marty sent a television crew from the European Parliament to record my evidence and a video presentation was made to the Parliament, and he called for a vote on his findings. Other than Romania and Bulgaria, the members agreed to what he had discovered. Then he moved on the Swiss legislative authority and his findings were submitted to the Swiss senate. Marty told them: "Youssef Nada's case dishonours Switzerland." The Swiss Foreign Minister protested. He then demanded that the Swiss government inform the United Nations Security Council that Switzerland would not be bound by its terrorism lists for any name who stayed more than three years without being indicted by the court. The Swiss government protested. Dick Marty then asked for a vote and his motion was unanimously approved.

'America believed that if Switzerland implemented the resolution, then other nations would follow and over-ride the UN Security Council. To stop that it lifted its veto against my name and agreed to remove it from the UN list, but not from its own list – which rather proves the case of Dick Marty who argues that the way the blacklist system is run violates international law and plays into the hands of terrorists. Switzerland is – so far – the only country to have adopted measures under which the government is obliged to lift sanctions against a blacklisted person if no judicial authority has been asked to examine their dossier and indicted them within three years.'

Dick Marty believes: 'The problem isn't with the lists as such, but in the way in which they are administered. Any state belonging to the Security Council has no problem in adding a name. All it has to do is to tell the sanctions committee (comprising fifteen Security Council members) that such and such an individual supports al-Qaeda or other terrorist network but doesn't have to provide any proof. The person finds himself on the list, without being informed or given a chance to put their case. They cannot find out the details of the accusation against them, which are declared to be State secrets, nor can they appeal to an independent authority to defend themselves. It is all totally arbitrary.

'All your goods are seized; you can't have a credit card or any bank accounts; and you are no longer allowed to pursue gainful employment. You are not given what is strictly enough to live on. Nor can you travel outside the country where you live. There is no time limit placed on these restrictions. For some people, this means economic ruin.

'The UN started to move as a consequence of the motion: a few names were removed from the blacklists. The UN also appointed an ombudswoman and she has already discovered that people who died some time ago still have their names on these lists.

'A lot of horse trading goes on in the sanctions committee, along the lines of "if you let me put my terrorist on the list, I'll let you put your terrorist on when the time comes". It's a scandal that they can work this way within the Security Council. Does the arbitrary way the blacklists are run widen the gap between the West and the Muslim world? Yes indeed, and governments, especially European ones, are not showing much courage about being consistent with the principles they preach. And that gives terrorism a certain legitimacy – the legitimacy to combat states which use illegal methods: blacklists, secret CIA flights, secret prisons.

'People have been kidnapped and held for years without trial in the name of the fight against terrorism. They are released nine years later, for lack of proof and with not one word of apology or a dollar in compensation. This creates a wave of sympathy for terrorists, which is extremely dangerous. It is especially disappointing that up to now, these measures have only affected Muslims. If a citizen of a Western Christian state was involved, that would get things moving.'

Dick Marty, quick and sharp in movement and mind, has a strong reputation and strikes a courageous figure. His participation in a human rights forum alongside the kindly and ebullient – and super tough – Milan prosecutor Armado Sparato tempted a packed audience to Lugano University in January 2012, despite sub-zero temperatures and a snowstorm. He was heavily guarded.

I was sitting with Youssef Nada toward the front of the audience when suddenly the auditorium erupted with about 30 environmental protesters screaming slogans and waving flags and stamping their way to the front of the hall. Dick Marty and the others watched without expression during the scuffles until security guards ejected the protestors. Later, Marty waved away the 'spot of bother'. It was nothing, said the security men: 'No one had a gun.' It was a vibrant display that no matter how good your intentions are you cannot please everyone. Especially in the time which elapses in the pursuit of justice.

Certainly, after swift initial action, the wheels of the world of justice do turn slowly. On 23 March 2011, I went with Youssef Nada, and his wife and Ghaleb Himmat, to the European Court of Human Rights. His case was that he had been improperly treated by the Swiss authorities.

Nada v Switzerland was heard in the magnificent Grand Chamber of the European Court of Human Rights in Strasbourg with a panel of

17 judges. The case challenged the implementation of UN sanctions 'on persons supposedly connected in some way to Al-Qaeda'. Court documents explained why the case was being made:

> ... *because of the passage of nearly seven years without providing either any specific allegations or any form of hearing in which they could be challenged, with the result that the applicant, Youssef Moustafa Nada, an Italian national was confined to a territory of 1.7 sq km and suffered serious interferences with his private and family life, as well as significant damage to his reputation.*
>
> *Nada was placed on the list of the United Nations Committee along with a number of organisations associated with him. On 30 November 2001 those names were added by the Swiss authorities to the list of people concerned by the anti-Taliban order.*
>
> *The order provided for the freezing of assets and financial resources of those concerned, and prohibited the provision to them of funds or financial resources. It further restricted their entry into or transit through Switzerland.*
>
> *Mr Nada requested the deletion from the list of his name and those of the organisations associated with him, as the Swiss investigation against him had been discontinued. His request and subsequent administrative appeals were rejected. Mr Nada was de-listed without any explanation or hearing in September, 2009.*

Jeremy McBride represented Youssef Nada with élan and presented his case: 'Campione d'Italia is something close to paradise. Rested on the shores of Lake Lugano, below the green slopes of the Southern Alps, the tiny Italian tax haven commune within the Swiss canton of Ticino is a place of extraordinary natural beauty. But to Mr Youssef Moustafa Nada one of its two thousand or so residents, it was more like something close to prison, after he was designated by the UN Security Council a terrorist banker.

'That was in October 2001, shortly after 9/11. Mr Nada, a wealthy

Italian businessman and a top figure within the Muslim Brotherhood, was suspected by the Bush administration of financing al-Qaeda. His bank accounts were frozen, as were those of his businesses, and his movement was restricted to the 1.6 km2 enclave – more than half of which is water – effectively placing him under house arrest. It wasn't until eight years later, in September 2009, that he was removed from the UN list of terror suspects and the sanctions against him lifted.

'Mr Nada has never been convicted of anything related to terrorism. He has never been accused; no official charges have been filed. Both the Swiss and Italian prosecutors have opened investigations, and both have closed them again for lack of evidence. He himself has always denied any involvement, but has never been able to refute the allegations.'

Because of the implications of the case in reference to activities by many Governments of blacklisting in the 'global war on terror', the Youssef Nada case took on worldwide significance, and the UK government had its own team at the hearing. The question being asked was: 'When was it right to go after terror suspects and ignore the law?' Or as the former American Secretary of State, Paul O'Neill put it: 'Set up a new legal structure to freeze assets on the basis of evidence that might not stand up in court.'

European counter-terrorism expert Gilles de Kerckhove defended the actions: 'It is not criminal law, it is an administrative sanction, the difference being that administrative sanctions, like a speeding or parking ticket, require less judicial safeguards. Those would only weaken the instrument. It is a delicate balance. It is also a political, a diplomatic tool.'

When it closed its investigative file on Youssef Nada, the Italian prosecutor's office said: 'Inclusions on blacklists are motivated principally by political choice.' And on 23 March 2011, Jeremy McBride made what is still a very relevant point: 'It has been nine years that the applicant has been waiting for a hearing before any court.'

More than a year from then, more than a decade on, Youssef Nada was still waiting for a judgment from the European Court of Human

Rights, and he remains pragmatic, saying: 'In the Muslim Brotherhood, I've learned to accept fate. I do what needs to be done and leave the rest to God.'

CHAPTER EIGHTEEN

SHOW ME
THE MONEY

'A nation that continues year after year to spend more money on military defence than on programmes of social uplift is approaching spiritual doom.'

Martin Luther King Jr

Youssef Nada has little time to concern himself with the prominent politicians (he finds it hard to get his tongue around the term 'world leaders') of the early 21st century, as former US President George W Bush and the now multi-millionaire Tony Blair, former Prime Minister of Great Britain: tweedledum and tweedledee, as it were.

I pointed out to him comments made by Blair on the BBC Radio 4 *Today* programme on 29 December 2011, that: 'Looking back now, and this should inform our judgements for the future, these situations, which you have people in power for 25 or 30 years, more in some cases it doesn't last. Even for a self-interested point of view we should be looking at how we engage in evolutionary change otherwise you will get revolution. I think it's better if we had been able to promote evolution of these countries so rather than revolution that will cause quite a lot of difficulties, not simply for us, but for people of these countries. Look at what has happened to Egypt's growth rates and tourist industry.'

Nada wasn't particularly enlightened by that. 'Anyone can attack Blair but he is yesterday's man, a waste of our time,' he told me. 'It doesn't work to have people in absolute power for thirty years. What is needed is an understanding of where we are and where we are going now that Blair's friends like Gadaffi have vanished from the stage. You don't have to cosy up to monsters – you have to negotiate with them: there is a huge difference.

'These dictators are not stupid. People who are dreaming – now that Gadaffi has gone, Mubarak has gone, and Ben Ali is no longer in Tunisia – that they will retrieve the monies which were stolen and smuggled out of their countries, will be lucky to get back ten per cent. Maybe less. These dictators and those around them cleverly got their money out so it couldn't be traced [unlike the British-army trained General Sani Abacha, president of oil-wealthy Nigeria for five years from 1993, during which time he and his family looted £5billion from the country until his mysterious death in the company of six teenaged Indian prostitutes and vials of poison].

'They will have entities and companies anywhere in the world, whether off-shore or on-shore, with bearer shares owned by whoever they are signed over to. No one knows who the real beneficiary – the ultimate beneficiary – is. You could, for example, be asking Switzerland for the money of Gadaffi, the bulk of which was smuggled out. And it was billions not millions. But it could be in the names of companies in which they had shares which could be sold at any time to any bearer. The ultimate beneficiary is the one to whom the bearer bond was last signed over to – and it could be anyone.

'Tony Blair said that 25 years or 30 years in power allows much time to make arrangements. 'In Egypt those of the Military Council (SCAF) which remains from the Mubarak era follow the lineage of Sadat and Nasser before him – that's 60 years and still counting of dictatorship.

There are the gold mines of Egypt but where is the gold from them – in Tutankhamun's tomb?'

Hatred of venal exploitation has indeed emerged as the united protest theme across the Arab world. The people of North Africa and the Arab Peninsula argue all the time over how much Ben Ali and Mubarak stole and what the Gaddafi dynasty siphoned off to New York and Paris and London. It is said the amounts soar up to US$100billion, and that's probably true, given the time in power and the extent of the energy wealth and the plundering of it.

The detestation of corruption, be it about a billion dollars or a licence for a street trader, is now central in the Arab world. It's as essential in the backdraft of the Arab Spring as it has become in the West, where bankers and hedge fund managers are equated as parallel with avaricious and wicked despots.

Another world is more and more being exposed, be it the arrogance or criminality of rulers. Youssef Nada points to the experience of one of his friends who went for a business meeting with Prince Khalid, one of the sons of King Faisal of Saudi Arabia: 'Prince Khalid was a governor of a large district of Saudi Arabia, and there was an important project in the area. My friend was a specialist. The appointment was for 9am but at 12.30pm he was still waiting. One of his team wanted to go to the bathroom. He opened the wrong door and found Prince Khalid standing in a smock with a paintbrush in his hand. He liked to paint, it was his hobby, and they had to wait for him! Time meant nothing to him.'

The story of Yehia Hussein Abdel-Hady, a valuation officer for Egyptian Government privatisation deals, was reported in 2011 and it told of how five years earlier he was summoned to his place of work, the Ministry of Investment in Cairo, and given a three-page document and ordered to sign it. The paperwork signed off the sale of Omar Effendi, a chain of 82 state-owned department stores, for 'the amount stipulated on the attachment'. There was no attachment.

Three days later all the shops and the land were sold to a Saudi Arabian businessman for US$99million. It was a tiny amount against their true value. Abdel-Hady said: 'The Government was in a hurry to sell, no questions asked.'

In 2011 and 2012, similar secret deals were being discovered as regimes changed and the hunt began for the dictators' hidden treasures. 'These economies operated under a cloak of opacity,' said Anthea Lawson of Global Witness, an anti-corruption research organisation in London. 'Corruption was the entire basis of these uprisings, and people were sufficiently furious to risk their lives and try and overthrow it.'

The extent – or rather, the known and estimated extent – of the wayward billions was only just becoming clearer in 2012. In Tunisia, the economy had been dominated by the extended family of President Zine el Abidine Ben Ali. His family owned houses in Paris, the Alps and the South of France. Switzerland froze US$69million of the family's bank deposits; the French and Swiss Governments impounded private planes.

Meanwhile, the hunt is still on for Gadaffi's wealth, with early discoveries including property in London's West End and shares in the Italian soccer club Juventus. Mubarak deposited these and other assets in dozens of countries, including the Gulf states and throughout Asia. Libya's central bank governor, Farhat Bengdara, who defected in March 2011, said that Gaddafi kept about US$500million in cash in Tripoli, as well as around 155 tons of gold bars, worth about US$7.5billion. An accounting of that had not been seen by early 2012.

In February 2011 the London-based *Guardian* newspaper estimated Mubarak's family fortune at US$40billion to US$70billion, including homes in California's Beverly Hills, in New York and Belgravia in Central London. If Mubarak was a vampire sucking his country dry, then the publication of that atrocious arithmetic was the stake in his heart. Yet, Anthea Lawson of Global Witness agrees with Youssef Nada about the chances of retrieving the missing millions. 'You can't just go on a fishing expedition; you have to know what you are looking for.'

The majority of nations require agencies trying to recover stolen assets to identify who hid them and where they are. That is complicated, as civil servants don't want to go to jail if they give details.

'The risk is that nobody knows where the money is and that people die and the documents are never recovered,' said Geneva lawyer, Pierre Schifferli in 2011. He helped recover billions embezzled by Nigeria's Sani Abacha and President Ferdinand Marcos of the Philippines. 'Marcos's money was so well hidden that not even his family members knew where it was.' Or so they said – suspicion and distrust is unlikely to vanish with any speed.

CHAPTER NINETEEN

NEW BEGINNINGS

'Great things are done when men and mountains meet.'

William Blake, 1789

VILLA NADA, CAMPIONE D'ITALIA, 23 JANUARY 2012

It wasn't long after lunch that Youssef Nada reached for the television control and flicked into the future.

Gosh, it was a loud and belligerent beginning to tomorrow's world.

Egypt's first freely elected parliament was in inaugural session in Cairo that Monday early in 2012. It was only two days before the first anniversary of the tumultuous events of Tahrir Square and the 'January 25 Revolution' as I sat with Youssef Nada watching the BBC's Arabic-language satellite broadcast of the event.

He didn't speak. His focus was on what was happening, his attention locked tight to the screen. The inauguration began with a prayer for the thousands who died during the revolution. Interim Speaker, Mahmoud al-Saqa of the Wafd party, who at 81 was the oldest member of the House, said: 'I invite the distinguished assembly to stand and read the *fatiha* [Muslim prayer] in memory of the martyrs of the revolution, because the blood of the martyrs is what brought this day.'

For decades, the Egyptian Parliament had been a rubber stamp, a sign-off on predetermined policy. This was an altogether different beast. Youssef Nada began a translated commentary as we watched the 'new boys', wearing bright yellow sashes, saying 'No to Military Trials for Civilians' in reference to those like him tried in military courts. One by one, members of the new assembly, answering a roll call, took the microphone to vow to protect the republican system, the interests of the people and 'to respect the constitution and the law'. Then, Mamdouh Ismail, an Islamist deputy from the Salafi Party, who have a quarter of the seats, intervened with: 'In whatever does not contradict God's law'. He was rebuked by the Speaker and when Salafi deputies tried to add similar phrases to their vows the Speaker's assistant cut them off. Those still determined to slip the phrase in began their vow with it.

The Salafi's electoral gains were the biggest surprise of the Egyptian election. Their strong showing is difficult for the Muslim Brotherhood which is wary of being drawn into more hardline positions. Unlike the Brotherhood, the Salafis wanted Egypt's new constitution – to be drafted by a committee selected by parliament – to stipulate the full implementation of Islamic law.

It wasn't long before the shouting began over procedures to choose the Speaker of the house. The Muslim Brotherhood's Freedom and Justice Party (FJP) had arranged with other principal political figures to appoint Saad al-Katatni (secretary-general of the FJP), to the job. Other candidates noisily insisted on the right to address the Parliament and present themselves to the assembly.

Katatni – the only prominent member of the Muslim Brotherhood never to have been jailed – was elected Speaker. His acceptance speech was politically sensitive and important. First, he thanked the Military Council (SCAF) for keeping its promise to hold elections, and said: 'We will not be content until all the aims of the revolution have been realised. We will avenge the martyrs through fair, effective and fast trials, and we will rebuild Egypt as a national, democratic, constitutional and modern state.'

A credible chamber is a way forward: the revival of an assembly that, as the 20th century dawned, held an independent voice which was heard against that of the monarchy and the British influence. All that went with Nasser's 1952 coup, and the impact of the man who put Youssef Nada in prison had never ceased.

This initial session of the revolution Parliament was the first step to changing that. In the past, Mubarak's party had always won sweeping majorities. The best performance by the Brotherhood was when it secured 20 per cent of seats in the 2005 election. In 2010, almost all the Opposition were defeated in a blatantly rigged poll.

Yet, it took until evening on that January day for Saad el Katatni to be elected Speaker by a vote of 399 to 97, a truly significant turn in the history of the Muslim Brotherhood. After 84 years of struggle in the shadows of monarchy and dictatorship, the Brotherhood, the fountainhead of Islamist ideologies around the world, had political power and democratic legitimacy. It was a marker of the Brotherhood's transformation from outlawed opposition to political establishment.

The new Speaker said: 'This is democracy that had left this hall for years, and now the people have grasped it. We want Egypt and the whole world to know that our revolution will continue, and we will not rest and our eyes won't sleep until the revolution fulfils all its demands.'

If the emotional resurgence was seen in the Parliament, the physical revival of the Muslim Brotherhood in Egypt took on a tangible form in May 2011 when they moved their offices from an apartment building on Cairo's Gezira Island to new accommodation in the city's Muqatam neighbourhood. Proudly, they put up their movement's logo in Arabic and English.

The FJP, which includes a minority of Christian Copts, says it wants a constitution that respects Muslims and non-Muslims, will not impose Islamic law, and is committed to a pluralistic and democratic Egypt. Their immediate problem was more economic than religious. Then, there are international politics. The Salafist al-Nour Party will want their way but so will the secularist, the nation's businesses and aspiring classes.

Yet it was the Muslim Brotherhood in charge of Egypt, the natural leader of the Arab nations. Moscow and Washington, London and Tehran and Tel Aviv watched every moment, every movement. In 2012 the Muslim Brotherhood took power in a world on the edge. You can't Google the future, but what was once described to me as 'the mess of the Middle East which delights America' was indeed that. A mess which, it can be argued, is the doing of others.

Meanwhile, as the Egyptian Parliament took control of itself, in America the race was on to find a Republican candidate to go up against Barak Obama for the next Presidency. The television debates were a fanfare of entertainment rather than insight. Some American commentators were reminded of weighing up uneasy relationships of the past. One, Steve Coll in *The New Yorker* of February 2012, recalled Eisenhower's State of the Union address in 1954, made less than a year after he had secretly ordered the CIA to overthrow Iran's Left-leaning government. In his speech Eisenhower celebrated 'the forces of stability and freedom' at work in Iran.

Coll wrote: 'In 1980, Jimmy Carter delivered his annual address amid the whirlwind of Iran's Islamic and anti-American revolution, which was inflamed in part by Iranians' memories of Eisenhower's coup. "We will face these challenges," Carter declared. "And we will not fail."

'Three decades on, Iran's theocrats have built a police state, spread violence across the Middle East, and acquired nuclear reactors. Iran remains a perennially grim subject of presidential oratory, and Barack Obama, while delivering his third State of the Union, added another entry: "Let there be no doubt: America is determined to prevent Iran from getting a nuclear weapon, and I will take no options off the table to achieve that goal."'

And Steve Coll made this grim point: 'Leaving options on the table is a not-so-oblique way of threatening war. On the same day, Israel's

Prime Minister, Benjamin Netanyahu, told the Knesset: "Only a combination of crippling sanctions and putting all the options on the table can make Iran stop" its nuclear drive.

'Meanwhile, three of the remaining candidates for the Republican presidential nomination – Rick Santorum, Mitt Romney, and Newt Gingrich – have been speaking approvingly about bombing Iran's atomic sites or assassinating its scientists.'

While the American politicking went on, the Obama administration turned around many, many years of mistrust and hostility as it began negotiations with the Muslim Brotherhood which it had so shortly before viewed as irreconcilably opposed to United States interests. The shift was an acknowledgment of a new political reality, the power of Islamist groups. It also reflected Washington's acceptance of what Youssef Nada has been saying – the Brotherhood's intent to build a modern democracy that will respect individual freedoms.

Certainly, America's public warming to the Muslim Brotherhood has boosted the Islamic movement in Egypt and given valuable international legitimacy to the Brotherhood. This emerging American relationship with the Brotherhood is part of a pattern which knits together the Middle East power shift following the changes in Morocco, Libya, Tunisia and Egypt – which has all happened in months, not years.

Senator John Kerry said after his visit to the Muslim Brotherhood leaders in Cairo: 'You're certainly going to have to figure out how to deal with democratic governments that don't espouse every policy or value you have. The Obama administration's outreach to [the Muslim Brotherhood] is like President Ronald Reagan's arms negotiations with the Soviet Union.   The United States needs to deal with the new reality. And it needs to step up its game.'

As Youssef Nada knows well, the Americans had never talked – even ever so quietly – to the Brotherhood. Yet, Hosni Mubarak was informed by his secret police that it was happening. He spoke with the American writer Mary Anne Weaver about it in 1994. Mubarak was another one lacking a crystal ball. He was adamant to Ms Weaver about one particular point: 'Your government is in contact with these terrorists from the Muslim Brotherhood – very secretly, without our knowledge at first. I can assure you these groups will never take over this country.'

CHAPTER TWENTY

VIVA NADA

'A week is a long time in politics.'
British Prime Minister, Harold Wilson, 1964

VILLA NADA, CAMPIONE D'ITALIA, 28 JANUARY 2012

'You have to call Rome!' shouted the Italian police commissioner. They alone can allow this to happen.'

'This' was the progress from Lugano, Switzerland, the few hundred yards across the border and into Italy for the Prime Minister of Tunisia, Hamadi Jebali. There was a confusion of language, of security cars, of Swiss and Italian policemen and Tunisian VIPs and their protection officers. No one wanted an international incident.

At the archway into the enclave of Campione D'Italia you can stand with one leg in Switzerland and the other Italy: such minor amusement can be a nightmare of jurisdiction for those in authority charged with the protection of a Prime Minister – especially a newly elected one.

The Ennahda Party and Hamadi Jebali, under the guidance of Youssef Nada's close friend Rashid al-Ghannusi, won an election victory in Tunisia. Now, at the conclusion of the World Economic

Forum's annual meeting in Davos, Switzerland, they were calling on Villa Nada this January Saturday in 2012 just as they had when they were outlaws, refugees from their homes and country.

When all the arrangements had been made and the armed policemen satisfied about who was going where and guarding whom, the cavalcade of bureaucratic acclaim escorted the Tunisian officials up the mountainside. What with the officials and the guards and the drivers it looked like a police convention outside Youssef Nada's home. There was little space to move around, and if you did there were officers in uniform and plainclothes to the left and to the right – everywhere, in fact.

It was similar to the scene at Villa Nada after US President George W Bush called Youssef Nada a 'financier of terror' and Swiss and Italian police surrounded and invaded his home on 7 November 2001. The difference this time was that a world leader was calling to pay his respects to Youssef Nada.

A strange moment?

'This is politics.'

GHOSTS OF
THE PAST

'Life can only be understood backwards; but it must be lived forwards.'
Danish philosopher-theologian Soren Kierkegaard, 1842

What became a mess of politics into the summer of 2012 was the future of Egypt. I was in Cairo when the Muslim Brotherhood Guidance Council decided by secret ballot to put forward the outspoken and influential businessman Khairat el Shater – one of their most high profile members – as a Presidential candidate. The vote was 56 to 52.

In the days up to that all but photo-finish vote the atmosphere had been overtly polite inside the Brotherhood's still sparklingly new headquarters in the Muqatam neighbourhood, overlooking the vast expanse of the city.

By then, their Freedom and Justice Party controlled almost 50 per cent of the new Parliament and a majority of the 100-member Constituent Assembly (CA), busily writing a new constitution. Following the revolutionary events of 2011 they had pledged not to put forward their own candidate for president, then in the first weekend of April 2012 they were. To many, including Nada and, clearly from the narrow vote, a good many of the Guidance Council, it was a mistake. Nada even went so far as describing it to me as 'a catastrophe'.

Indeed, it seemed like an own goal: it appeared the Muslim Brotherhood wanted total control – not the power sharing they had pledged – and were now focused on political gamesmanship rather than the good of the Egyptian people. Opposition groups were swift to insist that the Brotherhood, so shortly before still outlawed on legislative order by Hosni Mubarak, was putting itself in a position to wield unchallenged power. Others jumped on it as an Islamic takeover of Egypt – the leading and most pivotal of all Arab nations.

Officially, Secretary General Mahmoud Hussein said the Brotherhood's change of tactic was because of the 'lack of an effective government that represents the public, threats to dissolve the Parliament, and the presidential candidacy of members of the former regime. The movement changed its decision after spotting real threats to the revolution and democracy.'

He said they had approached some exceptional contenders from outside the Brotherhood but they had declined. Nada was not pleased. He was adamant with his view: 'We are an organisation built on religion and ethics and this does not allow defying promises. We have straight, honest rules to follow and should not be involved in political zigzags. We promised Egypt we would not present any Presidential candidate from the Muslim Brotherhood and our religion and values dictate on us to fulfil our promises. From the beginning they should not have promised the nation they wouldn't put forward any candidate before knowing if a good and neutral contender was available. Such decision must be within the authority of the Guidance Bureau not the Shura Council. And if the Shura Council does get involved in a decision which might harm the Brotherhood it must not be done by simple majority of four votes but by at least two thirds.

Shortly before Khairat el Shater's Presidential candidacy was announced on 1 April by Supreme Guide Mohamed Badei, I sat sipping tea in the Brotherhood's offices with Youssef Nada's long-time colleague and fellow 1950s jail inmate, Mahdi Akef. He had served as the Brotherhood's Supreme Guide until 2010 when Mohamed Badei took over. There was, he admitted, a great deal of pressure. There was the problem of SCAF which continued – and given its full title, the Supreme Council of the Armed Forces, can always do so – to dominate as it 'oversaw' events. The two groups were in a face-off over the future of Prime Minister Kamal El-Ganzoury, with the Brotherhood calling for his resignation.

The army could also complicate el Shater's aspirations by citing his criminal record. As a young dissident in the 1970s, Khairat el Shater, who was 62 in 2012, fled Sadat's Egypt to live in England. He returned to Cairo in 1984 and became active in business (making millions in textiles and furniture business) and in the Brotherhood. On 31 March 2012, he resigned his position as deputy to Supreme Guide Mohamed Badei and a member of the Guidance Council to become a presidential candidate.

With his wealth, el Shater has financially supported the Muslim Brotherhood, and Mubarak's government prosecuted him several times for 'giving money to an unlawful organisation'. In 2008 he was harshly sentenced to seven years in prison. Only when Mubarak's rule ended with the Arab Spring three years later was he pardoned from the remaining sentence, by SCAF's leader, Field Marshal Mohamed Hussein Tantawi.

Yet, as we sat talking, it became clear that for the ebullient Mahdi Akef the upcoming presidential election and the decision to go ahead with el Shater was simply another hurdle to leap in the worldwide long game.

'The Muslim Brotherhood has existed for many years in this battle for rights – through the 20th century and into the new millennium,' he said. 'We have survived and helped to make the world a more peaceful place by the work of good men like Youssef Nada. They have risked their lives. Youssef carried out missions, but only ever with the full backing and instruction of the Supreme Guide and the Brotherhood, around the world. Iran, Yemen, Iraq, Afghanistan, he's worked his miracles everywhere. He is the person the whole world – not just all the Muslim world – must listen to. He speaks the truth and not lies, for peace not war, for discussion together and not violence against one another.'

I asked Mahdi Akef if there was another international person who could match in status to Nada. He looked a little bewildered. I suggested that Youssef Nada was something of a Mandela figure. The former Supreme Guide and respected intellectual of the Muslim Brotherhood brought his fist down on his desk with a bang as his face flushed: 'Mandela! He was the President of a country who worked for one nation's rights. Youssef Nada is bigger than ten or twenty Mandelas. He is a champion of goodness – the man presidents listened to. Everyone should be privileged enough to hear the words of Youssef Nada. The world would benefit – especially the Americans.'

There are, as always, the Americans. They had been increasingly making clear their interests. When the US Embassy in Cairo invited the Brotherhood leadership to meetings with visitors from Washington, it was emphasized that the US dignitaries must come to their offices. And they did – without question. Mahdi Akef maintained the White House was acutely aware of what was happening in the region. Vast amounts of dollar bills were being waved around – influence, aid, help and all other manner of other temptations on offer for a Muslim Brotherhood who followed an American master's voice. Yankee-accented Fausts were in all the wrong places, as if in a bad production.

Mahdi Akef was boisterous at the thought of compromising deal-making: 'That is never going to happen. Egypt is full of natural resources and good people. Yes, the economy is in terrible shape, there is poverty and hardship but that is what we want to reverse. That is our goal. When the corruption is gone we will be able to look after ourselves and Egypt can speak for itself in the world. We had goldmines here which were sold to special connections for nine million American dollars. The real value was nine *billion* American dollars. That is but one small item of the corruption that has stripped this country for generations. We will work with whichever nations will help Egypt prosper. We are here to represent the people and not special interests.'

But what of the 'special interest' of the Muslim Brotherhood in the future of the Middle East, in Indonesia and Malaysia and around the globe? Clearly, with the Presidency and the Parliament under the Brotherhood's Islamic umbrella, few could doubt their influence and power – even if control is restricted by SCAF – in the Arab nation historically the champion of the region, the one the West must work with or against.

Their Freedom and Justice Party (FJP) which numbers a minority of Christian Copts, has constantly insisted it wants a new Constitution that respects Muslims and non–Muslims. The FJP maintains it will not impose misunderstood Islamic law and is committed to a pluralistic and democratic Egypt. Yet, the FJP and the Muslim Brotherhood are merging into an altogether new political landscape.

And they are not alone in the new revolution of political Islam. The more orthodox and hardline Salafi movement snaps at their heels every day. It trumped their presidential announcement when Hazem Salah Abou Ismail registered his presidential candidacy papers – 150,000 powers of attorney – 24 hours earlier than their candidate.

By that hot Friday evening of 30 March 2012, traffic around Cairo was bottlenecked. Abou Ismail's supporters lined the streets across the Egyptian capital, starting from Asad Ibn El-Forat Mosque in Dokki, through the Sixth of October Bridge and down Salah Salem Road in Heliopolis, the headquarters of the Presidential Election Committee. This people's march of endorsement was to prove the powers of attorney had not been forged – the Egyptian property world's favourite scam – as there were more people than proxies.

It wasn't provable either way if the crowds had been paid for. The leaflets were expensively published and campaign banners and posters with the long-bearded Abou Ismail smiling out at the voters. Many on the streets questioned who was paying for this Salafi bid for the Presidency. Most agreed vast amounts of financial support were from Saudi Arabia who endorse the Salafi doctrine – but always want, with their endeavours, to keep their American 'friends' happy.

From their gleaming Muqatam (FJP) HQ – the sign emblazoned on their entrance gate above the photograph of a newly sprouting plant reads in Arabic and English: 'We bring goodness for all people' – you can look across the city to the Cairo Tower landmark. Nasser built it with American blackmail dollars donated after he grabbed power and became the man to talk to. In so many ways, the ghost of Kermit 'Kim' Roosevelt and his grandfather's policies continue to hover over Egypt and the Muslim Brotherhood. And 'Roosevelt's folly' is a not-too-subtle aide memoire.

FAME AND CHANCE

'The problems of victory are more agreeable than those of defeat, but they are no less difficult.'

Winston Churchill

CAIRO, JUNE 2012

With the legacy of Kermit Roosevelt as a useful euphemism for the tactics and political agenda of America in the Middle East it requires recalling that Egypt is a nation ambushed by and dictated to by history.

By instinct if not heritage, Colonel Gamal Abdel Nasser was yet another pharaoh, a leader intent on absolute control and power. That authoritarian practise of government has persisted ever since: even after Hosni Mubarak was deposed and the subsequent guilty verdict against him for being an accessory to murder during the peoples' uprising of January, 2011. As Mubarak was sentenced on June 2, 2012, to life imprisonment for not preventing the killing of protesters during the people's uprising, one of the early questions asked on the streets and in the coffee shops of Cairo was just how lavish and luxurious his beachfront jail cell would be.

Mubarak's cronies, the military men he trained and rewarded in cash and medals, would be in charge of his 'punishment'. I was told that his military cronies had started creating a jailhouse 'villa' for him even before he left power. The handling of the 'democratic election' was that premeditated.

And Ahmed Shafiq, the former air force commander whom a shaken and disorientated Mubarak in the elapsing days of his rule appointed the nation's Prime Minister, had the Army's support in his run to become President of Egypt. He was the candidate for military control. For the status quo.

His prime opponents, as with Colonel Nasser sixty years earlier, were the Muslim Brotherhood.

A week is a long time in politics but in the Middle East time and events move even more extravagantly. Both backward and forward. As was soon to become disquietingly clear. The Egyptian junta's honeymoon with democracy never got down the aisle never mind marriage or consummation.

At the beginning of June, 2012, the Presidential race in Egypt with its worldwide implications from Beijing to Washington to a squeezed Europe was openly confrontational with the old enemies facing each other.

It was the world's worst nightmare. Or good against evil. It was this or that depending through which political prism it was being seen. I believe it was an inevitability of history.

The clock has been ticking irrevocably toward this High Noon between past and future.

The sudden Muslim Brotherhood decision to put forward a Presidential candidate — and it being the surprise Khairat el Shater — was swiftly countered by the Supreme Council of the Armed Forces. In a swift, chess move, they changed the game: they castled. They simply disqualified Shater and nine candidates from other groups from being eligible for the election. There was no appeal afforded against that. Shater was eliminated because of his 'criminal record' — the six-year prison term given to him by Mubarak's military court. Hazem Salah Abou Ismail of the Salafists was dismissed because his late mother had dual Egyptian–American citizenship – which he denies.

A lawyer and television cleric, Abou Ismail has an enthusiastic, ultraconservative following. They said his ban by Egypt's Electoral Commission was part of an American and Israeli plot against him. Shater saw what he described as fraud also as equally sinister: 'The military council is not serious about the handover of power but is looking for a figure that it can control from behind the curtains.' Shater accused the ruling SCARF of trying to fix the election by eliminating strong Islamist candidates. He called the Mubarak-appointed judges who comprise the Electoral Commission a gang.

Yet, the Muslim Brotherhood were going to confront them and the past they represented. Their new choice for the future President of Egypt was Mohamed Morsi, 60 in 2012, a committed Islamist, a member of the Brotherhood hierarchy in Cairo and a thoughtful man. The professor of engineering joined a dozen other candidates in the first round of Presidential voting. The result was a puzzle for many.

It was to be a run-off election between him and Ahmed Shafiq whom to so many Egyptians was the embodiment of the Mubarak era. He was against the 'Arab Spring' and an ardent Mubarak devotee. He is no man-of-the-people. He was derided as 'the pullover' for often being seeing wearing a navy blue sweater. But with SCARF support, the power of Egypt's 'deep state', he was never a pushover.

These two men were left from a field of 13 candidates who fragmented public opinion. Their three closest rivals, sharing about 50% of the vote, were the shoot-from-the-lip Abdel Moneim Aboul Fotouh who had left the Muslim Brotherhood to run for the Presidency; the Left-leaning journalist Hamdeen Sabahi; and Amr Moussa who served as Egypt's Foreign Minister under Mubarak. The people's choice was not clear cut but you could argue from the results that a majority were intent on living in a democratic nation rather than a dictatorship. Pre-election punditry that it was one or other – Islam vs the Military – was wrong; conventional wisdom about the make-up of the 21st Century centre of the Arab world was no more. The Copts made it clear that they would support Shafiq.

Morsi got 26% of the vote; his candidacy benefited from a more conservative constituency because of the disqualification of Abou Ismail but if he got the Salafists on his side then Ahmed Shafiq was helped by ghost votes. Ahmed Shafiq, 70 in 2012, found 24% electoral support. He had automatic backers with Egyptians who never supported the revolution and the Armed services and the police. Although…Egyptians serving the military and police force are forbidden from voting. Still, thousands of soldiers appeared to do just that – or help eligible voters give their support to the correct candidate. Ahmed Sahiq had the State with him – by order, by directives to vote for him.

But he was legitimately liked by a middle-Egypt fed up with chaotic public services and a nation and economy going nowhere but down. He had appeal to the Christian minority who were fed daily on scary stories of their place in an Islamist society of the Muslim Brotherhood. There was also an attraction in him being a military man – someone who could bring security back to the streets.

That, of course, that would also take the nation back to Mubarak. Or Sadat. Or Nasser. It's not the names that matter, only what they represent. During the election campaigns Ahmed Sahiq made clear his hardliner stance on the Muslim Brotherhood provoking memories of the days when Brotherhood members were jailed or monitored by State security. Especially before any elections.

The electoral confrontation – and this the country's first democratic presidential contest – was to elect a Mubarak clone or the man from the Muslim Brotherhood who could change their entire way of life. None of this was for the sensitive. 'Shafiq would be just like Mubarak, nothing more, nothing less,' said the businessman Magdy Mohamed adding: 'All of the democratic and judicial gains that Egyptians have accomplished would vanish. They might allow

Mubarak to go free.' A university student, Amr Shalabi, said: I have no choice now but to choose Shafiq. We can't allow the Brotherhood to take power.'

In the beginning it was that black and white. Soon, we had the enigma wrapped in the mystery, Egyptian style: whoever won couldn't win.

For whoever became the President would be in one of the hottest seats of power in the world. The pressure from inside Egypt, from around its borders and internationally would continue to be immense. The divide between the Islamists and those suspicious and fearful of them would remain.

It was in an attempt to bridge that divide that Mohamed Morsi who had been ridiculed by his opponents as a 'second choice' candidate, an understudy, grew into his Muslim Brotherhood mission. He had asserted himself in the first round of voting defeating the much higher profile Brotherhood 'face' Abel Moneim Aboul Fotouh. Voters had taken to him by the day, charmed by his manner against the more strident style of others. He was certainly more self assured, more like a winner. Now, he had to widen his appeal, broaden his church. He promised to work for everyone. Even the military. He offered a regiment of ideas. His tolerant thinking was directed to the many fearful of what might emerge from an Islamist-led Egypt.

But for the world, the hurdle of Palestine will always be present. Mohamed Morsi has been critical of Israel and its treatment of the Palestinians. The Muslim Brotherhood indicated it will act as an umbrella over Hamas and the rival Western supported Fatah faction hoping to merge them and renew pressure on Israel to recognise a Palestinian state.

Yet, he and his Presidential rival Ahmed Shafiq , said they would respect the peace treaty with Israel and Egypt's alliance with America. There will be fewer hazards for the new President in domestic rather than international affairs.

Mohamed Morsi said that under his administration, Christians

(10% of the population) would enjoy the same rights as Muslims and he would hire Coptic Christians as advisers in what he described as 'the institution of the presidency'. He did not oppose the construction of churches or Christian political parties" 'Copts are Egyptians who have the same rights stipulated in the law – most importantly, the freedom of belief and worship. We are ordered to protect churches like we do mosques.'

Further echoing the philosophy of Youssef Nada, he said the rights of women would be protected with no imposition of any dress code (*see appendix*) including the Islamic headscarf: 'Women have a right to freely choose the attire that suits them.'

Mohamed Morsi, who got his PhD at the University of Southern California (USC), vowed to work with a political cabinet: 'I am committed to the presidency being an institution. It will never again be an individual.'

He said he would form a coalition government with the parliamentary parties. He then reached out to the uniformed men who have ruled Egypt for sixty years. The young revolutionaries from the streets, from the horrors of Tahrir Square, have vocally called for the imprisonment and execution of the men from SCARF. But the Muslim Brotherhood candidate in a vain attempt to keep the peace offered: 'There is not a single Egyptian who doesn't like the military. The military played a glorious rule in protecting the revolution. There were mistakes, yes, but also positive steps. Among those positive steps is the elections held under the protection of the police and military.'

He said the government would not necessarily be led by a Prime Minister from the Brotherhood's political partner, the Freedom and Justice Party: and he was open to candidates who'd lost in the first round of Presidential voting to join him in office: 'I want there to be vice-presidents who are not from the Muslim Brotherhood or Freedom and Justice. I want aides and advisers who are capable of imparting real experience and real advice. I want counsellors in all fields.'

His victory would change all. It would endorse the Muslim Brotherhood's world status and strengthen the Brotherhood's place in Egyptian life and politics where they already controlled the parliament. For the military that was a most fearful thought. It would also most likely result in an almighty confrontation between the military who have enforced their will since 1952 and the Muslim Brotherhood who have pledged to accept what they are unable to change by peaceful means. Before the final count there was talk of Army-led coups, bloody street protests - a miserable and deadly continuation of unease and injustice and unaccountable death — no matter which of the two contenders won.

And on Thursday, June 14, 2012, on the eve of the Presidential run-off the military staged their 21st-century version of a coup d'état. It was a blinder.

When the 'Arab Spring' had bloomed in 2011 and the world became excited I initially found Youssef Nada's lack of enthusiasm difficult to understand. I quickly understood when he explained that after a lifetime of experience he knew that this was only the first tiny step. He was convinced the military would, after a cosmetic period, once again take firm control. The answer would be to understand it, accept it, and those with a passion for change would have to redeploy.

Events happened with a momentum and shape which he had so precisely forecast. It didn't cheer him.

'It's sad,' he told me, ' for the Army simply went by the instruction book and divided all the opposition — they were squabbling with each other — and ruled. They had plotted for the moment — they never left the stage these men of Mubarak. The time curtain falls and another thick curtain of forgetfulness was extended.'

Indeed, when SCARF made their play, those of the Left, the liberals and the Islamists, the stalwarts of Tahrir Square and public rebellion, were a lost group, mistrustful of each other. As the strongest opposition party the Brotherhood suffered most, targeted by the military's propaganda machine and tripped at times by their own fledgling grasp of power. Across the world the millions of Muslim Brotherhood followers had watched Egypt's political transition and followed all the manipulations, the twisting and turning and reversing of the rules. They all too well knew the background, many of whom had the scarred bodies and minds as testimony.

Still, there were those dismayed when the nation's constitutional court, stuffed with Mubarak appointees, dissolved the only recently elected parliament saying it was unconstitutional: 48 hours before the first presidential run-off elections ever. 'It's the worst possible outcome imaginable,' said monitor Shadi Hamid adding: 'This was masterfully played and took us by surprise.'

For the Muslim Brotherhood who had the largest share of parliamentary seats the loss in this cleverly calculated counter-revolution by the old guard was clearly greatest. The Brotherhood had expected such a tactic and it was the main reason they broke their promise not to field a presidential candidate. It harmed their credibility but – and as event proved – it left them with a player in the democratic arena. Albeit it not a very level one.

There are a host of parallels with events in Algeria in 1991, when after Islamists won a democratic poll the Army suspended a second-round of elections, introduced emergency laws which gave them special powers and a decade of chaos and death began. There was torture, the arrest of elected officials and a horrific guerrilla war.

By Presidential Election Weekend in Cairo, June, 2012, the military had given themselves emergency powers of arrest and the parallels were more apparent. The new laws meant the Army could do anything they wanted to contain and keep control. And which they would most readily do. They also knew the Brotherhood would accept events rather than provoke a situation which could lead to death or injury of anyone. They'd been checkmated by the military.

The court which dissolved parliament is Egypt's highest and once was known for its independence. But under Mubarak the State intervened with his arrangement of senior judges loyal to him. Politics came before protocol. Or justice. The judges didn't make a snap decision to dissolve parliament. It has pronounced on politically sensitive issues, including the legitimacy of electoral rules or whether laws comply with constitutional provisions derived from Islamic law. It was always believed that this was to engineer that Mubarak's son Gamal took over power from him.

The constitutional court ruling meant that whomever won the election would have no legislative body with which to work: It also disbanded the 100-member assembly formed to write a new constitution which would define and control Presidential power. If you know the result in advance that doesn't really matter.

It was a pantomime: the Presidential run-off involved a Muslim Brotherhood candidate whose parliamentary power base of had been dissolved by the supporters of his opponent. Who also insured they had a candidate: in a separate decision, the court also affirmed the rejection of a law passed by the Islamist-dominated parliament that would have barred former ranking officials of the Mubarak regime from running for higher office. This upheld the candidacy of the Army President of choice, Hosni Mubarak's former Prime Minister, Ahmed Shafiq.

After the ruling and the change of the game, Mr Shafiq praised the court for its historic decision. He would, of course. Prolonging the transition and all but stopping it in its tracks has been an uneasy move for the military rulers of Egypt. The economy is a mess. Millions are starving. The future is bleak. Where are the resources to send the nation forward? And what are they?

Hope, as much as anything, for that's what evolved following the long, long days of perplexity. Finally, on 24 June 2012, what once had seemed impossible happened. From this limbo, Mohamed Morsi of the Muslim Brotherhood, the decades-outlawed, persecuted and pilloried organisation, became the first democratically elected President of Egypt in more than seven thousand years. The result also defied decades of dictatorship and much of the world's opinion makers. The first civilian leader won 51.73% of the vote against the soon-to-be-self-exiled

Ahmed Shafiq's 48.27%. Tahrir Square went wild. Images of the jubilation, the riotous celebrations, went worldwide electronically. It was a special moment. It was history. So much remains uncertain but that Sunday afternoon in Cairo it felt as if there had most definitely been a revolution. It wasn't easy and it wasn't quick. Youssef Nada was happy. Within 24 hours he had an emotional telephone call from President Morsi. Later, he said to me: 'This is politics. I told you that you must learn patience.'

With Youssef Nada's story, we've also learned the struggle for the ultimate prize of decency of life is a perilous pageant.

APPENDIX 1

With all the many problems and questions, myths and predictions which have encircled the Muslim Brotherhood throughout its existence one subject almost always gets mentioned: its attitude to how women should dress. It goes directly to the place in society of men and women. As such it so much part of the 21st century discussion from East to West. The world has changed since University of Kansas scholar Dr Jeffrey Lang published his book *Struggling to Surrender* in 1994. But Youssef Nada believes Dr Lang's interpretations are correct and points to his work as a contribution to understanding.

Lang states:

In pre-Islamic times, the customary attire of the Arab tribal woman consisted of an ornamental head covering that hung down her back and showed her hair in front, a loosely worn tunic that was cut low in front leaving her breasts in view, and a skirt tied at the waist, together with various pieces of jewellery, such as rings, earrings, arm and ankle bracelets.

This style of dress, which was not only alluring but also

compensated for the intense desert heat, could still be found among certain Bedouin women in Arabia up to the turn of this century and was photographed by certain European travellers. The Koran's instruction to the believing women to draw their head coverings (*khimar*, plural, *khumur*) over their bosoms (24:31) and to put on their outer garments when they were in public (33:59), imposed, with the minimum of inconvenience, a modest standard of dress for Muslim women. As 24:31 goes on to say, they can resume the customary attire in their own homes in the presence of their immediate families and household servants. It becomes clear from the Prophetic traditions associated with these verses, in particular those related to (33:59), that sexual abuse is the concern here. And since society is always more apt to exploit women sexually rather than men, special emphasis is placed on the dress of the former. Over time, jurists elaborated a strict dress code for Muslim women. However, the wearing of the *khimar* as described in 24: 31, when combined with an outer garment of the kind mentioned in 33:59, probably closely approximated later elaborations. The earliest records of juristic discussion on this matter, going back to the generations of the Prophet's Companions and their successors, centred on the debate of whether a woman had to veil her face in public, or if it was appropriate for her hands and face to show? The latter was the majority opinion and has remained the standard ever since, but this does not mean that all women in the Islamic world recognize a single canonical attire, for there is considerable variation. For example, many Egyptian women cover their hair but allow their necks to show; Malaysian women sometimes wear pants underneath a long bib; Saudi ladies wrap one end of the head-covering loosely around the neck several times; and Iranian women frequently wear their scarves low on their foreheads so that their eyebrows cannot be seen. However, there is a nearly universal acceptance that only a woman's face and hands may be seen. This is not to imply that there are no dissenting opinions, for one can easily imagine the hardships encountered by Muslim ladies travelling and living in non-Muslim societies. To date, the strongest and most obvious argument for greater flexibility comes from Muhammad Asad:

Although the traditional exponents of Islamic law have for centuries been inclined to restrict the definition of 'what may (decently) be apparent' to a woman's face, hands and feet-and sometimes less than that-we may safely assume that the meaning of *illa ma zahara minha* is much wider, and that the deliberate vagueness of the phrase is meant to allow for all time-bound changes that are necessary for man's moral and social growth. The pivotal clause in the above injunction is the demand, addressed in identical terms to men as well as to women, to 'lower their gaze and be mindful of their chastity': and this determines the extent of what, at any given time, may legitimately − i.e. in consonance with Koranic principles of social morality-be considered 'decent' or 'indecent' in a person's outward appearance...

Hence, the injunction to cover the bosom with a *khimar* (a term so familiar to the contemporaries of the Prophet) does not necessarily relate to the use of a *khimar* as such but is, rather, meant to make it clear that a woman's breasts are not included in the concept of 'what may decently be apparent' of her body and should not, therefore be displayed...

The specific time-bound formulation of the above verse [33:59] (evident by the reference to the wives and daughters of the Prophet), as well as the deliberate vagueness of the recommendation that women 'should draw upon themselves some of their outer garments (*min jalabibihinna*)' when in public, makes it clear that the verse was not meant to be an injunction (*hukm*) in the general, timeless sense of this term but, rather, a moral guideline to be observed against the ever changing background of time and social environment. This finding is reinforced by the concluding reference to God's forgiveness and grace. The cogency of Asad's argument is somewhat diminished by his assertion that the restriction against a woman baring her breast is timeless, for if one 'covering' has eternal validity, why not the other? The charge of eclecticism will surely be raised, and indeed whenever a new interpretation is advocated in light of changed circumstances, such a charge has to be expected. The vagueness of the verses on certain points definitely provides room for different cultural adaptations and, as already shown, there have been many. But the issue at hand is one of extent. So far, on matters like these, I and other writers have advocated that those involved try to discern the overall direction of the Koran when responding to a given verse. For instance, as remarked previously, Muslims no longer insist upon gathering up horses in preparation for battle, even though that is the explicit dictate of 8:60, because it would not advance the larger objective of making adequate preparations for war. Therefore, in the present case, we might first determine whether or not the Muslim community should observe at least some minimal standard of modesty in dress. Probably all believers, based on 24:31, will concede this much, as does Muhammad Asad in his commentary on the passage. They would also most likely agree that the dress code inherited from the earliest Muslim community and handed down from one generation to the next was certainly appropriate in the past and in conformity with the injunctions of the Koran.

It then might be asked, at what stage did it become advisable or allowable for Muslims to assume Western norms. It would be hard to find a moral or psychological justification for such a change. In fact, in Islam at the Crossroads, Asad himself urged Muslims at the early part of this century not to adopt Western standards? In a revised edition that appeared a half of century later, he made no apology for that view and held that it was appropriate in its time. But, he stated, in the years since-then, the Muslim people had so absorbed Western cultural values that to attempt to return to earlier norms would be as senseless as the original adoption of Western styles. In his opinion, it would amount to no more than 'another act of sterile and undignified imitation: in this case, the imitation of a dead and unreturnable past'. In other words, the social mores, for better or worse, have in fact changed as an inevitable consequence of encountering a more powerful civilization. As a result, what was considered as exploitive or indecent dress in the past is simply no longer considered so today. Many Muslims will not be persuaded by this argument, for it is a main part of the believer's perception that religion sets moral standards for society and not the converse. Furthermore, even though in practice women often do not conform to the traditional dress code, this very code, as an ideal, is upheld almost universally by Muslims of both sexes; recently the global Muslim community has even witnessed the reappearance of traditional women's dress on a large scale. Finally, the traditional dress of women conforms to the spirit of the Koran and fourteen centuries of custom, and would deter what Muslims view as the sexual exploitation of women in the West.

I therefore feel that the case for any real revision on this matter is not entirely convincing. On the other hand, there is a desperate need for the community to exercise sympathy and understanding toward those who are grappling with this problem, in particular Muslim women living in the West. The difficulties and hardships-emotional, social, employment-wise-encountered in conforming to this code vary from individual to individual, and the approach of the Muslim should be conciliatory and accommodating rather than accusatory and reproachful. The utmost allowances must be made so that Muslim women are not dissuaded from community participation. Muslim men should also show the greatest sensitivity and propriety in this regard. It was not long ago that I witnessed the absurd spectacle of Muslim women, fully dressed, languishing at a picnic table under the hot summer sun while their spouses frolicked in the sand and waves amidst American sunbathers. It will be some time before American and European Muslim women find fashions that harmonize with their culture and religion. But if the demand should grow, then this will surely happen. For now, I would suggest a community attitude on this matter in line with the evocation that concludes 33:59, which reminds the reader of God's forgiveness and compassion. Perhaps this is, as Asad suggests, an acknowledgment of the future difficulties that Muslims will meet in this area and a call for clemency on the part of believers in their efforts to surmount them, for truly 'God does not burden any soul beyond its capacity' (2:233). And they ask you for a judgement concerning women. Say: 'God gives you [believers] a judgment concerning them'. (4:127) And they would continue to ask up to the present. Throughout history, religion has not been kind to women, for male-dominated orthodoxies fused cultural biases and aversions with dogma, law, and scriptural commentary. Twentieth-century society was bound to inquire into them, for how can God Himself have rendered such a low judgment concerning the character and place of women? Western Muslims, detached and/or severed from the cultures that have kept and preserved Islam, are discovering in the Koran and Islam a different view of women from the one they had harboured in the past. It is true that the 'male and female are not the same,' and any honest reading has to accept this as a Koranic precept. But this is not to say that one is more naturally intelligent or pious than the other. Rather, it means that their personalities profoundly balance and augment each other in ways that are well-suited to all the changes that society will experience. Equally true – and this accords with the Koran and the traditions – is that there is something in the characters of the two sexes that allows men to assume leadership and dominance more readily than women. Yet this reality does not imply that women are not fit to lead, learn, and participate, for I believe that Islam's textual sources are clearly open to this possibility. One thing that it does mean is that society must be alert to the abuse of women, because throughout the Koran one finds repeated injunctions and warnings against such mistreatment. A verse such as God has indeed heard the words of her who disputed with you concerning her husband and complained [about him] to God, and God hears the conversation between the two of you. Truly God is All-Hearing, All-Seeing (58:1), which addresses a common injustice committed by men of seventh-century Arabia, must, because of the obvious cultural specificity of the following verse, be read as a universal warning, to be forever heeded by the Muslim community. A faithful interpretation of Islam by modem Muslims most probably will not agree completely with twentieth-century feminists' platforms, nor will it agree with many of the views about women found in earlier Muslim scholarship. Once again, as on so many issues, the Muslim community finds itself forced into being a people of the middle way' (2:143) in its struggle to work out what it means to be a Muslim man or woman in the modern world.

CHAPTER ONE

APPENDIX 2:
DOCUMENTS DOSSIER

Origin: Embassy Cairo

Classification: CONFIDENTIAL

Destination:

Header: VZCZCXYZ0000PP RUEHWEBDE RUEHEG #1976/01 2920752ZNY CCCCC ZZHP 190752Z OCT 09FM AMEMBASSY CAIROTO RUEHC/SECSTATE WASHDC PRIORITY 3905INFO RUEHTV/AMEMBASSY TEL AVIV PRIORITY 1967RUEHJM/AMCONSUL JERUSALEM PRIORITY 1218RUEATRS/DEPT OF TREASURY WASHDC PRIORITY

Tags: EFIN, KN, PTER, ECON, PGOV, EG

CONFIDENTIAL CAIRO 001976 SIPDIS E.O. 12958: DECL: 10/12/2019 TAGS: EFIN, KN, PTER, ECON, PGOV, EG SUBJECT: TREASURY DAS DANIEL GLASER, S MEETINGS WITH MINISTRY OF FOREIGN AFFAIRS AND THE CENTRAL BANK Classified By: MINISTER COUNSELOR DONALD A. BLOME REASONS: 1.4 (B) and (D)

1.(SBU) Key points: Egyptian officials are unsure how funds destined for Hamas enter Egypt. The GOE is unhappy that the United Nations delisted Youssef Mustapha Nada from its UNSCR 1267 consolidated list of individuals or entities associated with Al-Qaida or the Taliban. At the request of the Palestinian Authority, the Egyptian Central Bank instructed all Egyptian banks to avoid doing business with the Hamas-affiliated National Islamic Bank on August 26, 2009.

2.(U) Treasury DAS Glaser met with Assistant Foreign Minister Coordinator for Counter Terrorism Ashraf Mohsen and Central Bank Governor Hisham Ramez on October 4 to discuss a broad range of terrorist financing and anti-money laundering issues in Egypt. Terrorist Financing in and through Egypt

3.(C) Mohsen asserted that he was not well briefed on the issues of funds destined for Hamas passing from Egypt into Gaza via tunnels. He surmised that money coming into Egypt destined for Hamas probably came via cash couriers, Arab tourists, and diplomats whose bags are not subject to search by customs officials. Mohsen stated that the GOE had no intention of creating a terrorist list of its own. He pointed out that, if the GOE proscribed Hamas domestically, no Egyptian official would be able to meet with Hamas about the peace process with Israel. Mohsen also worried that listing Hezbollah would 'legitimize' the organization and boost its prominence in Egypt.

4.(C) DAS Daniel Glaser requested information on Abdel Moneim Abdel-Fotouh and several other Muslim Brotherhood (MB) members arrested for conspiring with foreign organizations and money laundering. Mohsen said the GOE could not share any information on the case until their court trial was over. According to Mohsen, the prosecutor general has yet to file the case. GOE Upset about Nada Delisting

5.(C) Mohsen indicated that his government was unhappy with the United Nations 1267 Committee's removal of Youssef Mustapha Nada from its UNSCR 1267 consolidated list of individuals or entities associated with Al-Qaida or the Taliban. Mohsen referred to Nada as the Muslim Brotherhood's most important financier and that the MB sees Nada's delisting as a symbolic victory. Hinting at U.S. complicity in the 1267 Committee's decision to delist Nada, Mohsen said he saw contradiction between Nada's delisting and the USG's request to discuss Hamas with the GOE. Central Bank Diligent in Monitoring Financial Transactions

6.(C) DAS Glaser also met with Deputy Central Bank Governor Hisham Ramez to discuss safeguards against terrorist financing and other anti-money laundering issues. When queried about funding for Hamas that transited Egypt, Ramez guessed that such funding probably came via wire transfers. (COMMENT: Neither Mohsen nor Ramez seemed to have a good handle on the issue of funding for Hamas that transited Egypt. END COMMENT.) On North Korea, Ramez stated that North Korean financial activity was not a big issue in Egypt. Besides, he added, the Central Bank exercised a hands-on approach to monitoring risks to Egyptian financial institutions. For example, the Central Bank examines every foreign exchange transaction in the Egyptian banking system on an hourly basis to maintain stable exchange rates as well as detecting possible links to money laundering or terrorist financing.

7.(C) DAS Glaser asked whether the Egyptian Central Bank received a letter from Jihad al-Wazir, Governor of the Palestinian Monetary Authority, requesting that all Central Banks in the region not allow the Hamas-affiliated National Islamic Bank access to financial institutions in their jurisdictions. Ramez acknowledged the letter and stated that the Central Bank on August 26, 2009, instructed all Egyptian banks to avoid doing business with the National Islamic Bank.

8.(U) The Department of Treasury cleared on this cable. Scobey

MINISTERO PUBBLICO DELLA CONFEDERAZIONE
PROCURA FEDERALA

Taubenstrasse 16

☎ +41 (0)31 322 45 79
fax +41 (0)31 322 45 07
e-mail claude.nicati@ba.admin.ch
Votre Réf.
Notre Réf. BA/D40/01/BTE Nic

Berne, 23th January 2002

Department of the Treasury
Mister George B. Wolfe
Deputy General Counsel
By fax: 001 202 622 19 11 and via Swiss
Federal Office of Justice

Al Taqwa / Nada Managment Organization; your letter from January 4, 2002

Mister Deputy General Counsel,

Dear Mister Wolfe,

Thank You for your letter dated from January 4, 2002. I have read it with interest.

When I was in Washington on the 26th of November 2001, I received the guarantee from the General Counsel to get all informations You have about Nada / Al Taqwa. I was more than disappointed when I received Your letter. This does not give more informations that I already have and the only explanations I received are so general and without details that I can not use these to go on with my investigations.

To be clear I shall quote the content of Your letter and take the extract to ask You some more questions. I repeat what is important for me is to have elements that I may use to do one or more steps further in investigations in Switzerland and in the rest of the world against this firm and the directory from Nada / Al Taqwa:

Ad page 1: "...involved in financial radical groups like the Palestinian HAMAS, Algeria's Islamic Salvation Front and Armed Islamic Group, and Tunisia's An-Nahda."

- What are the demonstrable facts for a correlation between AL TAQWA and groups like ARMED ISLAMIC GROUP, ISLAMIC SALVATION FRONT and AN-NAHDA?
- Do You have informations about MOKDAD LAZHAR, born 13.03.1956, in connection with the Bank Al Taqwa??

Ad page 2: "in 1997, it was reported that $60 million collected annually for HAMAS from all parts of the world were moved to account with AL Taqwa"

- What does that means exactly?
- Who gave You this information?

- Is that a secret information?
- Do You have the demonstration from this information?
- On which Bank account?
- At which date?

Embassy of the United States of America

Bundesanwaltschaft / MPC

EINGANG

Zuordnung / Charkation

TO: Bundesamt fur Polizei, Terrorism Taskforce

FROM: Federal Bureau of Investigation, Terrorist Financial Review Group
           United States Department of the Treasury, Operation Green Quest

DATE: April 12, 2002

RE: ON SITE REVIEW IN BERNE OF RECORDS SEIZED RELATING TO AL
           TAQWA BANK and YOUSSEF NADA

From April 2, 2002 to April 12, 2002, the Bundesamt fur Polizei, Swiss Federal Office
for Police, Terrorism Task Force, hosted a delegation of agents and analysts from the
Federal Bureau of Investigation (FBI) and the United States Department of the Treasury
(DOT), allowing them full access to review the records seized by the Swiss Federal
Police during searches executed in November 2001. The searches were conducted in
conjunction with an investigation into alleged ties to terrorism concerning Youssef Nada
and his businesses Al Taqwa Bank and Al Taqwa Management.

The Swiss Federal Police were extremely helpful in this endeavor and provided full
unrestricted access to the seized documents, timely responses to any and all questions
posed by the delegation regarding the seized documents and an excellent work space
to review these documents. The assistance provided to this delegation, both
professionally and personally, was exceptional in every regard, and the delegation
wishes to express their sincere appreciation for such cooperation.

The delegation consisted of the following individuals:

   SA H. Dandridge Myles, FBI Terrorism Financial Review Group, 001-202-324-
   8836

   SA Thomas A. McCabe, FBI Terrorism Financial Review Group, 001-202-324-
   8521

   Analyst Lise Herbert, FBI Terrorism Financial Review Group, 001-202-324-9929

   Analyst Kelly Emerson, FBI Terrorism Financial Review Group, 001-202-324-
   3814

   SSA Todd Nevins, Treasury Department, Operation Green Quest, 001-770-994-

Page 1 of 4

4191

Programs Officer Jennifer Houghton, Treasury Department, Operation Green Quest, 001-202-927-6702

SA C. Steve Howard, Treasury Department, Operation Green Quest, 001-202-927-6926

GOALS

The delegation's goal was to review the documents seized in order to determine if sufficient financial ties to terrorism existed in order to request a Mutual Legal Assistance Treaty (MLAT). The method employed by the delegation was to review the documents and to extract any individual names, company names, addresses, telephone numbers, email addresses, and bank account numbers located in the documents and to process this information through the Terrorist Financial Review Group and Operation Green Quest criminal databases. Any responses or matches would be reviewed by the delegation, and if sufficient ties existed to terrorism, the delegation would then recommend that an MLAT request be produced and provided to the Swiss Federal Police. The delegation would provide the Swiss Federal Police with their findings and further investigative needs would be determined at that time.

REVIEW

The delegation was provided with access to seven cabinets of general business documents, including but not limited to invoices, stockholder balance statements, business correspondence, bank records and background information. Additionally, the delegation was provided with access to various videotapes and electronic media seized from the locations. These documents were in Arabic, Italian, German, French, and English. The records were seized from the Lugano office of Al Taqwa Management, the residence of Ahmad Huber, previously known as Albert Huber, the residence of Youssef Nada, the residence of Ali Ghaleb Himmat, and the Vaduz office of ASAT Trust.

The delegation performed a cursory review of all of the documents with the exception of the electronic media. After a cursory review was performed, the delegation then proceeded to review the documents in a detailed manner, extracting any names, company names, addresses, telephone numbers, email addresses, and bank account numbers. The documents were prioritized and bank records and stockholder records were reviewed in their entirety. Approximately seventy percent of the remaining records were reviewed by the delegation in detail.

The delegation provided a daily report of the extracted information to the Swiss Federal Police and to the FBI and Treasury offices in the United States. Each day at 11:00 a.m. the delegation met with the Terrorism Task Force at which time they would provide the

Page 2 of 4

U.S. Department of Justice

Federal Bureau of Investigation

Washington, D.C. 20535-0001

June 26, 2003

BY LIAISON

**ALI GHALEB HIMMAT,
YUSEF MOHAMAD NADA,
AND THE AL TAQWA MANAGEMENT ORGANIZATION**

(S) Per your request, dated 03/25/2003, the FBI
conducted a search of its records for information pertaining to
Ali Ghaleb Himmat, Yusef Mohamad Nada, and the al Taqwa
Management Organization. The information found in our databases
is the same information which you have provided to us. We
currently have no ongoing investigations on the above
individuals.

(S) With regard to the 141 pictures which you would
like to have circulated among the prisoners at Guantanamo, this
may be a possibility, provided you narrow the scope of the
parameters as to which detainees should view the photos. For
example, people captured in the same location where the meeting
took place, or members of an organization with whom the meeting
related, or specific Guantanamo detainees that you have knowledge
of that you feel should view the photos.

DEPARTMENT OF THE TREASURY
OFFICE OF PUBLIC AFFAIRS

EMBARGOED UNTIL
2:00 PM June 26, 2003

Contact: Taylor Griffin
(202) 622-2960

Written Testimony of David D. Aufhauser
General Counsel, Department of the Treasury
Before the Senate Judiciary Committee
Subcommittee on Terrorism, Technology and Homeland Security
June 26, 2003 2:00 p.m.
The United States Senate

The Threat of Terrorist Financing

Chairman Kyl and distinguished Members of the Subcommittee on Terrorism, Technology and Homeland Security, thank you for inviting me to testify today about the threat posed by those who fund terrorism and what can be done to keep that money from getting into the hands of terrorists.

I want to take a moment to emphasize that the terrorist financing strategy of the United States government does not target any particular faith or sect. We are not at war with a religion, but rather with terrorists who sometimes masquerade as its champion. It is a difficult challenge to distinguish between an austere, uncompromising and intolerant view of faith from extremism and fanaticism that purposely seeks the blood of children.

Terrorist supporters also corrupt otherwise legitimate companies to either raise or move funds for terrorists. Such activity, as with the abuse of charitable organizations, is particularly nefarious since this may occur without the knowledge of other shareholders, employees, or customers.

To date, the United States has taken strong action to shut down such front companies and businesses which have become corrupted by the influences of terrorist financiers and to strip away the otherwise legitimate holdings of those individuals who finance and abet terror. For example, we worked closely with our partners in the Caribbean and Europe for nearly a year to unearth the insidious network of financial houses and investment firms used by the European and Caribbean-based al Qaida supporters, Youssef Nada and Ahmed Idris Nasreddin. These companies were then publicly designated, shut down, and acted against by the United Nations for their ties to al Qaida in a joint action between the U.S., Italy, Switzerland, Luxembourg, and the Bahamas. We have also publicly designated a network of honey shops and bakeries in Yemen that funded al Qaida's operations as well as the front companies for the European-based al Qaida supporter, Mamoun Darkanzali.

We continue to monitor, analyze, and investigate the links between businesses, in the United States and elsewhere, and terrorist groups. Using Bank Secrecy Act data and analysis provided by the Financial Crimes Enforcement Network (FinCEN) and other relevant law enforcement resources, we are able to target suspicious business activities and anomalous transactions. This type of methodical investigative and analytical work will continue to uncover networks of businesses used to generate and funnel money to terrorist groups.

8

Testimony of Steven Emerson
Executive Director, The Investigative Project
Before the House Financial Services Committee
Subcommittee on Oversight and Investigations
May 18, 2004

The Investigative Project
5505 Connecticut Ave., NW, #341
Washington, DC 20015
Phone 202-363-8602
Fax 202-966-5191
Email: Stopterror@aol.com

31/03 2005 DO 13:35   FAX   ☎008/016

Introduction

Madame Chairwoman, Ranking Member Gutierrez, Chairman Oxley, Ranking Member Frank, and all Members of the Committee, thank you for inviting me to participate in this hearing. I commend you on assembling the best panel of private-sector experts on money laundering issues that I have seen at a Congressional hearing in the past two years. They are some of the most influential, knowledgeable, and dedicated experts in the United States and, indeed, the world. I want to thank Jon Levin and Dana Lesemann of The Investigative Project for their work in preparing this testimony.

We are here today to examine whether the Riggs case represents the exception to the rule or the tip of the iceberg. Riggs Bank's failure to file Suspicious Activity Reports (or "SARs") in deference to its clients' desire for secrecy is the single most serious breach ever in the first line of U.S. financial controls against terrorism, and the bank officials who participated in these willful violations should be held personally responsible. SARs are integral to identifying and interdicting illegal assets in the United States. I urge this Committee to conduct a thorough review of the examinations conducted by financial regulators of Riggs and other major financial institutions to see what the regulators knew or should have known of gaps in anti-money-laundering systems.

In at least one instance that I can discuss, a major financial institution cut ties with a terrorist-linked bank upon being advised to do so. In 2000 and 2001, Citigroup was participating in joint ventures with al-Aqsa Bank, which has ties to Hamas. When informed by the Israeli government of those ties, Citigroup contacted the United States Treasury for guidance and subsequently terminated its relationship with al-Aqsa Bank. The question is this: What is the true paradigm? Is it Citigroup's taking the initiative with the Treasury Department or is it Riggs Bank's failure to comply with government mandates? The answer to this question will be critical to determining how you formulate effective measures to interdict terrorism-related transactions in the future.

For those companies that do defy U.S. regulations or fail to prevent their employees from doing so, the recent $100 million fine against Switzerland's UBS AG is a crystal-clear illustration that any short-term profits produced by defying U.S. law will ultimately be overwhelmed by the repercussions of being caught. UBS likely avoided even greater censure by demonstrating that its violations were not part of a greater disregard for financial controls but were isolated actions taken by employees acting contrary to company policy.

However, al-Qaeda has established its own banking system outside of European and U.S. law. Al-Taqwa Bank was created by the Muslim Brotherhood in 1988 to move and safeguard large quantities of cash for terrorist causes; it was finally designated a terrorist entity by U.S. authorities in 2001.

Al-Qaeda and other terrorist organizations have also found innumerable cracks in the financial structures of western nations and exploit the lack of regulation in third-world countries to obscure the sources and destinations of their funds. How has the private sector responded to the revelation that al-Taqwa was a terrorist front? Were private-sector institutions aware of al-Taqwa's links to terror and did they turn a blind eye before the government's designation? Did al-Taqwa's business partners cooperate with U.S. and European investigators once they were made aware of al-Taqwa's links to terrorism? These questions will require your attention and oversight; the answers will guide your approach to regulation of this industry.

As far as maintaining oversight over domestic transactions, the U.S. must continue a multi-pronged approach to countering terrorist money trafficking in the formal international financial

2

According to President Bush, Bank al-Taqwa is "an association of offshore banks and financial management firms that have helped al-Qaeda shift money around the world."[27] Al-Taqwa was founded as the first step in "establishing a world bank for fundamentalists" and to compete with Western financial institutions.[28] Al-Taqwa's connections to al-Qaeda led the Bush administration to freeze al-Taqwa's assets on November 7, 2001.[29]

In January, 2002, the Treasury Deputy General Counsel wrote to Swiss official M. Claude Nacati that, "Bank al-Taqwa...was established in 1988 with significant backing from the Egyptian Muslim Brotherhood, and it has long been thought to be involved in financing radical groups like the Palestinian HAMAS, Algeria's Islamic Salvation Front, and Armed Islamic Group, and Tunisia's An-Nahda."[30] The Deputy General Counsel also wrote that, "[a]s of October, 2000 Bank Al Taqwa appeared to be providing a clandestine line of credit for a close associate of Usama bin Laden."[31] Al-Taqwa reportedly has offices and activities from Panama to Kuwait.[32]

Unlike al-Aqsa Bank or Beit al-Ma'al, al-Taqwa Bank was able to function entirely on its own, without relying on the patronage of a larger organization. By avoiding interaction with the legal financial community, terrorist organizations evade government regulations such as SAR reports entirely. Indeed, although it is not yet clear whether Riggs Bank made a simple business decision that not filings SARs would be beneficial to its standing among its target clientele or in fact instituted procedures to defy federal regulations, al-Taqwa and other terrorist institutions exist specifically to design means of circumventing government controls.

Al-Qaeda and other terrorist organizations have diversified means of obtaining cash, both legally and illegally, which must be passed from its multitude of sources to many fewer end-users without identifying the carriers, the means of passage, or the receivers. All of the produce of terrorist schemes involving counterfeit baby formula, CDs, and DVDs, schemes to profit on un-taxed cigarettes and other products, credit card fraud, smuggling, and a slew of other petty crimes must be laundered. While hawalas and suitcases full of cash have served to pass significant quantities of cash, al-Qaeda's financial apparatus is integral to the smooth operation of al-Qaeda's network of members and affiliates.

Indeed, Osama bin Laden came to prominence among the Afghan Mujahideen precisely because of his talent for moving men and money around the world without governmental interference. Every government victory in interdicting terrorist finances today is being examined by our enemies for lessons-learned, which are then incorporated into the organizations and companies replacing those we have shut down.

---

[27] "President Announces Crackdown on Terrorist Financial Network," November 7, 2001, http://www.state.gov/s/ct/rls/rm/2001/5982.htm.
[28] Bodansky, Yossef, "Iran's Pincer Movement Gives it a Strong Say in the Gulf and Red Sea," Defense & Foreign Affairs' Strategic Policy, March, 1992.
[29] Executive Order No. 13224, September 23, 2001. 31 CFR Part 595-597, in Annex dated November 7, 2001.
[30] Letter from George B. Wolfe, Deputy General Counsel of the U.S. Department of the Treasury, to M. Claude Nicati, Substitut du Procureur General, Switzerland, January 4, 2002.
[31] Letter from George B. Wolfe, Deputy General Counsel of the U.S. Department of the Treasury, to M. Claude Nicati, Substitut du Procureur General, Switzerland, January 4, 2002.
[32] "Money Laundering Probe to Look at Possible Bin Laden Link," Agence France Presse, September 23, 2001, and Executive Order No. 13224, September 23, 2001, 31 CFR Part 595-597, in Annex dated November 7, 2001. Various sources have referenced al-Taqwa activity in Liechtenstein, Italy, Malta, Panama, Switzerland, France, Kuwait, the United Arab Emirates, and the Bahamas...

BIBLIOGRAPHY

Aburish Said K, *Nasser: The Last Arab* (Gerald Duckworth, London, 2004); *Arafat* (Bloomsbury, London, 1999).

Ahmed, Leila, *A Quiet Revolution, The Veil's Resurgence from the Middle East to America* (Yale University Press, New Haven and London, 2011).

Ambrose, Stephen E, *Eisenhower: Soldier and President* (Simon & Schuster, New York, 1992).

Asbridge, Thomas, *The Crusades* (Simon & Schuster, London, 2010).

Akyol, Mustafa, *Islam without Extremes, A Muslim Case for Liberty* (W W Norton, New York, 2011).

Al-Awadi, Hesham, *In Pursuit of Legitimacy: The Muslim Brothers and Mubarak 1982–2000'* (Tauris Academic Studies, London, 2004).

Beattie, Kirk, *Egypt during the Sadat Years* (Palgrave Macmillan, London, 2001).

Bergen, Peter L, *The Osama bin Laden I Know* (Free Press /Simon & Schuster, New York, 2006); *Holy War Inc* (Weidenfeld & Nicholson, London, 2001).

Besson, Sylvain, *La conquête de l'Occident: Le projet secret des Islamiste'* [*The Conquest of the West: The Islamists' Secret Project*] (Seuil, Paris, 2005).

Braithwaite, Rodric, *Afgantsy, The Russians in Afghanistan 1979–1989* (Profile Books, London, 2011).

Catterall, Peter, *The Macmillan Diaries 1950–1957* (Macmillan, London, 2003); *The Macmillan Diaries Vol II: Prime Minister and After: 1957–1966* (Macmillan, London, 2011).

Coll, Steve, *Ghost Wars: The Secret History of the CIA, Afghanistan and bin Laden from the Soviet Invasion to September 10, 2001* (Penguin Books, New York, 2004).

Chandrasekaran, Rajiv, *Imperial Life in the Emerald City: Inside Bagdad's Green Zone* (Bloomsbury, London, 2007).

Cox, Caroline & John Marks, *The West, Islam and Islamism: Is Ideological Islam Compatible with Liberal Democracy?* (Institute of Study of Civil Society /Civitas, London, 2003).

Dalin, David G, & Rothmann, John F, *Icon of Evil, Hitler's Mufti and the Rise of Radical Islam* (Random House, New York, 2008).

Daniel, Norman, *Islam and the West* (Oneworld Publications, reprint, 2009).

El Baradei, Mohamed, *The Age of Deception: Nuclear Diplomacy in Treacherous Times* (Bloomsbury, London, 2011).

Esposito, John L, *The Islamic Threat: Myth or Reality?* (OUP, New York, 1992); *The Oxford Encyclopaedia of the Modern Islamic World* [4-vol. set] (OUP, New York, 2001).

Feiler, Bruce, *Generation Freedom* (Harper Perennial, New York, 2011).

Fuller, J F C, *The Decisive Battles of the Western World, 480 BC–1757, Volume One* (Granada Publishing, London, 1970); *Decisive Battles of the Western World (from the Defeat of the Spanish Armada to Waterloo) Volume 2* (Weidenfeld & Nicholson, London, 2001); *Decisive Battles of the Western World (from the American Civil War to the end of the Second World War) Volume 3* (Weidenfeld & Nicholson, London, 2001).

Ghazanfar, S M, *Medieval Islamic Economic Thought: Filling the Great Gap in European Economics* (Routledge, London, 2003).
Gheissair, Ali, & Seyyed Vali Reza Nasr, *Democracy in Iran: History and the Quest for Liberty* (OUP, New York, 2009).

Hattersley, Roy, *Campbell-Bannerman* (Haus Publishing, London, 2006).
Hersh, Seymour M, *The Samson Option: Israel's Nuclear Arsenal and American Foreign Policy* (Random House, New York, 1991).
Howarth, David, *The Desert King, A Life of Ibn Saud* (Collins, London, 1964).

Johnson, Ian, *A mosque in Munich: Nazis, the CIA, and the Rise of The Muslim Brotherhood in the West* (Houghton Mifflin Harcourt, Boston, 2010).

Kepel, Gilles, *The Roots of Radical Islam* (Saqui, London, 2005); *Allah in the West* (Polity Press, Cambridge, 2004).
Kocher, Victor, *Terrorlisten: Die schwarzen Löcher des Völkerrechts* (Promedia Verlagsges, Vienna, 2011).

Lacey, Robert, *Inside the Kingdom* (Hutchinson, London, 2009); *The Kingdom* (Harcourt Brace Jovanovich, New York, 1981).
Lia, Brynjar, *The Society of the Muslim Brothers in Egypt, the Rise of an Islamic Mass Movement, 1928–1942* (Ithaca Press, New York, 2006).

Mackey, Sandra, *The Saudis: Inside the Desert Kingdom* (Houghton Mifflin, Boston, 1987).
McCarthy, Andrew C, *The Grand Jihad: How Islam and The Left Sabotaged America* (Encounter Books, New York, 2010).
McGeough, Paul, *Kill Khalid, The Failed Mossad Assassination of Khalid Mishal and the Rise of Hamas* (Quartet Books, London, 2009).
Mitchell, Richard P, *The Society of the Muslim Brothers* (OUP, New York, 1993).

Naylor, R T, *Satanic Purses: Money, Myth and Misinformation in The War on Terror* (McGill/Queen's University Press, Montreal, 2006).

Norwich, John Julius, *The Normans in the South 1016–1130* (Faber and Faber, London, 2010); *The Kingdom in the Sun, 1130–1194* (Faber and Faber, London, 2010).

O'Sullivan, Edmund, *The New Gulf: How Modern Arabia is Changing the World for Good* (Motivate Publishing, Dubai, 2009).

Pargeter, Alison, *The Muslim Brotherhood: The Burden of Tradition* (Saqui, London, 2010).
Phares, Walid, *Future Jihad* (Palgrave Macmillan, 2005).
Qutb, Sayyid, *Milestones* (Islamic Book Service, New Delhi, 2001).

Rogan, Eugene, *The Arabs: A History* (Allen Lane, London, 2009).
Roy, Olivier, *Islam and Resistance in Afghanistan* (Cambridge University Press, Cambridge, 1990).
Rubin, Barry, *The Muslim Brotherhood* (Palgrave Macmillan, London, 2010).
Rutherford, Bruce K, *Egypt After Mubarak: Liberalism, Islam and Democracy in the Arab World* (Princeton University Press, New Jersey, 2008).

Seale, Patrick, *The Struggle for Arab Independence: Riad el-Solh and the Makers of the Modern Middle East* (Cambridge University Press, Cambridge, 2010).
Shawcross, William, *The Shah's Last Ride: The Fate of an Ally* (Simon & Schuster, London, 1997).
Skovgaard–Petersen, Jakob, & Bettin, Graf (editors), *Global Mufti: The Phenomenon of Yusuf al-Qaradawi* (Hurst and Company, London, 2009).
Silvers, Robert B, *The Consequences to Come: American Power After Bush* (New York Review Books, New York, 2008).

Simpson, William, *The Prince: The Secret of the World's Most Intriguing Royal: Prince Ban Dar Bin Sultan* (Harper, New York, 2007).

Thesiger, Wilfred, *Arabian Sands* (Longmans, Green and Co Ltd, 1959).

Vidino, Lorenzo, *The New Muslim Brotherhood in the West* (Columbia University Press, New York, 2010).
Vitalis, Robert, *America's Kingdom: Mythmaking on the Saudi Oil Frontier* (Stanford University Press, London/New York, 2009).

Weaver, Mary Anne, *A Portrait of Egypt: A Journey through the World of Militant Islam* (Farrar, Strauss and Giroux, New York, 2000).
Wright, Lawrence, *The Looming Tower: Al-Qaeda's Road to 9/11* (Allen Lane, London, 2006).

Yallop, David, *In God's Name* (Jonathan Cape, London, 1984).
Yamani, Mai, *Cradle of Islam* (I B Tauris, London, 2005).

ACKNOWLEDGEMENTS

'The greatest revolution of our generation is the discovery that human beings, by changing the inner attitudes of their minds, can change the outer aspects of their lives.'

Philosopher William James, 1883

Normally, debts are disagreeable but I am happy to have them with so many brave and diligent professionals who helped me tell the story of Youssef Nada and his lifetime with the Muslim Brotherhood. I can only salute Youssef Nada himself as a heroic figure who has worked to make life better for as many people as possible. And thank him so very much for his time, perseverance, patience and the kindness from him and his family and friend and associate Ghaleb Himmat.

My friend Nafil Al Mansouri believed Nada's place in the world needed documenting, not for glorification but as part of history, and encouraged me to pursue it. I agreed that his story did need to be on record as a balance to the dogma which so often results in fear and hysteria. Barry Williamson, a veteran of the Arab world, helped me circumvent the many logistic problems including desert driving, as other adept friends did through the equally twisting and tricky corridors of power in Washington and Cairo, Geneva, Zurich, Paris and Strasbourg. The Muslim Brotherhood's former Supreme Guide Mahdi Akef and his staff at their Cairo headquarters took time to speak with me during the fraught Presidential elections. And I must thank Mohamed Mori, who as I write is the new President of Egypt. The families I met in Alexandria were generous with their information and hospitality. The young in Tahrir Square were so in love with love, with bringing change to their lives, that it cheered the heart while troubling the mind over the risks they were taking and the injury and death so many endured. I have not been too specific with names for each day brings another surprise in this particular world and discretion can benefit.

More public can be the warm gratitude to the ground-breaking John Blake and his publishing team especially Allie Collins and Liz Mallett who believed this controversial book could make a difference and enthusiastically ran with the challenge. Salutations to them all.

Douglas Thompson, Cairo, June, 2012